THEODORE FRANCIS GREEN

BROWN UNIVERSITY
BICENTENNIAL PUBLICATIONS
Studies in the Fields of General Scholarship

192671

8-90

THEODORE FRANCIS GREEN

THEODORE FRANCIS GREEN:

The Rhode Island Years, 1906-1936

by
ERWIN L. LEVINE

BROWN UNIVERSITY PRESS
Providence, Rhode Island

Library of Congress Catalog Card Number: 63–18096

For my son, Dana—

Long the object of my love,
And subject of my hopes and dreams.

Preface

THEODORE FRANCIS GREEN, the son of Arnold and Cornelia Burges Green, was born in Providence, Rhode Island, on October 2, 1867. He was educated at Brown University, from which he received his A.B. degree in 1887 and his A.M. in 1888. From 1888 to 1892 Green studied at Harvard Law School and the universities of Berlin and Bonn, where he was a classmate of Konrad Adenauer. After being admitted to the Rhode Island Bar in 1892, Green taught Roman Law at his alma mater, Brown University, until 1897. Commissioned a Second Lieutenant during the Spanish-American War, Green commanded a provisional company of infantry. In 1906, he formed the law firm of Green, Hinckley, and Allen, remaining at its helm until its dissolution in 1923, whereupon he entered the partnership of Green, Curran, and Hart. Green was head of this firm until 1926, after which he continued in private practice.

Theodore Francis Green's family is deeply rooted in colonial America. Its revolutionary character is embodied in the service of Jonathan Arnold, a great-great-grandfather who was a member of the Continental Congress at the same time that another great-great-grandfather, William Greene, was governor of Rhode Island. During the nineteenth century, two members of the Green family, James Burrill, Jr., a great-grandfather, and Samuel Greene Arnold, a granduncle, served in the United States Senate. Still another of his great-granduncles, Tristram Burges, was a congressman from 1825 until 1835. Theodore Francis Green, then, came by his politics naturally.

Yet politics was only his avocation, not his vocation. He earned his living from his extensive law practice, his real estate holdings, and his wise investments, not from his political contacts.

It has been the plan of this writer to adhere as closely as possible to the political aspects of Green's career between 1906, when he first sought an elective public office, and 1936, when he became a successful candidate for the United States Senate. His non-political activities have been treated only when they seemed necessary to an understanding of Green's political activity.

The story of the politics of Theodore Francis Green must necessarily be viewed in the larger perspective of the politics of the state of Rhode Island. Rhode Island is, in fact, a splendid laboratory for the student of politics, and this study, it is hoped, is in some measure a contribution to the analysis of "the art of the possible."

Much of the research for this manuscript was done in Green's private collection of personal and political correspondence. Extensive use was also made of the *Providence Journal* and several other newspapers, particularly in the formative stages of the project. Personal interviews were held with persons whose reminiscences could bring to light that which was unknown before. I am greatly indebted to Edward J. Higgins, Green's administrative assistant and confidant for more than thirty years, for his invaluable assistance. Untold thanks are also due several members of the faculty of Brown University, particularly Professors Guy H. Dodge and Elmer E. Cornwell of the Political Science Department, Professor Elmer Blistein of the English Department, Professor Robert O. Schulze of the Sociology Department, and Professor James Blaine Hedges of the History Department, whose advice on the revision of the original manuscript was so graciously given and gratefully accepted. In addition, it is appropriate to single out Mr. David Jonah of the John Hay Library for his kindness and help, and Professor Forrest McDonald of the History Department. My gratitude, as well, goes to my former colleagues, Alexander Prisley and Frederic J. Fleron, Jr., who suffered through many months of office deprivation and my interminable garrulousness.

The preparation of the manuscript was aided by a grant from Skidmore College in 1962.

ERWIN L. LEVINE
Saratoga Springs, N.Y.

March 1963

Contents

Chapter **I**

The Political Heritage of Rhode Island

We live in a changing world. It is always changing. Growth means change in character. Progress means change in position. Life itself means constant change. Changelessness means death. ——THEODORE FRANCIS GREEN

CONTEMPORARY Rhode Island is essentially a product of two historical strains. On the one hand it is in the democratic tradition epitomized by Roger Williams' quest for civil freedom and religious purification following his banishment from Puritan Massachusetts in 1636. The concepts of religious freedom and the separation of church and state, so ingrained in our American democratic heritage, were born in Rhode Island in the seventeenth century. Thomas Wilson Dorr, too, exhorted the state in the 1840's to democratize its government and even resorted to force in what has since been called the Dorr Rebellion. Thus the fight to expand the suffrage and broaden the electorate, characteristic of Jacksonian democracy in the first half of the nineteenth century, is also deeply imbedded in the democratic side of Rhode Island history.

The enlightened fervor so necessary for the maturation of democracy, however, was neither consistently nor energetically perpetuated by most of Rhode Island's sons. The other vein in the state's dual nature is exemplified by the political corruption, economic avarice, and moral decadence so apparent by the end of the eighteenth century. In the early nineteenth century the state was still mostly Yankee in stock. Native-born, Protestant, and for

the most part Anglo-Saxon in origin, these people resisted giving
the suffrage to the growing number of newer Americans who
formed a great part of the influx of immigrants entering the state
after 1820. The Yankees continued to retain a political system
that permitted them to resist the intruders. Hence "the formation and retention of a constitution with its antiquated property
qualification, its all-powerful assembly and its undemocratic system of representation." Hence, too, the "sort of dictatorship or
bossism" that gave Rhode Island a well-deserved and "unsavory
reputation in politics."[1]

The franchise for selecting all elected officials was at that time
limited to those who possessed property valued at one hundred
and thirty-four dollars. In addition, the eldest sons of these free-
men, or freeholders, also had the right to vote. A conflict over extending the suffrage to those who did not possess property gave
rise to the dispute over two proposed constitutions. The first,
called the People's Constitution, was written by a committee of
non-freeholders and submitted to the people for their approval
in January, 1842. This constitution, having only age, sex, and residence requirements and containing no property qualifications
for voting, was overwhelmingly accepted by the people, most of
whom were of course non-freeholders. Thereupon, on January
13, the new constitution was proclaimed at a convention of non-
freeholders as the basic law of the state. Another constitution,
written by a committee of freeholders appointed by the state
legislature in November, 1841, and known as the Freeman's Constitution, retained property qualifications as a condition for the
franchise. This constitution was submitted to the voters in March,
1842, and was rejected by a small margin. The Rhode Island Supreme Court, however, declared the People's Constitution illegal, on the ground that it had not been promulgated by a body
legally called to do so by the legislature. The ensuing legal controversy developed into the abortive Dorr Rebellion.[2]

The political unrest which evolved out of this dispute had at
least one salutary effect. Although the property qualification was
retained in the constitution eventually adopted in Rhode Island
in 1843, the privilege of the "eldest sons" was stricken out. The

new constitution also granted suffrage rights to *native* male citizens who paid a poll or personal property tax of at least one dollar. Nevertheless, even they could not vote for the Providence City Council "or upon any proposition to propose a tax, or for the expenditure of money in *any* town or city" unless qualified under the one-hundred-thirty-four-dollar rule. The foreign born were still most closely contained within a restrictive proviso. Under no conditions could such an individual vote in a general election unless he had at least one hundred thirty-four dollars' worth of property, was male, twenty-one years of age, and had at least one year's residence in the state. *Native* citizens, without property qualifications, however, could vote in general elections, provided they had two years' residence in the state and had paid a poll tax of only one dollar. If they also had property valued at one hundred and thirty-four dollars, they needed only one year's residence in the state. Both native and foreign-born citizens who had property at the stated value could vote in the Providence City Council elections.[3]

During the 1850's, as part and parcel of the "know-nothing" movement of the era, there was much opposition throughout the nation to extending the suffrage to the foreign born. Occasionally an attempt was made to grant the franchise to more citizens. True enough, the Civil War made possible the extension of the suffrage to foreign-born residents of Rhode Island who had enlisted from the state and fought for the Union. This concession, however, did not occur until 1886, some twenty years after the war. Most endeavors to dispense with the property qualifications continued to meet with defeat at the hands of the state legislature or by the narrowly drawn electorate in the ratification process. Not until 1888 was there any real success along these lines; in that year the legislature passed the Bourn Amendment, deleting the term *native* from the constitution and thus permitting the foreign born to vote in the general elections after having satisfied other minor requirements. The same amendment, however, further extended the property qualification by making it apply not only to those voting for the City Council of Providence, but also to those who cast ballots for the city council of "any city."[4]

In other words, by 1900, all civil officers of the state and local governments were elected by male citizens, provided residence and registration requirements had been fulfilled, but in the five cities of the state the city councils were elected only by those male citizens having the usual property qualifications. Between 1896 and 1900, close to 60 per cent of the resident citizens of Providence were thus disfranchised in city council elections. This resulted in the city councils' being controlled by the Republican Party, which was, in turn, for the most part synonymous with the "property vote." The mayors of the five cities were usually Democratic, the councils Republican.[5]

The population of Providence increased tremendously throughout the nineteenth century as great migrations of foreign born flowed into the industrial northeast. Rhode Island politics, nevertheless, remained dominated by the oligarchic commercial and manufacturing interests, the heirs to the landed aristocracy that ruled the state in its early history. As one Brown University professor, writing about the times, put it, "There never was a time when the whole body of the people were allowed a voice in government."[6]

The Irish made up the largest percentage of the newer Americans; they were followed by the Italians, English, Canadians, French-Canadians, Russians (mostly Jews), Swedes, Germans, and Scots, in that order. Most of the immigrants were Catholic, their rate of literacy fairly low and, by and large, there was ethnic cohesion in living areas as well. Although gradually outnumbered by these newer Americans swelling the north and south sides of Providence, the Yankees still managed to control the Providence ward committees to such an extent that during most of the nineteenth century they constituted almost all the Republican ward committee membership and always had at least a sizeable majority of ward committeemen in the Democratic Party.[7]

Throughout the nineteenth and into the twentieth centuries the Rhode Island Senate was dominated by the Republican Party because of the continued employment of the rotten-borough system of representation. The Senate was composed of thirty-eight senators elected on the basis of one from each town and city in the state.

This meant that, in 1900, the twenty-eight smallest towns and cities, having only 18 per cent of the total population of the state, elected twenty-eight senators, a majority of nine. The ten largest towns and cities, having approximately 82 per cent of the total population, elected only ten, or 27 per cent, of the upper house. Even at that, in 1906 Republican control was so powerful that in four of the ten largest cities and towns—Newport, Warwick, Cranston, and East Providence—Republicans were elected to the State Senate.[8]

As a rule, the House of Representatives in the Assembly was also Republican in composition. The balance was slightly weighted in favor of the Republicans, since Democratic strength was concentrated in the larger cities and towns. In 1906, for example, Providence sent twelve representatives, all Democrats and elected at large rather than by individual districts, to the lower house. This represented about 17 per cent of the total seats, whereas the city of Providence had approximately 40 per cent of the state's population.[9]

In the first decade of this century the governor of Rhode Island could do little. The state constitution gave few powers to his office. He had practically no control over administration, nor did he possess the power to veto legislation. The governor could recommend, but he could neither direct nor negate. Neither could he give orders or investigate any department or administration or demand reports from any officer, unless so authorized by the Assembly. What few insignificant appointive powers he did have were subject to the restrictions imposed by the Brayton Law, passed in 1901. Under this statute the Senate had to approve almost all appointees of the governor. If it failed to do so after three days, the Senate then had the legal right to select its own nominees for the particular positions being filled. Thus the important factor of patronage rested in the Senate's collective hands, in reality the Republican Party bosses', and not in the governor's.[10]

The power to govern actually reposed with an autocratic Assembly. As the Senate, heavily Republican, had to approve all measures passed by the lower house and in addition possessed the real power of appointment, in effect it controlled the state.

State administration was a labyrinth of overlapping departments, commissions, and boards, with little supervision and no co-ordination. Responsibility of administrators was to the legislature, not to the people.

Rhode Island politics at the beginning of this century, then, was essentially undemocratic at best. "Republican politicians in Providence found it easy to bribe or coerce enough Irish Democrats to demoralize or defeat the plans of the Democratic organization; and the maintenance in office of 'yellow-dog' Democrats, paid by the Republican machine and known to be subservient to its wishes," was a recognized feature in politics. Italians were also cultivated by the Republicans and, for whatever reasons, were "easy victims of coercion and bribery." The two largest groups of newer Americans were still unorganized, and thus their potential voting power was ineffective. The Republican Party had at times attempted to cater to the new immigrant groups, while the Rhode Island Democratic Party, because of a lack of funds, had great difficulty in reaching many non-English-speaking people.[11]

Civic pride in Providence was weak, "partly because of the limited elective franchise and beggarly representation in the assembly, and also through causes common to all of the larger cities of the United States, such as rapid growth and an influx of an alien population ignorant of governmental institutions." Bossism was common throughout the state. Many townsmen were transients, of foreign birth as well, and "largely unfamiliar with local traditions and usual courses of action. Under such conditions local bossism and corruption" became rampant.[12]

Political reform was in at least some people's minds at the turn of the century. A few hearty souls agitated for a more modern and democratic constitutional structure, in keeping with the growing importance of the newer Americans. Rhode Island, nevertheless, was still politically backward. The state had not reformed its elective system even to the extent of adopting the direct primary in nominations for office. Political manipulators continued to make extensive use of the party caucus, which selected delegates to the state and city conventions, and in those days, just as is often the case today, an "active minority" managed to control the politics of the caucus.

A new weekly newspaper, *The State,* appeared on the Rhode Island scene in 1906. The paper's lead story vowed that it would scrutinize and report the doings of the Rhode Island government in order to bring about a better and more qualified public opinion. Political reform at the local level had to begin by rejecting "any man whose conduct was not conspicuously and positively above suspicion." The rotten-borough system could be wiped out only by having the people "go out into the country and ask the country people to vote against *their* traitors." *The State* declared that its efforts would be directed toward making the people more cognizant of the dangers inherent in bossism, particularly within the Republican Party. The weekly pointedly rebuked the politics of the *Providence Journal,* charging that the *Journal* was in "direct cahoots" with the Republican Party and had purposely helped select weak candidates from that party. Moreover, the *Journal* had allegedly suppressed various facts, had hired halls away from Democrats seeking to rally the people for reform, and had even corralled the "Saloon vote." Notwithstanding the probability of journalistic exaggeration, this was indeed the era of stuffed ballot boxes, of the marking of ballots of illiterate voters on behalf of the political machine, and of the wholesale bribery of voters.[13]

The boss of the Republican Party in Rhode Island was Charles R. Brayton. A large, affable, almost blind man with a magnetic personality, Brayton was well suited for his position. His Civil War record, his Masonic connections, and his constant alertness to the political complexities of the state made him quite attractive to those who sought public office. He specialized in buying the voters of the small towns, which elected his personally chosen delegates, who in turn took their orders directly from him. His post of operations was in the State House office of the High Sheriff of Providence, who was thoroughly dominated by the boss. Brayton's technique was to sit in an armchair in the High Sheriff's office and issue orders, in good military fashion, as the members of the Assembly—sometimes Democrats as well as Republicans—

filed in like so many private soldiers to receive orders or report on proceedings in the chamber. His visits to the State House were timed to coincide with the opening and adjournment of the Assembly's sessions. The *Providence Journal* once epitomized "General" Brayton's role in a cartoon. The drawing depicted Brayton leaving a padlocked State House, after having deposited on it a sign giving his home address in case of emergency; the cartoon's caption read "General's Assembly Adjourns." Brayton made his living by serving as an able, efficient, and allegedly corrupt lobbyist for such clients as the New Haven Railroad, and as both lobbyist and chief counsel for the Consolidated Railroad and the electric car system in and around Providence.[14]

These were the conditions that Theodore Francis Green faced when he began his long career in Rhode Island politics. They were, indeed, the external reasons why, in his thirty-ninth year, he entered politics at all. The internal reason was that by heritage, education, and temperament he was in the other half of the state's tradition: the democratic and liberal tradition of Roger Williams and Thomas Wilson Dorr.

For one thing, in essence and in spirit Green was a dissenter. His entire political life was oriented toward progress and democracy, which in Rhode Island were synonymous with dissent. His attitude is revealed by his admiration of Thomas Wilson Dorr. Once on Rhode Island Independence Day (Rhode Island declared its independence from Great Britain two months before the rest of the colonies in 1776) Green unveiled a portrait of this famous revolutionary and gave a speech lauding Dorr's personality and democratic qualities. In speaking of Dorr, he was speaking of himself when he said that Dorr had refused to defend "the existing political or social or economic conditions as the be-all and end-all of society, but strove instead to better the conditions of those less fortunate than himself." Green, in the twentieth century, fought to free the people from political tyranny and economic want, just as Dorr had fought in the mid-nineteenth century.[15]

And Green was also a restless soul, who entered politics as much to prove himself worthy as to do good for the people; this was rooted in his family tradition, particularly on his mother's side, where Dorr's stand had long been defended. While Green was by no means blind to the degenerative side of democracy, he had no fear of revolution; perhaps he even craved it. In any event, he did not view changing conditions, as some viewed them, as the advent of anarchy. Indeed, what was far worse was that "Yankees [had] become Tories, the Revolutionaries [had] become reactionaries." Political conditions in his native state, where were first established the "foundation stones of our republic, soul liberty and the complete separation of church and state," had now fallen so low that Rhode Island, along with Pennsylvania, was generally regarded as the most corrupt of all the states.[16]

Finally, Green had deep-rooted humanitarian and democratic feelings. To him, the essence of democracy was not "merely to live on the past, but to build for the future," in which all people would have an opportunity to earn a living wage, to improve their station in life, and to live decently. To build for the future, men must have knowledge, that "glowing, fluctuating, widening and ever-changing part of the blood stream of humanity." Tolerance, too, was necessary, because of the strains generated in a nation as heterogeneous as America, in a state as heterogeneous as Rhode Island. In seeking these ends, Green believed, it was clearly the obligation of persons of good background, good inheritance, and good education to lead the way. Thus it was almost inevitable that Green should, sooner or later, enter a fight to end corruption and misrule in Rhode Island.[17]

He entered the fight in 1906. In that year he cast his lot with a short-lived reform group, the Lincoln Party, because he had decided that the rule of the boss-ridden Republican Party could no longer be tolerated. (In some respects, the Democratic Party was scarcely better, the principal difference being that the Republicans controlled every branch of the state government.) In his decision Green was joined by many other men born to the manor, men who held a "patrician disdain for greedy businessmen"[18] who pulled the strings of government behind the facade of a political party. The Goddards, the Sharpes, the Metcalfs, and the

Watermans were only a few of the famous old-stock Rhode Islanders who were linked with Green in his effort to obtain honest
government.

Seeking to create a reform party distinct from either major
political party, Rhode Island aristocrats had banded together
not long after the turn of the century, to try and wrest control of
government from the hands of the avaricious and dishonest. In
the attempt to accomplish this herculean chore, many either fell
by the wayside in cynical despair or joined forces with the small
nucleus of reform-minded Democrats in order to further their
aims. It was difficult as well for the aristocratic reformers to distinguish between Democrats truly interested in honest reform
and those who gave the impression of having such desires but who
in reality were merely tools of the opposition party. What made
Theodore Francis Green stand out from so many of his kind was
the fact that he continued in active association with the Democratic Party of his state long after the others had deserted it. By
so doing, he not only set himself apart from his own class, but
joined a group who for years viewed him with a certain amount
of suspicion; his new associates in politics could not understand,
or refused to, that Theodore Francis Green was apparently continuing in Rhode Island politics simply because he was genuinely
interested in furthering the cause of the people.

Chapter **II**

The Novice Lawmaker

Mr. Green has not been identified with politics.

———Providence Journal

T HE OCCASION for the formation of the Lincoln Party, under which Theodore Francis Green began his political career, was the senatorial election of 1906–1907. The term of Republican Senator George Peabody Wetmore was about to expire and—the Seventeenth Amendment, providing for the direct election of senators, not having yet been adopted—the General Assembly, meeting together in Grand Committee of both houses, would elect his successor. Much therefore depended upon the political composition of the legislature that would be elected in November, 1906. In April an informal committee of three Democrats, led by former Governor Lucius F. C. Garvin, submitted to the Democratic State Central Committee a series of resolutions recommending the calling of a party convention for the express purpose of choosing an opponent to Senator Wetmore—or to Samuel Pomeroy Colt of the United States Rubber Company, a prominent Republican who had decided to challenge Wetmore.

The Democratic State Central Committee unanimously agreed and issued a call for a state convention, the first ever held by either party in Rhode Island for such a purpose. Democrats gathered in Providence's Old Music Hall in May and duly nominated Colonel Robert Hale Ives Goddard, a wealthy, upstanding Rhode Islander. Though Colonel Goddard's political inclinations were generally toward the Republican Party on national issues, he was one of the many outstanding citizens of the state who were appalled at the extent of Charles R. Brayton's control of Rhode Island's government. Goddard accepted the nomination

and Frank E. Fitzsimmons, chairman of the State Central Committee, appointed a special committee whose principal task was
to secure the election to the General Assembly of men who
would unequivocally commit themselves to vote for Goddard
when the time came in 1907. In this drive to cast off "the yoke
of political slavery and establish democracy in Rhode Island,"
the Democrats were warmly supported by *The State,* the *Providence Journal,* and a number of independents. They joined ranks
to aid the Democrats' efforts to get voters to register, and when
registration ended on June 30, a large increase in the total number of registered voters was noted. Then late in July the Goddard Campaign Committee, hoping to attract to its side larger
groups of independents and anti-Brayton Republicans, announced
the formal adoption of the name Lincoln Party for its organization.[1]

The Lincoln Party made it clear that its fight would be solely
for the election of Goddard; it proposed to ignore the contests
for statewide officers and support only General Assembly candidates—which in practice meant Democrats running for that body.
The organization worked separately from the Democratic State
Central Committee, though some men were members of both.
Among its leaders were several leading Democrats—notably Pawtucket's popular young Mayor, James H. Higgins, who became
the Democratic candidate for governor—and a number of prominent Republicans. The bipartisan nature of the group created
many problems of campaigning; to circumvent them, it was decided to attack Brayton and "bossism" rather than the Republicans themselves. At the Goddard ratification rally—a common
event in those days—speeches centering upon the theme "down
with Braytonism" were made by independents and members of
both major parties: Democrat Higgins; Henry D. Sharpe, a prominent manufacturer; Professor William MacDonald of Brown
University's History Department; Everett Colby, leader of Republican reformers in New Jersey; and William Gammell, long
a staunch Republican in Rhode Island. Among the newcomers
on the stage that evening was Theodore Francis Green, who had
said Yes when his friend and colleague, Richard Comstock, had

asked him to run for the General Assembly on what came to be the combined Lincoln-Democratic Party ticket.[2]

The regular Democratic State Convention to select state and congressional candidates was set for October 3, a full two weeks earlier than usual, in order to allow more time for campaigning and building their case against the Republicans. A crusading spirit began to pervade the urban communities of the state as the Democratic Party received added support from several ministers and from the infant labor unions, which were incensed over the refusal of the Republican-dominated General Assembly to pass an eight-hour-day act. Although only the Central Trades and Labor Unions officially endorsed the Democratic Party in the state, practically all the local branches of the various unions publicly condemned the Republicans. The Democratic State Central Committee was well aware that, in view of this spirit, they should choose a competent slate of candidates for statewide office, and that the city and town conventions, which met shortly afterward, should select good candidates, particularly from Providence, for the General Assembly. Accordingly, the Central Committee embarked on a drive to have the local caucuses "clean house" and make certain that a "ticket worthy of the support of the independent element" was nominated. An important factor in previous Democratic local caucuses and conventions had been the presence of "renegade" Democrats, those who wore the Democratic label but who, in reality, had close working agreements with the Republicans in their communities. These older, more conservative Democrats preferred to continue the *status quo,* in which they were the minority party, for through it they retained their local power and compensated themselves well in the process. The younger Democrats, who dominated the State Central Committee, claimed to be the true Democrats, charging that the "renegades" were "made up principally of hirelings in the pay of the Republican machine leaders." It was the young Democrats who led the fight for Goddard, and it was they who sought a slate of good and honest Assembly candidates which would appeal to independents and anti-Brayton Republicans alike.[3]

The Democratic State Central Committee worked feverishly to

purge and root out the corrosive elements in the party. Throughout the Providence wards and in several other cities and towns,
appeals were issued to further the ascendancy of "true" Democrats in the selection of delegates to state, city, and town conventions. The Central Committee, which worked closely with Goddard's outside backers, was victorious in most of the ward caucuses in Providence. Elsewhere, attempts to purify the Democratic
Party were less successful, for in several cities and towns the Central Committee's zealous interference stirred up resentment
among local Democratic leaders, not all of whom were "renegades."[4]

A few days after the rally, the Democratic State Convention endorsed the selection by the nominating committee of Mayor Higgins for governor, chose the rest of the statewide ticket, renominated Congressman Daniel Granger from the First Congressional
District, and named former Governor Garvin as the candidate
from the Second District. Democrats also passed the important
resolution pledging "the vote of every Democrat elected to the
General Assembly to Robert H. I. Goddard for the United States
Senate." During the next week, the various city and town conventions met to choose candidates for the legislature. Providence
Democrats held their city convention on October 10. A few dis-
contented Democrats, desiring to nominate candidates in opposition to the list previously agreed upon in individual ward caucuses, raised cries of a Democratic brand of "Braytonism." Otherwise, "the convention was harmonious and the nominations practically unanimous." Richard B. Comstock of Providence's Second
Ward nominated Theodore Francis Green of Providence as candidate for eleventh representative, or representative-at-large.
Jesse H. Metcalf, former member of the General Assembly and
one of Rhode Island's most influential citizens, was nominated
for twelfth representative. Later, Metcalf was to be a rival of
Green for power in the state.[5]

The Lincoln Party's decision to ignore the statewide officers in
the coming election caused some difficulty for Democrats in the
eventual composition of the ballot. As in the case of the ballots of
the preceding year, the individual columns in which each party's

candidates were listed were headed by the party emblem and, immediately below it, a circle in which straight party voters could place a single cross instead of having to place crosses opposite the names of each candidate's name in the list below. In its column, since it had decided to ignore the statewide contest, the Lincoln Party listed only General Assembly candidates—and these were the same as those of the Democratic Party. However, if a Republican or independent voter wanted to vote for Lincoln candidates for the Assembly but preferred to cast his ballot for the Republican statewide ticket he would have to be extremely careful. If he placed his mark in the Lincoln Party circle (showing his preference for the Lincoln Assembly candidates) and then in the Republican circle (casting his vote for the Republican statewide candidates), he would have been voting in reality for two sets of Assembly candidates, thus invalidating the entire ballot. In counting the votes, clerks in the pay of the Republican machine might very well invalidate *only* the Assembly part of the ballot and count in the votes for the Republican statewide nominees. This possibility caused great consternation to some, and the *Providence Journal* printed instructions showing how to cross over on the ballot and avoid this eventuality by simply voting for each individual candidate. The newspaper also pointed out that the straight ticket circle could be used, provided one set of General Assembly candidates had their names crossed off by the voter. The effort was vain, for the instructions were even more confusing than was the ballot.[6]

The Republicans nominated Governor Utter for re-election, along with the entire list of state officials. At their state convention, they ignored the coming battle between Senator Wetmore and his potential adversary Samuel Pomeroy Colt. Green's opponent for the Assembly was nominated by the Republicans in their city convention in mid-October. George L. Pierce, who was born in Seekonk, Massachusetts, in 1837, had had a great deal of political experience. A grocer by vocation, he had been a member of the Providence Common Council, an alderman, and a state representative as well. (Editorially, the *Journal* blasted the Republicans for renominating a group of assemblymen, "not one of whom on a single occasion at the last session showed that he represented anybody but Brayton. They did not represent even themselves, let alone the citizens of this big city. They ran to the Sheriff's Office almost for permission to breathe.")[7]

The campaign became more and more lively as October wore on. Not to be outdone by labor unions and white ministers who called for Brayton's destruction, the Reverend S. W. Smith, pastor of the Negro Congdon Street Baptist Church, directed one of his sermons against boss rule in the Republican Party. It will be remembered that after the Civil War Negroes in the North invariably voted Republican. Reverend Smith had sought to be a Republican candidate for the General Assembly, and Brayton had obstructed his nomination. Rankled by this, Reverend Smith told his flock:

> It seems that the Republican Party has no use of the negro. They have refused the negro every request except the insertion of a plank in their platform praying the South to stop their wholesale slaughter of negroes. Charles R. Brayton has everything under his control. He is against right, and as long as he is in power we need not look for anything. We must throw off the yoke of bondage.
> Governor Utter is all right but he is in bad company. The Republican machine is rotten to the core and we are going to help defeat it. What chance have we under the present regime? We are going to agitate. We will not equivocate. We will be heard. We were not heard at the caucus, but we will be heard at the polls. We want all our voters to rally. We must put at least 800 voters in a solid phalanx against bossism.[8]

Appeals to ethnic and religious groups to vote a particular way were common at this time, and subtle manipulation as well as overt entreaties were the norm. Indeed, bloc voting on ethnic rather than economic lines was a cardinal fact in Providence politics. In 1906, Democrats worked hard and effectively to equate the issue of "bossism" with its evil effects on individual groups, whenever such political charges might acquire votes. Thus, for example, Democrats attempted to swing votes of Providence Jews, as well as Negroes, to their side.[9]

On October 25, at What Cheer Hall, a Democratic rally, publicized by posters written in Yiddish was sponsored by Jewish leaders of Providence's Third Ward. Addresses were made by

James Williams, a prominent Rhode Island Democrat; Congressman Daniel Granger; Charles Marnet of New York, an immigration expert and agent of the Jewish Immigrant Aid Society; and John Hogan, the Democratic candidate for third representative opposing Republican Jacob A. Eaton, a Jew and the only new candidate on the Republican General Assembly ticket. For the most part the speeches dealt with the theory that the Jewish vote should be Democratic, not Republican. James Williams even attacked Eaton as not "a representative Jew and not an honor or credit to his race." Jake Eaton had been selected as the Republican candidate to oppose Hogan, said Williams, because "the boss of the Republican party wanted to catch the Jewish vote and at the same time wanted a Jewish office-holder whom he could mold to his liking as the potter fashions clay." Williams then went on to equate Russian tyranny over the Jews with Brayton's tyranny over Rhode Islanders—"for tyranny is all of a piece wherever it exists."[10]

Again and again, at rallies throughout the state, Democrats hammered away with charges of boss rule and corruption in Republican ranks. They viewed 1906 as presenting their best chance to elect a Democratic Assembly since 1902, when Democrat Lucius Garvin, now a candidate for Congress, had won the governorship and Democrats had come within twelve seats of a majority in the Grand Committee of the General Assembly. The uprising against Brayton at that time, however, had been purely of local nature, being confined to Providence, Pawtucket, and the Blackstone Valley. The chances were now good for Democratic victories in other areas of the state. Too, with Goddard as the focal point for anti-Brayton voters, reform forces were more united than ever before. The Wetmore-Colt struggle for the Republican nomination for the United States Senate also added to the hopes of anti-Brayton reformers.[11]

Theodore Francis Green, running for political office for the first time and against an experienced politician besides, took only a minor role in the campaign. He rarely appeared at rallies with the better-known Democrats and confined his speech-making to small gatherings. His wit and eloquence did not go unnoticed, however. At Central Falls, in late October, Green delighted voters by urging them to elect as governor James Higgins, a man "with a backbone" who could and would throw Brayton out of the State House, and to reject Utter, a man "with a wishbone" who simply could not. A week later, at a rally of the Lincoln and Democratic parties in East Greenwich, Green turned a Republican argument to good advantage. Republicans had often reprimanded Goddard for having taken the name Lincoln for his party. Defending Goddard's right to use the President's name, Green said: "Col. Goddard was brevetted twice by President Lincoln for gallant and meritorious service, and who is there who dares deny him the right to use that martyred President's name in the service of his State now?" He then went on to tell veterans of the Civil War and their sons to resent deeply any who told them to vote against Goddard, and he brought the audience to a high pitch of enthusiasm by an eloquent plea for "old soldiers" to vote for Goddard, whose Civil War record Green carefully outlined. Green's speech was so well received and his manner so obviously attractive that it brought him his first major appearance in print: a heading on the lead story of the morning *Providence Journal.*

The *Providence Journal* supported the Lincoln Party ticket for the Assembly. *The State* went further, advocating the election of all Democratic candidates for office. "A *cross* in the *circle* under the *star* [the Democratic emblem on the ballot] means the removal of the disgrace of Braytonism and the election of Robert H. I. Goddard for United States Senator." The *Issue,* the official newspaper of the Rhode Island Temperance League, also urged the election of all Lincoln Party candidates, and it individually endorsed Green. The *Journal* foresaw victory for Higgins but felt that the outlook for the reform candidates was not favorable. On the other hand, *The State,* with undue optimism, predicted a landslide for the entire Democratic-Lincoln Party ticket and the total destruction of Braytonism.[12]

The weather was fair on election day, November 6, and a relatively large vote was cast. James Higgins was elected Governor, 33,195 to Utter's 31,877, but the rest of the statewide offices were carried by Republicans. Democrat Daniel Granger was re-elected to Congress from the First Congressional District, defeating his Republican challenger, Mayor Elisha Dyer of Providence, by only 816 votes. Dr. Garvin, running for the seat from the Second District, lost to the Republican incumbent, Adin Capron. Providence elected a Democrat, Patrick J. Murphy, as Mayor, but the Board of Aldermen and Common Council remained Republican.

The Providence wing of the Democratic-Lincoln Party fusion ticket swept into office with the election of the entire Assembly list, placing Rathbone Gardner in the State Senate and winning all twelve of the city's seats in the lower house. Green received 12,738 votes, fifth in the field of twelve, to his opponent's 9,607. Overall, Republicans captured twenty-seven of the thirty-eight seats in the Senate, but they won the House of Representatives by only two seats, thirty-six to thirty-four. Two members who had been elected on independent tickets, Ray G. Lewis of New Shoreham (Block Island) and Howard R. Peckham of Middletown, could very well deadlock the selection of the Speaker of the House, who had the power of choosing the membership of the House committees.[13]

Early in December, the newly elected Democratic members of the legislature gathered in caucus to prepare for the coming legislative session. For the first time in a number of years the Democratic contingent was strong enough to require some sort of organization to direct matters, and that fact occasioned considerable personal opportunity for Theodore Francis Green. The Democrats decided to establish a joint House and Senate committee to shape policy on pertinent questions put to it by Democrats in the Assembly, and Green, who had begun to acquire a reputation as an independent thinker and orator, was made a member. Other members of the committee were Senators James L. Jenks of Pawtucket and John A. Remington of Central Falls and Providence Representatives Lewis A. Waterman and John W. Hogan, who had trounced Jacob Eaton in the Third Ward by an almost two to one majority.

Green's name was also brought up at the December meeting

as a possible candidate for Speaker of the House. If the Democrats could convince the two Independents, Lewis and Peckham, to vote with the Democratic Party in the organization of the House, a tie would result. Were the Democrats then able to swing one or more Republicans to their side as well, they would be able to select the Speaker, whose power was almost boundless. It was thought that Green, because of his personal and social background, could possibly bring a few Republicans into the Democratic camp. The Republican leadership was well aware of the danger of defections of disaffected representatives who feared being overlooked by a Republican Speaker "handing out the committee plums." If a secret ballot were used instead of an open roll-call vote, political insubordination was entirely possible in the selection of the Speaker. (Being the Democratic candidate for the speakership would be advantageous for Green even if he should lose, for he would then be considered the spokesman for the Democratic opposition, a platform from which he could expound his own personal views and thus gain political recognition and fame in the state.)[14]

A week later the Democrats met again and issued a statement of their goals for the coming session. They would, they said, press for the granting of the veto power to the governor, for a corrupt practices act, for reapportionment of the House, for abolition of property qualifications for voting, and for restoration of the appointive power to the governor. The party policy committee, of which Green was a member, was assigned the task of drawing up the bills. The Lincoln Party, at approximately the same time, merged with the Rhode Island Citizens' Union, a small and relatively insignificant organization devoted to the advancement of good government in the state. The new group, styled the Lincoln Union, resolved to "continue the work of its predecessors in the cause of good government and in opposing corrupt machine methods in the political life" of the state.[15]

On New Year's Day, as the 1907 legislature met for the first time, Theodore Francis Green was again singled out as an excellent choice for Speaker, but after much consideration the House Democrats finally chose John W. Hogan as their candidate. Neither

Hogan nor Roswell B. Burchard of Little Compton, Republican candidate for Speaker, took part in the voting. Uncommitted Representatives Lewis and Peckham voted with the Republicans, as did Albert N. Luther, who had been nominated to the Assembly by the Democrats but also endorsed by the Republican Party. Most of Luther's votes on legislative matters thereafter went to the Republican side. Burchard thus won the speakership, thirty-eight to thirty-two, and adding the votes of Burchard and Hogan to the total, the *Providence Journal* correctly observed that the division of the 1907 House of Representatives would probably "be drawn upon the line of 39 to 33, a Republican majority of six."[16]

The newly elected governor, James H. Higgins, was also sworn into office on New Year's Day. While Higgins was being inducted "with fitting pomp," General Charles R. Brayton "established himself in his accustomed place in the office of High Sheriff Hunter C. White, and there was kept advised of the progress of affairs in the House and Senate." Brayton thereby served notice that he intended to keep his finger on the pulse—or the jugular vein—of the Assembly, Democrats, Lincoln Unionists, and reformers notwithstanding. On the second day of the session the heavily Republican State Senate quickly adopted its usual set of rules. The House of Representatives would be much slower to adopt its rules because the Democrats vowed to challenge every item which tended to favor the Republican machine. At the very start, House Democrats complained that Speaker Burchard had not called the chamber to order at eleven in the morning as required, but had done so at 12:07 P.M. This seemingly trivial complaint would return in due time to plague the Republicans.[17]

Green had the honor of introducing the first legislation in the House when he proposed an amendment to the state constitution giving the veto power to the governor. The measure also provided for the requirement of a two-third's vote of both houses in order to override the governor's veto. Green explained that his proposed amendment was a "verbatim copy" of its counterpart in the United States Constitution. James Harris of Smithfield, representing the views of his Republican colleagues, stated that more time was required for consideration of such an amendment.

Although the proposed amendment had been introduced in substantially the same form for the past three years, it was laid temporarily on the table by a roll-call vote of thirty-nine to thirty-
three, a ratio Green and his Democratic cohorts were to hear
many times during the 1907 legislature. (A decent burial of the
amendment would have to wait until March, when the Speaker
gently deposited it in the Committee on Special Legislation,
there to expire with the end of the session in April.) Lewis Waterman then proposed a bill in effect repealing the Brayton Law
of 1901, which permitted the State Senate to select its own appointive nominees three days after the governor had submitted
his candidates. Waterman's bill would have abolished this right
and returned the appointive power to the governor, leaving the
Senate only the right of confirmation. This, too, was tabled by a
vote of thirty-nine to thirty-three.[18]

On both these measures roll-call votes had been requested by
John W. Hogan, who relied on Rule 26 of the 1906 House. This
rule, still in effect until new rules were adopted, provided for a
roll-call vote when one-fifth of the members so requested. When
Hogan demanded a roll-call vote on Green's veto resolution,
Speaker Burchard, who was serving his first term in the chair,
did not appear to be sure of his grounds. Hogan thereupon pro-
ceeded to lecture Burchard as to his duties under the rules. The
Journal, covering this first day of proceedings, said that "the
Democratic leadership in the House appears to be between John
W. Hogan and Theodore Francis Green of this city."[19]

On the next day, before the Governor's inaugural address,
Green attempted to introduce a resolution which would have excluded paid lobbyists from the floor, thus freeing members "from
the importunities of persons advocating or opposing matters of
legislation." As the lower house was then about to draw for floor
positions of seats for the legislators, Green's resolution was rejected by the Speaker as out of order. After the drawing, which
was by lot, the Republican majority voted for a quick adjournment in order to meet with the Senate to hear the Governor's
inaugural address. Green's resolution was forestalled again.
"After the House adjourned," wrote a political reporter, "a well-

known Republican politician, not a member of the General Assembly" asked Green if his resolution had been a bill to "aid lobbyists." Green informed him that it was a bill on "paid lobbyists" at which the Republican said, "Oh, paid lobbyists. Hell, that doesn't include me—I haven't been paid yet!"[20]

On the third legislative day, Democratic representatives tried to alter House Rule 11. This rule read as follows:

When any member is about to speak in debate, or to deliver any matter to the house, he shall rise from his seat and respectfully address himself to 'Mr. Speaker,' and shall not proceed until he has been recognized.

Obviously this rule gave the Speaker power to control the speaking order of the assemblymen, and even to refuse to recognize anyone if he chose. John W. Hogan accordingly introduced an amendment to the rule which would have struck out all the words following "Mr. Speaker" and have substituted the words "and the presiding officer shall recognize the member who shall first address him." Hogan's proposal was defeated on a straight party vote.[21]

Rule 30, specifying that any motion or resolution directed at forcing a particular bill from a committee was to be voted upon without debate, was even more vexing to the Democrats. Democrat Joseph McDonald proposed that all bills be reported out of the committees every Tuesday, and that the right of debate be limited to thirty minutes on all such bills. This would have rendered it impossible for a committee to pigeon-hole a bill indefinitely. Republicans voted this down by a roll-call vote requested by the Democrats. In the debate on this proposal, Green blasted the Republicans for their opposition to fair debate. "We see from this discussion," he said, "that the whole spirit of these rules is to prevent debate—why should the gentlemen on the other side be desirous that committees do not report? . . . These rules were introduced with the idea of preventing discussion. . . . We on this side of the House are anxious to have our position on this matter known. Why are the members on the other side so anxious that their position on this matter shall not be publicly known?"[22]

Later that afternoon, a caucus of House Democrats selected
Green as Secretary of the Democratic Steering Committee, a
seven-man group which hoped to keep Democratic assemblymen
aware of all the ways and means to thwart the Republicans in the
General Assembly.[23]

The first real break in Republican ranks in the House occurred
on the fifth legislative day. Democrat Joseph McDonald introduced an amendment to Rule 32, the list of standing house committees. McDonald's amendment added a Committee on Labor
Legislation to the thirteen permanent committees. Aware that
labor wanted a voice in the General Assembly, and cognizant of
labor's position in the 1906 campaign, seven Republicans broke
with the party and voted for the amendment. Theodore Francis
Green took an active part in the debate which finally led to the
passage of the amendment. He charged that Republican arguments against formation of a labor committee were only "flimsy
pretexts," and that actually Republicans were not in favor of protection of living beings on any scale—they had even, he said, bot-
tled up in committee conservation measures that would have
"protected squirrels and lobsters." During his tirade he won a
reprimand from Speaker Burchard by accusing Republicans of
being under boss rule, and daring them to break ranks and vote
with the Democrats. Of the seven Republicans who did vote with
the Democrats in favor of the amendment, four were new members, two of whom were the Independents Albert N. Luther and
Howard R. Peckham. A Committee on Labor Legislation thereby
became one of the standing committees by a vote of thirty-seven
to thirty.[24]

Another battle over the adoption of the rules took place on the
following day. John W. Hogan introduced an amendment to
Rule 39 which would have required any committee to report to
the floor all bills within a month after having had them referred
to it. Republican Samuel W. K. Allen of East Greenwich moved
that the House refer Hogan's proposal to the Committee on Rules
and Orders after the Speaker appointed the House committees.
There, of course, the bill would have remained for the entire
session. Green defended Hogan's amendment on the grounds
that the House was entitled to know the opinion of the minority

on any committee. Tongue in cheek, Green said: "For example, if the Committee on Fisheries considered the question of the protection of the lobster, and the minority of the committee decided that as self-preservation was the first law, the lobster ought to be protected, the House ought to know the opinion." Green then went on to argue that Republican leaders Allen, James Harris of Smithfield, and Elmer Rathbun of West Greenwich were in the habit of moving resolutions to committees when it appeared that the Republican majority might not have its way in the event of an immediate vote. "Their position is consistent with that theory," said Green. The proposal before the House was so simple that it scarcely required referral to any committee for further study, but in line with usual Republican practice, Allen had recommended that it be so referred. Despite Green's argument, the motion to refer Hogan's amendment passed by the familiar thirty-nine to thirty-three vote.[25]

Democrats now tried to obstruct Brayton's influence on House members by attempting to amend Rule 46, concerning admission of persons to the floor of the House. This rule, in effect, granted authority to the Speaker to admit to the floor anyone he desired. Thus it was more or less customary to have an open floor in the House. Green introduced an amendment to Rule 46 which would have provided that "all lobbyists shall be excluded from the floor and lobby of this House, and the Speaker is given authority to enforce this rule." Green went on to say that he

did not wish to be understood as taking the position that all lobbying was bad. Just as parties are represented before courts by paid attorneys, so persons advocating measures before legislative bodies may with propriety be represented by paid attorneys. But while this may be a proper proceeding, it should be borne in mind that it may be a very improper proceeding. The safeguards thrown around the representation of parties by paid attorneys in courts are not thrown around the similar representation before legislative committees. There are provisions for disbarment of attorneys for unprofessional conduct in court. There are no such provisions regulating lobbyists, and so it frequently happens that they are among the most corrupt of persons.[26]

After a fierce debate, Green finally asked for a roll-call vote on his amendment. One Republican, Everett A. Codlin of Westerly (who had also voted with the Democrats to establish a labor committee) cast his vote for Green's proposal, but Green's attempt to restrict Brayton and his agents by legislative decree went down to defeat, thirty-five to thirty-one.[27]

The lower house referred one more important rule to the Committee on Rules and Orders. Rule 49 required the Speaker to compel the retention of all members present and, at the request of any nineteen members, to compel the attendance of absent members with a warrant calling on the Sheriff and his deputies to enforce his ruling. The rule remained on the record, and later on political fireworks ensued because of it.[28]

That afternoon Assembly Democrats caucused to discuss an amendment to the state constitution abolishing property qualifications for voting for the city councils. As it turned out, the discussion that day covered another significant aspect of Rhode Island politics. Supervisors were often used to mark ballots of illiterate voters when so requested. Republicans usually held these jobs under Democratic labels, and thus ballots had often been marked on behalf of Republican candidates when in reality the illiterate voters preferred Democrats. To offset this, Green proposed a proviso to the amendment under discussion, requiring that every voter personally mark his own ballot except when he was blind or physically incapacitated. This recommendation worried some Democrats in the caucus, who genuinely feared that its adoption would unfairly disfranchise many illiterate voters. Green, fighting for his proposal, claimed that if a voter were so illiterate that he needed assistance to mark his own ballot, he would never know whether the supervisor had marked it correctly for him. Green believed that knowing the party label at the top of the party list was all that was necessary for an illiterate voter to identify a candidate. Intelligence, not education, was the criterion. The caucus could decide nothing definite about the matter and resolved to reconsider it at a later date. The committee of Democrats who proposed the amendment at this January caucus was composed of Senators Jenks of Pawtucket and Remington of Central Falls and Representatives Hogan, Waterman, and Green, all of Providence.[29]

On January 15 the Grand Committee, the upper and lower houses meeting together, took up the election of a United States senator. Three days earlier, Frank E. Fitzsimmons, chairman of the Democratic State Central Committee, had sent letters to all Democratic assemblymen, impressing upon them the necessity for constant attendance so as "to assist in redeeming the pledge made to the people" to support the candidacy of Colonel Goddard. Incumbent Senator George Peabody Wetmore and his challenger Samuel Pomeroy Colt were both nominated by the Republicans. Theodore Francis Green placed in nomination the name of Goddard on behalf of the Democratic Party. Green's speech was well thought out and capably delivered. He accused the Republican Party of permitting "subterfuge and intrigue" in Rhode Island. Disgusted with bossism and determined to root out organized corruption, Green said that honest Republicans and the Democratic Party had united in May to support a Republican, Robert H. I. Goddard, for the United States Senate. Green vowed to throw down the gauntlet "before the retainers of the over-lord, the partisans of the boss." If elected, he went on, Goddard would sustain good government and be an honest senator representing the people of Rhode Island faithfully. Goddard was a rich man, he said, but he was not ostentatious as were his wealthy opponents. Furthermore, Goddard's wealth had been acquired by honest work, whereas the Republican contenders had inherited their wealth. The selection of Goddard would be in accordance with the people's will, because "the members elected as pledged to Col. Goddard represent towns containing 49,260 voters," which was five-eighths of the total electorate.[30]

To be elected, a candidate had to have a majority of the votes cast in Grand Committee. The Democrats continually held fast, and the eight Democratic state senators combined with the thirty-three representatives invariably gave Goddard forty-one votes. Because Wetmore and Colt almost evenly divided the Republican vote, no one had a majority. As it turned out, indeed, the Grand Committee never did select a senator to serve with incumbent Senator Nelson Aldrich in the session that began on March 4, 1907, for all three groups refused to budge.[31]

Meantime, the Democratic minority stood little chance to pass reform legislation. They introduced a succession of bills for the general welfare, including an employer liability bill and bills calling for the direct election of United States senators, for constitutional initiative, and for electoral reform, only to see them referred to one committee or another for killing. In every committee, the Republican majority was under direct orders of Burchard, who in turn drew his directives from Brayton.

Governor Higgins, in keeping with his campaign pledge, began in late January to press for the ejection of Brayton from the State House. He called the State House Commission together and formally objected to the use of the State House grounds for the continued pleasure of Brayton. The Governor urged the Commission, which was charged with the maintenance of the area, to take action. The Commission, however, decided that it had no jurisdiction in the matter. Brayton, to calm things down for a while, moved his base of operations from the Sheriff's office to the House Clerk's.[32]

Theodore Francis Green thereupon decided to aim his own fire at Brayton, and he began a steady assault on the Republican Party boss. The Jamestown Tercentennial Commission was then in the process of erecting an exposition in Virginia. Rhode Island had properly decided to construct a building to house Rhode Island historical exhibits and reminders of her place in early American history. Green introduced a resolution "for the maintenance of the dignity and honor of the State of Rhode Island, in connection with its participation" in the Virginia exposition. In effect, the resolution admonished the Executive Secretary of the Rhode Island Exhibition, George N. Kingsbury—who had often been used as a go-between at the Capitol for Brayton and various Republican members of the House—to ignore Brayton. Green's motion was the source of considerable irritation to Republicans, and Allen, one of Green's most vociferous antagonists, claimed that the resolution was insulting. Green answered that Allen might well declare "to whom it is insulting," and he was promptly declared out of order by Speaker Burchard. This time the Republicans wanted an immediate vote, and over Hogan's motion to commit the resolution, Burchard ordered the measure voted upon immediately. Green's proposal was laid on the table, and thereby effectively killed, by a thirty-eight to thirty-one vote. (Kingsbury himself, appreciating the directness of the arraignment, even though it was aimed at himself, pronounced Green's resolution "a corker.")[33]

In the second month of the session Green brought into play Rule 49, which required the retention of all members of the House upon the request of any nineteen of them. On February 5, a severe snow storm hit Rhode Island, and fifteen Republicans and three Democrats were kept from reaching the Capitol on time. When both houses met in Grand Committee to vote for United States senator, as was required every legislative day, only ninety-three legislators were present, and thus only forty-seven votes were necessary for a majority to elect.[34]

Not only did the storm give the Democrats a chance of electing Goddard; it also gave them a temporary one-vote majority in the lower house. Burchard delayed calling the house to order until the Senate was ready to meet in Grand Committee. Thus he opened the session at 12:07 P.M., and before the Democratic majority could move any resolution, the State Senate was announced at the door for the purpose of casting ballots for United States senator. As it happened, just enough Republicans were present to prevent Goddard from obtaining a majority. To avoid any possible recurrence of the events which had almost led to the election of Goddard, Brayton later advised Wetmore and Colt backers in the Assembly to seek quarters in hotels, at the candidates' expense, whenever severe storms seemed likely.[35]

Immediately after the joint vote was taken and the Senate retired, Theodore Francis Green arose on a question of personal privilege and stated that he wished to invoke Rule 49, compelling the members of the House to remain in the lower chamber. If the Republicans could be kept in the House, there would still be a quorum and thus Democrats could seize the opportunity to pass some reform legislation. Green stated that he had twenty signatures on the necessary petition; Speaker Burchard, ordering the signatories to stand, counted only nineteen, but that was enough to invoke the rule. Attempting to stall for time until some Republicans could show up from the Rhode Island hinterland, Burchard ruled the petition out of order on the ground that it was not dated. Up popped Green again and said that he had had the petition "drawn up ready for such an emergency as this" and he could very easily date the paper. This he did and Burchard, after conferring with Republican Allen, announced that insofar as he could he would compel the retention of all members in the chamber. First, however, he ordered the House Clerk to read the previous day's *House Journal* in its entirety, a rare practice. Green interrupted the reading and asked Burchard to order the Sheriff of Providence County, as required by Rule 49, to compel the presence of all members. Burchard, growing increasingly angry, said that he himself would keep those already in the chamber at their places. As the reading of the *Journal* began again, in strode three Republicans who had been delayed by the storm, and now with a thirty-three to thirty-one majority the Republicans quickly adjourned the session. Had the Speaker called the House to order at eleven in the morning, as he was theoretically supposed to, the Democrats might well have managed to put some of their reforms on record, though it was certain that the Senate would have negated their efforts.[36]

Undaunted, Green again levelled his aim at Brayton on the day after the storm. The House Finance Committee had recommended passage of a $30,000 appropriation in addition to the regular outlay for the Rhode Island Exposition Commission of the Jamestown Tercentennial. With this extra money, it was argued, Rhode Island would have a larger part in the Virginia celebration. Green introduced an amendment to this appropriation, requiring that the commissioner give "satisfactory assurance that he will not permit his office there to be used in the manner in which the High Sheriff's Office in the State Capitol is now used."[37]

Green's amendment immediately touched off an acrimonious debate. Green conceded that Rhode Island should be represented at Jamestown, but said that "a good deal was likely to be expended for champagne," and he saw no reason for such a large appropriation. Are we, he asked, "to provide for an occupant of the Sheriff's Office a summer office, as well as a winter residence, such as he now inhabits in the Sheriff's Office?" The money might be better spent, he concluded, in search of a cure of tuberculosis or for placing a portrait of General Nathanael Greene in some conspicuous place. Zenas Bliss, Cranston Republican, answered that the money would be well spent and the interests of the state properly looked after in Jamestown, and Green's amendment was defeated thirty-seven to twenty-eight. The appropriation was approved with the added stipulation that only that part of the $30,000 actually necessary would be spent by the commission.[38]

Green never missed an opportunity to agitate Speaker Burchard. Not long after the incident over the extra $30,000 for the Rhode Island building at Jamestown, Green requested that an eight-page bill dealing with orchard inspection in the state be read aloud to the assembled representatives. He pointed out that he did not really want to take the time of the House on such a trivial matter, but asserted that before the bill was referred to the agricultural committee, he wanted to make certain that there was no $30,000 hidden appropriation for some kind of orchard commission.[39]

The Assembly Democrats came in for praise from *The State* during the session, but the reforming weekly did point out that they had been somewhat lax in fighting to force the Speaker to call the House to order promptly at eleven in the morning. Only Green made this point a continual issue. Two weeks after this mild reprimand by *The State,* this problem came into sharp focus. Burchard had been calling the House to order very close to the noon hour and had indeed often called it into session after twelve. On February 28, House Democrats finally insisted that the chamber could not legally convene after the noon hour. On that day Burchard had brought his gavel down on the Speaker's table at 12:04 P.M., and Democrat Francis Rattey then moved that the Speaker take heed of Rule 1, which set eleven as the time for the call to order. After Burchard ruled Rattey's motion not well taken a second motion was made and seconded by Green. After a

bitter debate over the point, Burchard prevailed and the motion
was defeated. The Democrats were determined, however, to teach
Burchard a lesson.[40]

Shortly before 11:15 on the next day, Green, seeing that the
House was not going to be convened within the hour, asked the
Recording Clerk, Charles H. Howland, to call the House to order. The clerk, taken by surprise, made no reply and Green again
asked him to convene the House. Again the clerk sat mute and
Green then demanded, "Mr. Clerk, will you or will you not call
the House to order?" Astounded, the clerk could only answer that
he would have to think it over and he remained sitting without
doing anything. Green thereupon strode to the Speaker's chair
and himself called the House to order. On the motion of Lewis
A. Waterman, seconded by another Democrat, James Murphy of
Central Falls, Green was elected Speaker of the House, pro
tempore. On motion of Burrillville's Democratic Representative
John Lace, seconded by Pawtucket Democrat Joseph McDonald,
Lewis A. Waterman was unanimously elected Reading Clerk, pro
tempore. Waterman then read the roll and seventeen Representatives, all Democrats, answered as present. Declaring that no
quorum was present, Green then stated that the chair could entertain only a motion for adjournment. McDonald so moved and
after a second by Jesse Metcalf, the House officially or semi-offi-
cially adjourned.

At 11:50 A.M., thirty-five minutes after the start of Green's temporary take-over, Burchard, followed by the Republicans, marched
into the chamber, mounted the rostrum, called the House to order, and asked Reading Clerk Raymond G. Mowry to call the
roll. Though there were many Democrats on the floor, only three
answered as present. Nevertheless, since more than thirty-six
members answered, there was a legal quorum, and to make sure
of it, Speaker Burchard ordered Mowry to read the names of
those who had responded to the roll call. Mowry read the name
of Hogan, to which the Providence Democrat violently objected,
saying that he had not answered the roll. Lewis A. Waterman,
who had also refused to answer the roll, immediately rose to his
feet to claim that the second session of the day was illegal. There-

upon Burchard asked him if he wished to be recorded as present, pointing out that if he were not present, he could not be granted recognition to speak and should therefore sit down. Waterman replied that he was only seeking information dealing with a parliamentary procedure, but Burchard refused to allow him to speak further. To repay the Democrats for their attempt to embarrass him, the Speaker even had Democrats recorded as present who were not on the floor at all, including Richard Herrick, a Woonsocket undertaker. As Mowry read the roll, Herrick (who had been listening from the outside hall) entered the chamber and began to object to the entire proceedings. Burchard simply ignored him. Meantime, Green and Waterman kept changing seats to harass Burchard even further.⁴¹

Although the Democrats had made their point, the outcome was general confusion. Had there been only one legal session that day or two? Legally it mattered little, though one observer noted in the *Providence Journal* that "sum iv th' Dimmycrats tried t' shtart a little house iv Riprisintives all be thimsilves." A few days later Green moved to place in the minutes of the *House Journal* of March 1 the entire proceedings of that day, in order to put on the record the fact that the Democrats had made a point of Burchard's failure to call the House to order on time. Waterman defended Green's motion, stating that the Democrats had not intended taking over the House as a joke, but to emphasize the "shameful conditions" that had been allowed to continue for so long; "nothing but heroic measures," he asserted, could have been employed. Unsurprisingly, Green's motion was laid on the table by a straight party vote. In the long run, however, Green did gain his point, for the proceedings of March 5, the day he made his motion, were included in that day's *House Journal* and these minutes told the story of March 1.⁴²

Some of Green's efforts were more serious and more successful. Two of his bills amending the election laws to make it easier to prosecute illegal voting were finally passed after being recommended by the Committee on Elections. Both bills went through the Assembly without much difficulty. One bill provided for a fine up to $1,000 and imprisonment up to two years for fraudulent voting. Any voter casting more than one ballot was subject to criminal action under this law. The other bill provided the same penalties for any kind of bribery of a qualified voter.[43]

One interesting aspect of the passage of these bills was that Green noted on his personal copies of the original bills that they were to be carefully checked against the final act, to ensure that the act as printed by the Secretary of State corresponded with the act passed by the legislature. This careful watchfulness on Green's part arose from his experience on the Committee of Engrossed Acts. A week earlier, he had objected to the custom of having bills approved by the legislature before they were actually printed and counter-read by the Committee of Engrossed Acts. He claimed that the committee was a sham, that it employed a clerk for $600 who more often than not permitted Republicans to take out bills which had not been properly certified. On the particular measure before the House at that time, that had occurred. When Green had objected, Representative Allen, one of Green's most consistent adversaries, claimed that a bill was first passed and then engrossed. He was quite wrong, and Green easily won this parliamentary point.[44]

Throughout the debates over the annual appropriations bill Green challenged every ambiguous wording that might be misconstrued, and item after item received his attention. Naturally, the Republican majority approved no changes in the text of the appropriations act, but Green's activities toward this end were no less consistent. For example, he moved that the Providence Sheriff's salary of $5,000 be inclusive of any and all fees paid him. It was commonly believed, with some measure of proof, that the deputy sheriffs had to "kick back" to the Sheriff a goodly portion of their salaries. The argument was that Sheriff White required each of his twenty deputies to contribute $200 annually to ensure their continued employment. Green proposed that all such "fees" be reckoned a part of the annual salary of the Sheriff. John Hogan also berated White for the manner in which he conducted his office. These efforts were futile; the item dealing with the Sheriff and his office passed by a straight party vote.[45]

Green's purpose in scrutinizing the appropriations bill was to make certain that all moneys appropriated would be carefully spent and not used "to provide a job for a political heeler." Another example illustrates his point. In the appropriation for the State Militia there was an item of $16,000 for "miscellaneous expenses." Green wanted to know how this sum was arrived at, inasmuch as there was no specific itemization in the bill. Zenas Bliss informed Green that the State Auditor determined how these funds were spent. Green charged that this was very "unbusinesslike," saying that "such an arbitrary power of spending money ought not to be given to any man, even though he be a more competent man than the State Auditor." Speaker Burchard then attempted to cut Green off by stating that he had been trying for some time to "discern some lucidity in the remarks of the gentleman from Providence" but did not think he could do so. Caustically, Green answered that he doubted if the Speaker would ever be able to do so.

Defeated in his effort to reduce this appropriation, Green then offered an amendment which required signed requisitions from all department heads who used any part of the money. Zenas Bliss, who was chairman of the Finance Committee, said that such a requirement would cause all sorts of abuses and that the whole idea was irrelevant. When the day ended, the Democrats had lost on all major parts of the appropriations bill. It was passed relatively unchanged from the original proposals put forth by the Finance Committee.[46]

Another matter considered by the 1907 session of the legislature was petitions for the constitutional initiative. Invariably, after being presented by a Democratic assemblyman, such petitions were referred to the Committee on Special Legislation, where they remained throughout the session. The proposals generally followed the same pattern. They usually requested that a small percentage of the voters be enabled to submit any constitutional amendment directly to the legislature; thus, for example, an amendment to abolish the rotten-borough system could have been petitioned by the people, promoting manhood suffrage and the "end of corporation rule." The Committee on Special Legislation did report out one bill proposing an amendment to the state constitution granting the initiative and referendum to the people. Despite many petitions supporting the amendment, the committee recommended indefinite postponement. Democrats spoke fervently for changing the constitution, arguing that the rotten-borough system enabled 3 per cent of the people to negate progress in the state. Joseph McDonald emphasized the fact that Roswell Burchard was Speaker of the House by virtue of only a slim 121 votes, as he came from Little Compton and had been elected without opposition, whereas a "member from Providence was placed in office by the votes of several thousands of electors." Francis X. L. Rattey scored the Special Legislation Committee for daring to recommend postponement of the measure and for failing to trust the people of the state. John Hogan told the Republicans that "you on the opposite side of this house fear the people and we on this side trust them." Green, too, defended the right of the people to have the initiative and referendum. But the House adjourned without taking any action, and on the following day it rejected the proposal by seven votes. As the *Providence Journal* had predicted, the constitutional initiative was "once more relegated to the obscurity that has been its lot in recent years."[42]

Democrats in the House also tried to abolish property qualification for voting. In late March they caucused to discuss such a bill that Green was to introduce. Most agreed that property qualifications should be abolished, but Green also included in his bill the provision that "a voter physically able to vote should not be permitted to receive assistance in voting." To overcome the resistance he had met when he made his proposal in January, Green expanded his arguments. Those who must receive assistance, he argued, fell into two categories. The first was the man who actually could not make his mark on the ballot "although he only needs to distinguish between an eagle and a star" so as to place a cross in the circle under the label. Such a voter was incapable of knowing whether the supervisor who assisted him had marked his ballot as the voter desired. Too, the supervisor could and often did inform employers how illiterate voters sought to vote. The second kind of voter needing "assistance," Green said, was he who had sold his vote and had to call the supervisor only to show that he had voted the right way. Green's proposal would eliminate this form of corruption. The Democrats were again divided on the issue, however, and after some argument they struck the controversial provision. The caucus then voted unanimously to submit the amended proposition to the Assembly. Again the effort was vain; when Green submitted the resolution it was promptly referred to the Committee on Special Legislation, where it expired.[48]

The most significant of all Republican proposals in the 1907 session came from Zenas Bliss, who introduced two resolutions. The first was a constitutional amendment providing for redistricting the state to increase the lower house to a hundred members, with a proviso that no city or town could have more than a fourth of the total representation. The purpose of the measure was not electoral reform, but maintaining tight Republican control over the legislature by limiting Providence's representation. Bliss' second measure would have given the governor the right to veto certain legislation, exclusive of appropriations, and would have required a three-fifths vote of both houses to over-ride a veto.[49]

The Committee on Special Legislation recommended passage of Bliss' veto power resolution but did not report out the proposal to increase the size of the House. Like all amendments to the state constitution, the veto measure required a vote of two-thirds of the House for approval. Green and others objected to Bliss' proposal on the ground that the governor should have the power to veto all bills and resolutions, and it failed to obtain the necessary majority.[50]

As the legislative session neared its end there was still a dead-lock over the choice of United States senator. The Democrats held their line firmly, and the Republicans continued to be split between Wetmore and Colt. The House voted for the final adjournment to take place on Tuesday, April 23, and after much maneuvering the Senate followed suit. If Rhode Island was to have its second senator, the Republicans would have to settle their differences in short order. Brayton dispatched letters to all Re-

publican assemblymen urging a decision, and the Republican
State Executive Committee issued a call for an emergency caucus. Even so, the Grand Committee could not agree and no candidate received a majority of the votes cast on April 23, despite
the taking of no less than twenty-five ballots. In sixty-three legislative days, eighty-one ballots had been taken, an all-time high.[51]

The Assembly adjourned a little past midnight on April 24. At
12:10 A.M., after the House had completed its own legislative
business and while its members were waiting for the Senate to
send word that it was also through, the Democrats held a mock
session. Green called the "House" to order and Tim Myers was
elected the House poet laureate. He read a poem, which Green
had written, entitled "The Labor Clerk," a satire on the attempt
of the Republicans to employ a permanent labor clerk for the
newly created Committee on Labor. The Democrats then nominated Charles Brayton for United States senator, "declaring that
was the only way he could be gotten rid of." After several other
comical actions, including an impeachment or two, the upper
house sent word that it had concurred in adjournment, and at
12:30 A.M. the 1907 legislature was at an end.[52]

It had been a meaningful session despite the absence of reform
legislation. For one thing, the House Democrats had their public
say on several important matters. For another, General Brayton
had been defied and defeated for the first time. The 1907 session,
said the *Providence Journal,* would be noted for the actual de-
thronement of Brayton. He had entered the Sheriff's Office on the
last legislative day to direct personally the contest for Colt, who
had been finally backed by the Republican State Executive Committee. Habit would normally have dictated obedience on the
part of the Republican legislators, but for once Brayton did not
have his way. "His chagrin was perceptible even to the casual
passerby who happened to glance into the Sheriff's Office."[53]

After the session Green traveled to Europe. While he was
there, he decided that he should devote more time to his law
practice, and that he should bide his time before embarking on
another campaign. But the experience had been instructive. The
insights he gained as a legislator proved invaluable for his later

political campaigns and his successful years as governor and United States senator from 1933 to 1960. The friendships he made among his Democratic colleagues also stood him in good stead for the years ahead. As personal accomplishments for Rhode Island in 1907, Green could claim only two minor acts dealing with fraudulent voting practices. Nevertheless, starting with his 1906 campaign, he had begun to learn the most difficult of all arts, the art of politics.

Chapter **III**

The Campaign Drive to 1912

No tears shed! ———THEODORE FRANCIS GREEN

DESPITE Green's announcement, Providence Democrats again nominated him for representative-at-large. Before the convention could approve the entire slate for the Assembly, however, Richard Comstock informed the delegates that Green had authorized him to say that because of pressing business engagements, it was impossible for him to accept the nomination. Accordingly, Comstock withdrew Green's name and substituted that of John C. Pegram. Jesse Metcalf's name was also withdrawn, ostensibly for the same reason that Green's had been, and Olney Arnold II, an East Sider of high social standing, was put in his place.[1]

Though not a candidate himself, Green did campaign vigorously for the Democratic ticket. The Democrats had nominated Governor Higgins for re-election; his opponent was the Republican Lieutenant Governor, Frederick H. Jackson. But again the important part of the race was for the Assembly. At the Democratic ratification rally in the latter part of October, Green admitted that the legislative results of the 1907 Assembly had been "pitifully meagre." On the other hand, he said, there had been other effects of "great and lasting importance." First, the people of Rhode Island were now interested in State House events as never before, and, second, the Democratic Party had proved that it could be relied upon for consistent action, wisdom, and restraint. Finally, there had been a lessening of the power of Brayton, who had been openly defied on the floor. Green appealed to all to vote once again for the entire Democratic ticket, which was

40

pledged to continue the fight against "boss" rule and to advance the cause of Goddard.[2]

Feeling that it was time to show that he did not possess the power Democrats had been accusing him of, Brayton sent an open letter to Frederick H. Jackson, promising not to occupy the Sheriff's Office during the ensuing legislative session. Brayton pledged his support to Jackson and vowed that he would do nothing that might give the Democrats reason to fling charges of corruption at the Republican Party. He did this, he wrote, to keep the party from being embarrassed even though he himself had done nothing unethical. He was "first of all, a Republican" and had attended the Sheriff's Office in the past to prove to Democratic Governor Higgins that he had a perfect right to perform his duties for his "clients," appearing in the State House on behalf of their interests "with the management of matters pending before the Legislature and its Committees." He had even attended the sessions, continued Brayton, at a great inconvenience to himself. Nevertheless, if Jackson thought his activities were harmful to the party, Brayton said, he would cease visiting the Sheriff's Office.[3]

Green took up the challenge. At a Democratic rally in Providence several days later, he pointed out that Brayton had promised only to give up his attendance in the Sheriff's Office, not the State House itself. Furthermore, Brayton had not promised to cease representing his clients on legislation before the Assembly, nor had he promised to refrain from consulting with its members on political matters. Green attacked the Republican platform as well, stating that the two reforms it called for, larger representation in the legislature for cities and towns and the veto power for the governor, were so ambiguously worded that it was impossible to know their real meaning. When Democrats had introduced similar bills in the 1907 session, Republican-dominated committees had buried them. Green went on to claim that Republicans probably did not even understand what they meant by enlarged representation. Zenas Bliss' bill granting the governor the veto power had been nothing more than a "bunco-veto" measure, for it withheld the power to veto resolutions, the method used for voting appropriation bills. Charging that the Republicans had changed only their candidate for governor, not their policies, Green called upon his fellow-citizens to rise up, enter the halls of the legislature, "overthrow the tables of money-changers and cast out them that sell and buy laws."[4]

Five days later in Harrisville, Green warned Democrats not to overemphasize Brayton's personality, for it was Braytonism, not Brayton alone, that had to be routed out. Conditions which made possible a renewal of bossism and corruption must be altered, and this could be done only by making fundamental changes in the state constitution. Realization of that ideal could come about only through a victory of the Democratic Party throughout the state. At another meeting Green emphasized the fact that though his election-fraud and bribery bills had passed the previous legislature, a Democratic victory was now needed to see to it that the laws were enforced.[5]

The outcome of the election was much like the outcome in 1906. Higgins was re-elected governor, increasing his plurality by 900 votes, even though, despite an increase in the number of registered voters, 400 fewer votes were cast than in 1906. Again, however, the rest of the statewide ticket was Republican, and again Republicans carried both houses of the Assembly, gaining five seats in the House and losing two in the Senate. Providence sent an all-Democratic representation to the House, but Pawtucket returned all Republicans, completely reversing its 1906 pattern. (Pawtucket was the home base of rigged elections and "strange" doings in the counting of ballots. James L. Jenks, defeated in his bid for re-election as state senator from that city, wrote Theodore Francis Green, a week after the election, that he had been "amazed at the return." Doubting that the returning board would bring about any reversal of the vote, Jenks only regretted that so many good votes would be lost for Goddard in the Grand Committee.)[6]

The 1908 legislature was notable for two things: it finally elected a United States senator, and it engendered a bitter battle over Bliss' constitutional amendments. The fight had taken on a new aspect in June of 1907, when Samuel Pomeroy Colt unconditionally withdrew as a candidate. In withdrawing, Colt gave as his reasons ill health, the press of business, and his desire not to disrupt party unity. With Colt out of the running, and the Democrats holding even less numerical power in the Grand Committee, Wetmore was finally elected United States senator over Goddard on January 21, 1908, with 68 out of the 109 votes cast.[7]

The proposed constitutional amendments would have granted the veto power to the governor and reapportioned and redistricted the membership of the lower house. These measures occupied much time and debate in the Committee on Judiciary, to which they were committed. Republican legislative leaders had decided that if the governor was to receive any effective veto power, the state would first have to be carefully redistricted. Dividing the state into 100 electoral districts would necessitate an artful gerrymander to ensure the continuation of Republican control in the legislature, which, in turn, would render the veto power meaningless. If the governor were a Democrat the Republicans could easily override his veto; if a Republican, he would be under the domination of the machine. Accordingly, Republican leaders combined these reforms into a single package, and as one amendment they were assigned to the Judiciary Committee for further study. Democrats, seeing through the scheme, charged the Republicans with duplicity and the matter was bitterly fought over on the Senate floor.

When the Republicans met in a state convention to select delegates for the coming national convention in Chicago, a tumultuous argument broke out over the issue of this amendment. Some of the more reform-minded Republicans fought for the separation of the two proposals into two amendments. The Brayton forces maintained control, however, and a motion to adjourn the convention was passed even as one of the advocates of two amendments was endeavoring to gain recognition. Later, House Republicans, meeting in caucus, also voted down the separation of the amendments, averring "no district system, no veto." But disagreement among Republicans was kept alive when their 1908 gubernatorial candidate, Aram Pothier, announced that he personally stood for the two separate amendments. To make the matter even more confusing, the Republican State Executive Chairman and the

Republican Providence Assembly candidates decided that for
campaign purposes they would back Pothier.[8]

That Pothier could differ with Brayton on this issue did not,
however, mean that the Boss had lost his touch. Indeed, the
choice of Pothier was a shrewd one. Democratic Governor Higgins having decided to retire, the Democrats nominated Olney
Arnold II to succeed him and attempted to win the French vote
by choosing the ex-Mayor of Woonsocket, Adelard Archambault,
for lieutenant governor. In a studied design to divide Democratic
loyalties, Brayton countered with Pothier, another Frenchman.
As one writer has observed, "The continued dominance of the
Democratic Party by Irish politicians had already produced grum-
bling among Franco-Americans, and the nomination of Pothier
postponed the consolidation of the ranks of the immigrant
groups."[9]

The 1908 elections were a Republican landslide. They swept
the state and the nation, and in Rhode Island they even captured
the mayorships of Providence, Central Falls, and Pawtucket.
Woonsocket split its vote, electing a French Democrat mayor but
giving Pothier a thumping victory over Arnold, whereas it had
voted for Higgins the year before, when no Frenchman was in the
race. Democrats also took a severe beating in the General Assembly, capturing only six Senate seats and only six of the seventy-
two seats in the lower house. The cause of reform seemed set back
on its heels.[10]

In the new legislature the Republicans closed ranks and passed
—and submitted for popular ratification—three constitutional
amendments which, though ostensibly reforms, were actually
blatant efforts to perpetuate Republican control of the state. The
first of these amendments increased the size of the House of Representatives to a hundred members and provided that every city
and town have at least one representative but that none have
more than a fourth of the total. Another feature of this amendment provided that, in cities with more than one representative,
House members would be elected by districts instead of all being
chosen at large, as had been the case. The second amendment
provided that the lieutenant governor, instead of the governor,

would preside over the Senate. The third gave the governor power, with a few minor exceptions, to veto all bills, resolutions, and votes, and permitted the legislature to override a gubernatorial veto with a three-fifths majority. The governor was also given a "pocket-veto" power much like that of the President of the United States. Surprisingly, these three amendments passed unanimously.[11]

It has been claimed that the amendments "developed directly out of the anti-Brayton sentiment" fairly common at the time, but in actual fact, Brayton probably engineered them. In any event, he was far from worried that ratification of the new amendments would harm his party. Indeed, at an address in October, 1909, the elated Republican boss stated that the redistricting amendment could be worked out "so that Democrats would never have more than 25 out of the 100 members in the House of Representatives." With utter frankness Brayton declared that Newport would have one district "so black with Democrats that we could never elect a Republican, but we would pack all of the Democrats into that district and the other three districts would always be Republican." Essentially the same thing, he added, could be done in Warwick, Pawtucket, and Valley Falls. In Providence, the Democrats would be "crowded into five districts," leaving twenty for the Republicans. The Republican Party could accomplish in the lower house what had been done with the Providence City Council, where Democrats rarely held more than two wards.[12]

Democratic leaders campaigned hard, but in vain, for the defeat of the redistricting amendment. In the 1909 elections, all three amendments carried and Republicans won all the statewide offices. Aram Pothier was re-elected governor—after pledging to use his new veto power to prevent gerrymandering in the redistricting—and Zenas Bliss was elected as the first lieutenant governor to preside over the State Senate. Democrats did gain two seats in the lower house—with the election from Providence of James J. Nolan and George F. O'Shaunessy, soon to be a political rival of Theodore Francis Green—but Republican majorities were still overwhelming.[13]

Democratic leaders, Green among them, now attempted to head off the expected gerrymander. Republican leaders were planning to place only two Democrats on a seven-man board to redistrict the state. After a brief debate in the legislature, a bill was passed setting up a nine-man board, but the Democrats failed when they attempted to make it mandatory for the governor to appoint five persons from the majority and four from the minority.[14]

Neither the Democrats' fears nor Brayton's confidence, as it turned out, was justified, possibly because Brayton himself fell ill during the year and died in September. At any rate, gross gerrymandering failed to materialize. As expected, Governor Pothier, on February 22, appointed a board consisting of six Republicans, two Democrats, and one Lincolnian, but he surprised the Democrats by the calibre of his choices. Democrats in the Assembly appeared satisfied with the Republicans chosen and found no fault with the other three. The *Providence Journal* congratulated the Governor "on his good judgment" in choosing "a representative body of self-respecting citizens" who would not be "political gerrymanderers." The Redistricting Commission speedily did its work; before the end of August its report was submitted to and passed by a special session of the legislature. In the reapportionment Providence received twenty-five seats in the lower house, Pawtucket ten, Woonsocket eight, Newport, Central Falls, and Warwick five each, and Cranston four. The *Journal,* complimenting the board for its fine work, stated that there had been no gerrymandering and that all the districts had followed natural lines.[15]

Curiously, this turn of events revitalized the reform impulse in the Democratic Party. Crushed by their defeats in 1908 and 1909, Democrats had feared that they could never make a comeback. When Brayton's scheme collapsed—and when Brayton himself died—they began to believe again that they might have a chance. Thus in 1910, for the first time in three years, they entered the campaign in earnest. Theodore Francis Green's part in that campaign was an unsuccessful bid for the Democratic nomination for Congress from the First Congressional District.

The First District—containing about one-third of Providence and all of the towns of the eastern shore—had been captured two years earlier by Republican William P. Sheffield, who had defeated Democratic incumbent Daniel Granger by the narrow margin of eighty-one votes. In mid-1910 Green's friends began to tout him for the position. He was not alone; George F. O'Shaunessy, one of the two Democrats from Providence in the State House of Representatives, was regarded as a major contender for the congressional seat, as was Green's friend Richard Comstock, though Comstock soon withdrew in Green's favor. In September, Mayor Patrick J. Boyle of Newport announced his candidacy.[16]

For a time, Green refused to commit himself, protesting that he had not as yet thoroughly considered the matter. His hesitancy derived at least in part from practical considerations. Providence, having fifty of the eighty-six votes in the First District convention, was all-important, and Green was sure of only the Second and Tenth Wards. O'Shaunessy had solid support from Providence's Seventh and Ninth Wards. Boyle's strength was apparently confined to Newport, where he had been elected mayor several times and where he commanded a tight organization. Another reason for Green's hesitancy was that he had not yet been completely accepted by all Democrats as being really one of them. The Democratic Party was strongly dominated by Irish Catholics and in some ways Green, although recognized for his ability, was viewed with suspicion by many of them. As one unnamed Democrat said, Green was probably the best possible candidate for Congress—and certainly far superior to O'Shaunessy, who was a newcomer to Rhode Island and was generally considered a "Tammany Hall" man—but "some Democrats maybe do not think he is sufficiently partisan."[17]

One Republican summed up the Democratic problem as follows. He discounted Boyle completely as not strong enough outside of Newport. Green, he surmised, would receive the largest independent vote of any candidate, but there was some doubt that he could hold on to the straight Democratic vote and also carry Newport. O'Shaunessy would also get the Irish Catholic vote and "some Italian and other votes that would probably not go to

Green." All in all, Sheffield had more to fear from O'Shaunessy than from Green. But it was generally conceded that Boyle had the balance of power in the state convention, and he could throw his support either way.[18]

Just before the convention in late September, Green finally announced that he was a candidate for the nomination but would "not make the slightest contest to obtain it." In addition to having the support of the party organization in Providence's Tenth and Second Wards, Green now had the personal blessings of ex-Congressman Granger and the *Providence Journal,* and just as the convention opened, it was rumored that the chairman, John J. Fitzgerald, was in league with him and that Boyle's contingent was ready to throw its weight to Green.[19]

The efforts were for naught: by a slim margin, O'Shaunessy won the nomination on the first ballot. Showing his characteristic humor and ability to bounce back from defeat with grace, Green noted on the top of an acceptance speech he had prepared, "Later —this speech was still-born. Dr. O'Shaunessy in attendance. No tears shed." He pledged his support, and during the campaign he spoke regularly for O'Shaunessy as well as the rest of the Democratic ticket.[20]

The election bore out the prediction of one of Green's backers that the First Congressional seat was "the only office the Democrats are sure of winning." O'Shaunessy unseated Congressman Sheffield by 1,851 votes. Otherwise, Republicans carried the state, re-electing Pothier, winning the other statewide offices, and capturing the Second Congressional seat. Even so, Democrats had reason to be encouraged. They cut Republican pluralities greatly, and they made a respectable showing in the Assembly races. Republicans took sixty-two of the seats in the new 100-member lower house, a much smaller percentage than they were accustomed to winning, and lost ground though retaining control in the Senate. Too, the redistricting worked out fairly, as Democrats won sixteen of the twenty-five assembly seats from Providence and Democrat Addison P. Munroe, a Providence grocer, won the Senate seat from Providence. Finally, the proceedings of the new Assembly demonstrated that the Republicans, without a boss to direct them, could no longer maintain strict party opposition to reform.[21]

Republicans had no difficulty choosing Henry F. Lippitt, a wealthy manufacturer, as the successor to retiring Senator Nelson W. Aldrich, but they were unable to hold together to defeat a proposed constitutional amendment changing from annual to biennial elections. Even on the Democrat's perennial proposal, a constitutional amendment to abolish the property qualification for voting, eight Republicans bolted the party and voted affirmatively with the Democrats. On still other issues, including an important tax bill, the Republicans proved unable to maintain strict party lines. Furthermore, House Democrats managed to prolong the session by parliamentary maneuvers and filibustering tactics.[22]

In the 1911 elections Democrats were split over the biennial-election amendment. Green himself—after turning down a nomination for alderman and accepting, with relish, an invitation from the almost exclusively Irish Executive Committee of the Democratic State Central Committee to take active part in the campaign—opposed the amendment on the ground that it was not well written. He felt that the biennial-election system, coinciding with national elections, would make it "more difficult to give state elections the attention they deserved," and would also lengthen the time it would take to secure a more important reform, the abolition of property qualifications. Despite such objections, the voters approved the amendment by a large majority.[23]

And, despite the death of Brayton and their lack of discipline in the legislature, the Republicans won another substantial victory in 1911. A week after the election Lewis A. Waterman, the defeated Democratic gubernatorial candidate, wrote a despairing letter to Green. "I do not regret the outcome so much for myself," he said, "but because it makes the outlook for decent government so dismal. It does seem at times as if Rhode Islanders were the easiest and most willing dupes in the universe. . . . Next year it is some other person's turn to make the sacrifice of time and energy."[24] Green would be that "other person" in 1912.

The background of Green's nomination for governor was a com-

plex struggle for power inside the Democratic party. Congressman O'Shaunessy sought to replace his erstwhile ally, ex-Mayor
George W. Greene of Woonsocket, as Democratic National Committeeman from Rhode Island. So bitter did the ensuing squabble
become that the Democrats, in an effort to prevent a convention
fight, resorted for the first time to a direct primary to choose between them and to elect delegates to the forthcoming national
convention. Theodore Francis Green sided with O'Shaunessy, as
did Chairman Frank Fitzsimmons of the State Central Committee, Mayor Boyle of Newport, and another Newporter, Peter
Goelet Gerry. (Gerry, the grandson of Elbridge Gerry—a signer
of the Declaration of Independence, vice-president under Madi-
son, and the man after whom the gerrymander was named—was
thus making the debut of a long and successful political career,
after having moved to Newport at Green's suggestion.)[25]

Green sought to be a delegate to the national convention because he wanted to support Woodrow Wilson, whom he warmly
admired, and though committed to O'Shaunessy, he wisely avoided
attacking George Greene personally. Instead, he talked of the
virtue of the direct primary—which O'Shaunessy espoused and
Greene opposed—and berated the Republicans for their refusal
to adopt it. (Green called the handpicked Republican delegates
to their national convention a "wonderful aggregation of old political hacks and young society beaux, who were there to take the
joy ride to Chicago"; a Republican newspaper retorted that Green
"almost fit into both those classes himself, being a bit too young
for one and a bit too old for the other.")[26]

Green won the gubernatorial nomination in 1912 largely because of the way he handled himself throughout this hectic contest. Everything seemed to go wrong—first O'Shaunessy lost to
Greene in the primary; then he lost an acrimonious struggle to
negate the voters' decision by claiming, in the national convention, that there had been fraudulent manipulation in the primary;
and to top it all, the Rhode Island delegation was pledged to
Champ Clark instead of Wilson—but through each apparent reversal Green gained ground. In campaigning for the primary, he
ingratiated himself with the O'Shaunessy faction without alienat-

ing the Greene faction. Selected as an alternate to the national convention, he impressed everyone with his personality, his wit and charm, and his ease as a mixer, despite the explosiveness of the circumstances. And because he was one of the state's earliest and staunchest backers of Wilson, he gained by Wilson's nomination.[27]

Another national event made it seem that the nomination would be a plum rather than the bitter pill it had been to Waterman in 1910. Ex-President Theodore Roosevelt, angered by his loss to President Taft at the Republican National Convention, bolted the party and accepted nomination by a special Progressive convention, and his candidacy as a Progressive promised to split normal Republican votes in state elections as well as the national election. It thus appeared that, for the first time in years, the Democrats had an excellent chance to carry Rhode Island. Accordingly, there were several aspirants for the Democratic gubernatorial nomination, notably Theodore Francis Green, State Senator Addison P. Munroe of Providence, and John J. Fitzgerald of Pawtucket, who had led the George W. Greene faction at the Democratic National Convention.[28]

Green, declining an appeal by Theodore Roosevelt's son to join the Progressives, worked hard for the nomination. A serious struggle threatened but failed to materialize, as one by one the other contenders dropped out of the race. The state convention, meeting on October 10, nominated Green without opposition, partly because of the events of the year and partly because he was the only prominent Yankee in the state who had remained loyal to the party through its lean years. Ex-Governor Higgins was nominated for the United States Senate, former State Senator Sumner Mowry of South Kingstown was nominated for lieutenant governor, Congressman O'Shaunessy was renominated from the First District, and Peter G. Gerry was selected as the party's choice for Congress from the Second District. For the new Third District, created when the state gained a seat through reapportionment after the 1910 census, the Democrats nominated former State Representative Francis X. L. Rattey of Central Falls.[29]

The Democratic platform urged the defeat of the "political-

commercial oligarchy" that ruled Rhode Island and called for
sweeping reforms. It declared in favor of redistribution of the
seats in the State Senate, the direct election of United States senators, adoption of the initiative and referendum, the granting of
the appointive power to the governor, and the abolition of property qualifications for voting. In contrast to its Republican counterpart, the Democratic platform also pledged the enactment of a
law establishing a fifty-four-hour work week for women and children, and another requiring all legislative committees to report
all bills submitted to them during a legislative session.[30]

The Republican State Convention chose, in the main, a seasoned
slate of vote-getters. As expected, Governor Pothier was renominated. Roswell B. Burchard, former Speaker and Green's old target in the 1907 House of Representatives, was nominated for
lieutenant governor. Former Congressman William P. Sheffield
was chosen to stand again for Congress from the First District
and former Governor Utter from the Second. For the new Third
District—which contained part of Providence, the cities of Woonsocket and Pawtucket, and the town of Cumberland—the Republicans nominated Ambrose Kennedy, an assemblyman from Woonsocket since 1910. Finally, they endorsed Judge Lebaron B. Colt
for the United States Senate. Their platform endorsed Taft and
the protective tariff and skirted most reform issues. On the controversial fifty-four-hour law, it promised only "giving special and
serious attention to the question," even though Pothier himself had
urged the convention to endorse the measure outright.[31]

The *Providence Journal* supported Green for governor. In an
editorial it called Green "an uphill fighter, a supporter of every
good public cause and a man who cannot be persuaded or intimi-
dated into any act which is against the interests of the people."
Moreover, it said, Green would be an efficient governor who
"would fill the office with great honor to himself and great benefit to the state." The editor and general manager of the paper
wrote Green that his chances were excellent and reminded him
that he had once introduced Green as "the next Governor of
Rhode Island."[32]

The Republican *Providence Tribune,* on the other hand, called the Democratic choice an unfortunate one. After Green's name, the *Tribune* always tacked the initials A.M. to signify the paper's disdain for his master's degree. An editorial called Green "an excellent young man who wore his trouser legs turned up like the college sophomore; from whose mental processes his own are not infinitely remote."[33]

Following the custom of the time, Green accepted his party's nomination by a letter to the chairman of the State Central Committee. He promised economy and efficiency if he were elected, but he paid greatest attention to expressing his independence from bosses and factions, and his freedom from obligations to any interests except those of the people. These assertions elicited sharp criticism from a well-meaning citizen of Rhode Island. In a personal letter, Luke O'Connor challenged Green's freedom from political bossism, charging that whether Green realized it or not, he had himself been the mere tool of political bosses. Republican political leaders, O'Connor asserted, controlled Pawtucket Democrats through John J. Fitzgerald, and it was Fitzgerald's stepping aside that had made Green's nomination possible. O'Connor added that it was people like Green, "Rhode Islanders to the bone," who permitted such deplorable conditions to exist. Stung to the quick, Green answered that he was unfettered by corrupt associations and that he would seek advice from wise counsel once he was elected. O'Connor, surprised that Green would even tender a reply, answered that he would accept Green's word that he would not be subject to dictation if elected, but suggested that Green never seek advice from anyone while carrying out the duties of his office. To do so, he said, would be infantile and would mean being influenced by others, if only indirectly.[34]

This exchange is cited as an early indication of a tender spot in Green's personality. He always wanted to be considered his own man, his own boss, his own master, and accordingly he was always wary of long intimate attachments to anyone. His desire along these lines is exemplified by his repeated praise of such independent spirits as Nathanael Greene, his idol Roger Williams, and the subject of his intense personal study, Thomas Wilson Dorr. These letters from O'Connor, safely kept by Green all his life, had hit a sensitive chord in his make-up.

Another illuminating letter Green received after his nomination came from a member of his own law firm. Rush Sturges told Green in a clear, incisive script that he felt qualified to pass on Green's personal characteristics. He did so not with malice, he said, but with a view toward aiding Green to see himself as others did. Sturges criticized Green for excessive use of sarcasm and "unnecessarily hostile" words to stress his points of view. Such use of the language, wrote Sturges, was rooted in Green's own thin skinned personality. Green jibed at people at times because he was not "kindly and sympathetic in matters of a personal nature."[35]

Green was besieged with advice as well as personal letters. Joseph McDonald, former Democratic Representative from Pawtucket, suggested that "it would be good politics to bring out as strongly as possible that the Republican Party of Rhode Island was practically a part of the mill equipment of the state and, as such, was financed by the manufacturers." From Brown University came letters from President Faunce; history professor and well-known advocate of political reform William MacDonald; the beloved Professor of English Walter Bronson (who jocularly wrote Green that he would not make public the fact that Green had authored the inscription to the undergraduates on the 1887 gate at Brown); and Zechariah Chafee, Brown University's great gift to those who champion free speech in America. Even some prominent Republicans—notably R. L. Beeckman—sent good wishes, though few offered support or advice.[36]

Green decided to focus his campaign on six major issues—the high protective tariff and its effect on Rhode Island, the fifty-four-hour-a-week proposal, the state's financial position, the continuation of property qualifications for voting and the rotten-borough system, the question of graft in Rhode Island's state government, and boss rule in the Republican Party.

Green attacked the high tariff policies of the Republican Party at a rally in Barrington, explaining that when a tariff was imposed on an import the tax was indirectly passed on to the consumer who bought it. He was careful to say that the Democratic Party did not advocate abolition of all tariffs, for before the passage of the Sixteenth Amendment, import duties were "the principal source of our national revenue." Still, said Green, a balance had to be struck. All agreed that consumers had to be taxed to put money into the national treasury, but they should not be taxed "to put money into the pockets of the manufacturers." Green was not against tariff protection for infant industries, but he was strongly opposed to enriching well-established manufacturers at the expense of both the government and the consumer. Too, Green saw other evils as being "attendant upon the tariff." It "encourages the formation of trusts," he said, "with the resulting elimination of competition and ruin of small dealers." Again, though manufacturers claimed that the tariff protected laborers as well as capitalists, such was rarely the case. Indeed, very low wages were often found in the most highly protected industries. Clearly, Green concluded, the tariff does not give "employees with one hand nearly as much as it takes away with the other."[37]

Green's attacks on the tariff were not unanswered. The Tariff Publicity League, an organization of manufacturers and businessmen in Rhode Island, directed the fight against the Democratic charges. Their main weapon was newspaper advertisements arguing that whenever tariffs had been reduced, wages had also declined. The League emphasized that under President Cleveland cotton mill wages in Rhode Island had decreased as the tariffs went down, and that under Republican protective tariffs cotton mill wages had, between 1899 and 1912, increased 40 per cent. (The League neglected to point out what Green's papers showed, that in the same period the cost of living had increased by 50 per cent.)[38]

Green was astute enough to realize that the intricacies of the tariff problem were too complicated for most voters to comprehend, and except in the Barrington speech he concentrated on his other five issues. The issue of the fifty-four-hour law centered upon the sincerity of Governor Pothier's claim that he supported it. The issue was hot: agitation against long working hours for women and children was rife in 1912. New York and Massachusetts had already enacted the fifty-four-hour week for women and children, and such a bill had been submitted in the Rhode Island House of Representatives, only to die in the Committee on Labor Legislation. Despite the obvious opposition of his party, Pothier had declared himself in favor of the law just before the state convention, and soon afterward he began to suggest that Republicans were generally for it. Three years earlier, he said, he had been instrumental in the passage of a fifty-six-hour law in Rhode Island, and only fear of placing the state at an economic disadvantage in relation to her neighboring states had prevented him from seeking a fifty-four-hour law. Now that the laws of Massachusetts and New York had eliminated that danger, he could safely advocate passage of the law in Rhode Island.[39]

Green lashed out at the Governor for this claim, labeling it "an act of hypocrisy." Green charged that Pothier had not supported the fifty-four-hour law during the 1912 legislative session; he said Pothier had never "lifted his little finger to get that bill out of the pigeon-hole of the Committee on Labor Legislation where it was locked up." Pothier's pretended friendship for labor, he implied, was transparently bogus. Throughout October at a series of noon rallies at factory gates, Green used the same arguments, accusing Pothier of being the tool of the mill owners and the Tariff Publicity League and charging that the Republican Party was controlled by big business in general and the textile manufacturers in particular.[40]

Another and more tangible issue was the state's finances. In several speeches Green attacked the handling of Rhode Island's finances during Pothier's administrations. He said that in 1911 the Governor had vetoed an appropriations bill on the ground that revenues were inadequate to support the expenditures, but in 1912 he approved an increase of about a million dollars in total appropriations, even though revenues had not increased. Such gross mismanagement, said Green, had resulted in burdening the state with a deficit of almost a quarter of a million dollars. The whole business, Green hinted, smacked more of corruption than of bungling.[41]

Pothier defended his position by claiming that increased expenditures for public institutions, highways, and harbor facilities had become necessary and could no longer be delayed. He asserted that the 1912 tax law would not only bring in additional revenue by increasing property valuation but would also, by establishing a state tax department, make tax collection more efficient. Furthermore, the tax law had also created a Board of Control and Supply which would supervise all purchases for the state. This board would retrench "expenditures without impairment of efficiency" and result in a saving of sixty to seventy thousand dollars a year.[42]

In the running exchange with Pothier over this issue, Green regularly implied that Pothier could not veto the 1912 bill because he had orders from the financial controllers of the Republican Party not to. Green sought to suggest this, in part, by interweaving the issue with his attacks on Pothier on other grounds. As to the property qualification for voting, Green argued that if the property voting registry was reliable proof, only about a fourth of Providence's voters could possibly own their own homes and only about an eighth of them had personal property valued at more than $134. Some "20,713 voters had not even $134 worth of real estate or money or belongings to be taxed on." This seemed highly unlikely to Green. Probably many of the disfranchised actually did have enough holdings to have their names on the tax rolls, he speculated, but had been kept off the lists by Republican tax assessors; only Republicans who always voted the straight Republican ticket found it easy to get on the rolls. "This terrible abuse of the tax assessor's power [constitutes] one of the chief reasons for the abolishing of the property qualifications for voters."[43]

A closely related problem was the rotten-borough system. In the State Senate only a small minority of the electorate was really represented. The twenty smallest towns of the state, having only 8 per cent of the total population, elected a majority of the Senate. When this system was coupled with property qualifications for voting, Green argued, it could be readily seen that average Rhode Island citizens were being trod upon by the property voter, who was more often than not a Republican.[44]

In his charges that the Republican Party was graft-ridden and that Pothier had general knowledge of it, Green got down to specifics. There were in the state more than fifty commissions and boards that were concerned with harbors, parks, fish and game, health, public roads, banking, and the like; Green charged that the appointments to many of the commissions and boards were tainted with graft. For example, there was established in 1912 a Commission on State Printing, consisting of the Secretary of State, the State Auditor, and one elector appointed by the governor. The elector acted as secretary of the commission at a salary of $2,000 per year; two days after the commission was established by the legislature, Pothier had appointed Jacob A. Eaton, a member of the Assembly and a candidate for re-election. Such dual officeholding was common: William C. Bliss had also been appointed to the Public Utilities Commission while at the same time he was a court clerk; Governor Pothier's secretary, Edward Tobey, had been paid more than $6,000 between 1910 and 1912 for clerical work at various conferences while he was still the Governor's secretary at a salary of $1,200; Ambrose Kennedy, Republican candidate for Congress from the Third District, was clerk of the State Redistricting Committee while a member of the governor's personal staff; and many assemblymen were on several commissions and boards.[45]

Green charged that graft was even more common in the building and maintenance of public roads. He pointed out that men with no qualifications for the positions had often been appointed inspectors on road repair work, and that politically influential barbers, mill hands, saloon keepers, and others drew pay without doing any work. For example, in 1910, the legislature had approved a $5,000 appropriation to improve a beachway in the town of Charlestown, and the governor appointed a three-man committee to direct operations. One of the three, a state senator from Charlestown and a physician by profession, received more than $6,000 in three years for "personal labor" on the beachway. In other instances inferior materials and shoddy work were standard practices in road building and repair.[46]

Green's last major campaign issue was that of boss rule. Brayton's eventual successor as figurehead in the Republican Party for the vested interests of big business and manufacturers in Rhode Island was Charles A. Wilson. Unlike Brayton, however, Wilson was chairman of the Republican State Committee and received a salary in that capacity from the committee. Green regularly used this fact in making Wilson the new whipping boy for the Democrats. Again and again, Green asked the Republicans, "Who hires the boss and what do they get in return?"[47]

Green used one other tactic in his campaign: a direct appeal to the state's various ethnic groups. At the urging of Robert Grieve, his campaign manager, Green spoke at Pontiac "to a large gathering of Swedes," paying tribute to their democratic ways. He advertised in the foreign language papers, particularly the Armenian, Italian, and Scandinavian; he also made special appeals to Negro voters, and sent Jewish voters a circular printed in Yiddish, urging not only his election but also that of "all Democratic candidates."[48]

Another event of the campaign, though superficially unrelated, had strong ethnic underpinnings. Republican Mayor R. P. Daignault of Woonsocket, through the medium of the *Woonsocket Evening Call,* did much damage to Green's bid for the governorship. Daignault stated that a number of years earlier some Woonsocket marsh land had been surface-drained by a channel construction running through land owned by the Green family. This particular land now contained a textile mill and Theodore Francis Green, as the representative of the Green family, had come to be manager of the property. The family had sued the city of Woonsocket for damages, and the city had to pay the family as well as reroute the drain. Daignault claimed that, on the other hand, Pothier had done much good for the city and had brought in industry and money, not taken it out. He asked Woonsocket residents to recall this on election day. Green attempted an answer to these charges; in a letter to the paper he said that he had been asked by the city fathers to bring the suit so that the matter might be legally settled. Without litigation, he explained, such could not be the case. Furthermore, the owners of the property, his family, had always paid their taxes, and they were as entitled as all other property owners to proper compensation for land used for public purposes. Despite Green's answer, he was the worse off in this predominantly French city, where he had already faced an uphill fight.[49]

Green received a break on the morning of election day, when there appeared on the front page of the *Providence Journal* a facsimile of a letter sent by the chairman of the Republican Second Ward Committee of Providence to registered Republican voters in Pawtucket, South Kingstown, and East Providence urging them to vote a straight Republican ticket. This might have been merely political advertising except that each letter, the *Journal* stated, contained a two-dollar bill for the recipient to "buy a few cigars" for friends. Here, then, was at least one outright attempt to hold on to voters by a small bribe. The sender of the "little something" had also admitted to *Journal* reporters that he had personally handed a number of two-dollar bills to voters. This was actually nothing new to Rhode Island citizens. At a meeting in July ex-Governor Lucius Garvin had told several persons that there was an association of about sixty people in North Smithfield who delivered their votes as a bloc for as much as twenty dollars apiece. The price was five dollars in West Greenwich and varied in several other small towns in the state. The *Journal* hoped that a storm of indignation would sweep the state on election day as a protest against this kind of blatant political corruption.[50]

This was not to be the case. The entire Republican statewide ticket was elected by the voters, though Rhode Island went Democratic in the presidential election for the first time since the formation of the Republican Party. A Democrat, Joseph H. Gainer, was elected Mayor of Providence by a small plurality over the incumbent Henry Fletcher. Patrick Boyle was successful in his bid for re-election as Mayor of Newport, but all other mayors elected in 1912 were Republicans. Woodrow Wilson received 30,412 votes, Taft 27,703, and Theodore Roosevelt 16,878. Obviously the election of Wilson electors in Rhode Island, as in so many states, had been caused by the Republican bifurcation.[51]

Democratic candidates for Congress from Rhode Island fared better. O'Shaunessy defeated Sheffield so decisively in the First

District that he would have won even without the help of the Progressive candidate. In the Second District, just two days before the election Congressman and former Governor Utter, the Republican candidate, had suddenly died, and the Republicans had substituted the name of Zenas Bliss, the retiring lieutenant governor. Peter Gerry, the Democratic challenger, gained a decided advantage from this as well as from the inclusion of the Progressive candidate, Claude C. Ball, and as a result Gerry edged Bliss by a scant 393 votes. In the Third District, Ambrose Kennedy soundly defeated Democrat Francis X. L. Rattey. The Republicans also lost ground in the state legislature, for the most part caused by the entrance of Progressive candidates.

The gubernatorial race was quite another matter. In spite of the fact that the Progressive candidate for governor, Albert H. Humes of Pawtucket, took 8,457 normally Republican votes, and in spite of the fact that Green actually received more votes than had Wilson, Governor Pothier was still re-elected, defeating Green by 34,133 votes to 32,725. Green actually received a smaller percentage of the total vote cast in 1912 than Waterman had received in 1911. In 1911 Waterman had had 42.97 per cent of the total vote cast and in 1912 Green had only 41.86 per cent. Green's loss occurred primarily in the Blackstone Valley area—Pawtucket, Woonsocket, Johnston, Cumberland, North Providence, North Smithfield, and Smithfield.

Several reasons for Green's defeat, particularly in the Blackstone Valley, are readily seen. More than likely, the tariff issue played a part: many mill hands in this textile area had been convinced by the simple Republican argument that a Democratic victory would mean fewer jobs. This was much easier for them to understand than the intricate arguments of the Democratic Party for a lower tariff. In addition, the concentration of voters of French extraction did not switch their support from Pothier to Green. It is doubtful that even had Green gone all-out to appeal to them, they would have done so. As it happened, Green had attacked the Governor's integrity in his handling of the state's finances, in his alleged knowledge about graft in the state, and in his changing stand on the fifty-four-hour law; this probably cost

Green many votes in Pothier's home territory. Green had assaulted one of their own and that simply would not do. Finally, the *Woonsocket Evening Call* gloatingly called Pothier's victory "a spendid tribute" and pointed out that Woonsocket and the Blackstone Valley "had a great big share in bringing about Governor Pothier's re-election." Robert Grieve believed that Pawtucket ballots had been greatly tampered with and Cumberland voters had been the recipients of a number of bribes. Bribery had also played a large part in Johnston and North Providence as well. There is little doubt that, in view of the fact that Pothier's margin of victory was only 1,408 votes, Green was indeed counted out by vote manipulation of one sort or another. Nevertheless, he did not receive as many votes as had been expected.[52]

Green issued a statement on his defeat for the morning papers and told Rhode Island voters that the cause of political reform had been lost in the state because of a corrupt machine, expenditures of enormous sums of money, intimidation, and threats to the workingmen of shutdowns and loss of employment. Still, discouragement was to be avoided and although "baffled for the moment, the self-respecting, liberty-loving people" of Rhode Island would rise to fight all the harder.

Green received many letters of condolence. Probably the one that meant most to him was a personal note from his sister Eleanor. "I want you to know in some definite way," she said, "how splendid in my eyes have been your personal sacrifice, your attitude of mind and heart, and your public fight for better things."[53]

Chapter IV

Mr. Green Looks to Washington

> The people seem to realize that great issues are at stake
> and that the appeal to support Wilson is based not on
> partisanship but on patriotism; that the reason they are
> asked to send Democratic candidates to Congress is not
> because they are Democrats, but because it is desirable to
> have in Congress those who will heartily co-operate with
> the President. ——THEODORE FRANCIS GREEN

FOR Green, there was gain even in defeat: simply by virtue of being the Democratic gubernatorial candidate in a year in which his party captured the White House, Green's political prestige assumed new proportions. Through Wilson, he had the rare good fortune to have a personal link with the national scene, and he had, as well, direct entrée into the offices of the state's two Democratic Congressmen, O'Shaunessy and Gerry. As the nominal party leader, he remained active by urging his fellow Democrats to campaign for greater registration of voters, the theory then being (as it is today) that a greater registration means a greater number of Democrats qualified to vote. Green also remained in touch with the Democratic National Committee, which asked his co-operation in raising money for the national party.[1]

But the most important immediate manifestation of his newfound prominence was that the Wilson administration, in seeking to fill various national and state positions by the time-honored practice of handing out political patronage, channeled part of its efforts through Green. Green received many inquiries, particularly from the State and Treasury Departments, and was often asked for his confidential opinions about Rhode Islanders under consideration for Federal appointments. For example, he warmly praised two bankers, Frank W. Matteson and Walter S. Hackney; his recommendations of three others were less than enthusiastic. He also supplied Peter Gerry with favorable information about two men being considered for the position of postmaster at Wickford, Rhode Island. On some occasions, Green actively solicited positions for people. He urged the State Department to appoint Olney Arnold II, the Democratic candidate for governor in 1908, to the consulship at Cairo (the practice of filling consular posts with young career officers had not yet become fully established). Arnold was approved by the United States Senate on President Wilson's recommendation in September, 1913.[2]

Green's energetic efforts as a Rhode Island agent for Democratic patronage placed him in a favorable position by giving him the opportunity to do favors for Rhode Islanders of immigrant stock. Catering to the Italian population as well as to East Side aristocrats, he helped two Rhode Island Italo-Americans secure positions as vice-consuls in Chungking and Siam. Green supplemented these activities with others designed to befriend the state's various ethnic groups. Thus, for example, he took several personal advertisements in *Le Jean-Baptiste,* a bi-weekly French newspaper with a circulation to homes of eight thousand French families in Rhode Island.[3]

Such activities would one day bear real fruit, but ethnic politics, then as now, was a tricky business because of the endemic friction between groups. One significant incident (to be repeated many times, one way or another, before the Democrats in Rhode Island were to weld a solid organization) illustrates the problems. In 1914 Judge Frank E. Fitzsimmons decided to retire as chairman of the Democratic State Central Committee. He had his eye on a political plum, the collectorship of customs in Providence, a position which was lucrative but did not carry much responsibility. But Guistino de Benedictis, the first Italo-American ever to have been a delegate to any national convention—having successfully backed George W. Greene in the 1912 Democratic presidential primary—also wanted the port job. De Benedictis was a leading Providence citizen with strong claims on favorable treatment: as a member of the campaign committee of the Democratic National Committee in 1912, he had been instrumental in inducing many Italians in Providence to switch their loyalty from the Republican Party to Woodrow Wilson. The Fitzsimmons backers prevailed in Washington, however, and de Benedictis lost the coveted position. This understandably upset the Italian population in Providence, many of whom, characteristically, felt personally slighted, and the incident became another source of Italian-Irish friction in the Democratic Party in Rhode Island. By appointing Fitzsimmons, Wilson missed his chance to cement further the allegiance of hundreds and perhaps thousands of newly won Democrats. Adamo R. Aiello, the only Italian Democrat ever elected to the legislature from Providence up to that time, expressed bitter disappointment at Wilson's decision. Italians in Providence felt little reason to place their faith permanently in the Democratic Party in 1914.[4]

There were other reasons why the Democratic outlook in Rhode Island was not bright for 1914, and why Green's personal outlook, despite his current prestige, was not any brighter. Democrats in the Rhode Island legislature accomplished little in the first session in 1913, although it finally passed a law limiting to fifty-four hours the work week of women and children employed in factories. Otherwise, no legislation for the betterment of the general welfare emerged from the Republican-controlled body. Too, James H. Higgins, declining the recommendation made by the Democratic State Convention in 1912, refused to stand for the United States Senate; and his replacement, Addison P. Munroe, was easily defeated in the Grand Committee by the Republican, Judge Lebaron B. Colt.[5]

The second session of the General Assembly in 1914 was punctuated by a fierce battle over abolition of property qualifications for voting, the most important single subject considered by the legislature. Green entered the fight by addressing an open letter to Governor Pothier, asking whether he intended to use his strong partisan influence in behalf of a constitutional amendment which would establish unrestricted manhood suffrage in Rhode Island. Reminding Pothier of his record of hesitancy in extending the franchise—as an assemblyman he had been slow to approve granting the vote to foreign-born citizens—Green alleged that the Governor was again using dilatory tactics in the issue of abolishing property qualifications. Just because the Governor had no power to veto proposed constitutional amendments, Green asserted, that did not mean that he could not take positive steps in the fight to lift suffrage restrictions in the state. Green challenged Pothier to send or deliver a message to the legislature "urging the necessity of submitting the question to the people." Green closed by stating his intention of making his letter public. The *Providence Journal* also condemned Pothier for not rising to the occasion and forthrightly speaking out for abolition of property qualifications. In an editorial, the paper charged that the Governor "could have whipped the Senate into line by a plain, outspoken statement to the people, or by a vigorous, ringing message to the Legislature." Pothier, confident of his strength, disdainfully ignored both Green and the newspaper.[6]

Not all the Republicans in the Assembly were as callous as the Governor, and two days later the amendment to abolish property qualifications, submitted by Providence Democrat Albert B. West, passed the lower house by a 59–38 vote. Many Republicans voted for the proposal because they believed that the people of the state had the right to express their opinion on the matter. On the other hand, as one Republican put it, many of those who did vote to submit the amendment to the people for approval, a requirement for all constitutional amendments, did so with strong reservations about the efficacy of abolishing property qualifications. And Republican senators apparently thought it not worth the bother of consulting the people, for they summarily killed the House-approved measure.[7]

West's successful championship of the amendment in the lower house stood him in good stead, and he was soon mentioned as a worthy candidate for the governorship. At a dinner sponsored by the minority legislators in June, he received expressions of support from many Democratic assemblymen. At the same festive occasion—and festive it apparently was, from all accounts—the name of Addison P. Munroe, Providence State Senator who had stepped aside to permit Green an unopposed nomination in 1912, was also advanced for the same office. It was plain that the political eruptions so typical of the state's Democratic Party had begun to emit the first sounds of summer's biennial activity.[8]

It was also plain that Green was not likely to be renominated as the Democratic gubernatorial candidate. On one important occasion, someone did suggest him as the probable candidate: on his return from a trip to Ireland (bearing and expounding the virtues of a shillelagh) Green attended, along with both Aiello and de Benedictis, a testimonial dinner for Frank E. Fitzsimmons, and the suggestion was made in one of the after-dinner speeches. But as the *Tribune* pointed out between jibes at Green's shillelagh, his defeat in 1912, a substantially Democratic year nationally, did him little good as a prospect for 1914. Furthermore, Congressman O'Shaunessy, while publicly calling Green an able lawyer and good man, did not think him a sufficiently aggressive candidate. O'Shaunessy and Green had never completely lost their mutual distrust after the convention of 1910, at which Green had been defeated by O'Shaunessy in the battle for the congressional nomination.[9]

In August, Addison P. Munroe announced his intention to seek actively the Democratic nomination for governor at the state convention. In a letter to the Democratic State Chairman, John B. Sullivan, Munroe said that his record as state senator and the large number of votes cast for him in previous elections showed him to be "an acceptable candidate to Democrats as a whole." Soon, still another name was brought up as an "excellent and outstanding" candidate. At the outing of the Tilden Club of Providence's Tenth Ward, Colonel Patrick H. Quinn, former chairman of the Democratic State Central Committee and then president of the West Warwick Town Council, was boomed as such a man. Green, however, was again in Ireland and Colonel Quinn declined to discuss the gubernatorial race until Green returned. Calling Green "a splendid man and a most loyal Democrat," Quinn stated that if Green desired renomination, he was for him. Furthermore, Green had not been "a fair-weather Democrat . . . had supported the party under all circumstances . . . and had great ability." Therefore, he would await Green's return.[10]

Arriving in Boston a week later, Green refused to discuss domestic politics until he knew more about the situation. Most of his trip abroad had been spent in Ireland, and, with an eye toward his fellow Rhode Islanders of Irish extraction, he expressed his appreciation for the hospitality which had been showered upon him in the Emerald Isle.[11]

Meantime, the Rhode Island trolley system had been falling deeper into debt, and the New York, New Haven, and Hartford Railroad, the parent company, had reached an agreement with the Department of Justice in Washington that Green be one of five trustees designated to take over the trolley system in the state. Green then wrote the Attorney General of the United States asking whether, in the event that he were elected governor, it would be proper for Green to hold the trusteeship. Several days later, Green made public a letter he had written to Quinn, stating that upon full study and upon the Attorney General's advice that the department did not want him to withdraw as trustee, he had decided not to seek the nomination for governor. He also indicated his personal confidence in Quinn and urged him to seek the nomination. Thanking Quinn for his friendship and for awaiting his return from Europe, he promised his full support for the Colonel in the November fight. Albert B. West also withdrew in favor of Quinn, leaving Munroe as the only other avowed candidate. Colonel Quinn immediately declared himself a candidate and became the odds-on favorite to win the Democratic nomination at the state convention on October 8. Munroe refused to withdraw, taking particular exception to Green's having refused to endorse him, after his own withdrawal on behalf of Green in 1912.[12]

At the Republican State Convention, R. Livingston Beeckman, State Senator from Newport and a longstanding friend of Theodore Francis Green, was nominated for governor, and Emery J. San Souci was nominated for lieutenant governor. The Republican congressional nominees were Roswell B. Burchard, who had been Speaker of the House during Green's term there, from the First District; Walter R. Stiness of Warwick from the Second; and Congressman Ambrose Kennedy of Woonsocket from the Third District.[13]

On October 8 the Democratic State Convention opened, with Green occupying the chair. In his brief opening speech to the delegates, Green reminded them that many charges of financial extravagance he had levelled at the Republicans in 1912 had proved to be accurate. He heaped praise upon President Wilson and urged the election of Democrats to all Rhode Island state offices, so as to carry into practice Wilson's principles. The convention then adopted its platform—again urging the abolition of property qualifications for voting and also advocating extension of the suffrage to women (a plank the Republicans had not adopted)—before getting down to the business of selecting candidates. The fight for the gubernatorial nomination was not even close: the delegates chose Quinn over Monroe by the lopsided vote of 147 to 27. Green's running mate in 1912, Sumner Mowry, was again nominated for lieutenant governor, and both Congressmen, O'Shaunessy and Gerry, were also renominated. Thomas P. Haven, another of Green's colleagues in the 1907 Assembly, was chosen to oppose Ambrose Kennedy in the race for Congress in the Third District.

The 1914 political campaign was slow in starting because of popular preoccupation with the outbreak of war in Europe. Rhode Islanders had another distraction as well: Brown University was celebrating its 150th anniversary, and the event took precedence over most others in Providence's leading newspapers. From all over the country scholars and other eminent persons, including Charles Evans Hughes, visited America's seventh oldest institution of higher learning; the days were filled with convocations of one sort and another, reunions of alumni, dinners, and parties, each of which received wide enough press coverage to keep politics off the front pages during the first half of October.

The Rhode Island Democrats, however, never got their campaign in high gear, and generally speaking, the campaign of 1914 was much duller than that two years earlier. The European war continued to be of far greater interest, and neither party waged a fight that could be termed at all spectacular. R. Livingston Beeckman, to offset the Democratic plans recommending the enfranchisement of women, stated his own approval of such action in a letter to the Rhode Island Woman's Suffrage Party. Colonel Quinn, a self-educated Irish-Catholic who held his rank by virtue of having once been a military aide to a Democratic governor, charged Beeckman, a wealthy man who had started with few family resources, with using his money for unethical if not illegal procurement of votes. Republicans in turn accused millionaire Peter Gerry of "financing the Democratic campaign." Democrats assailed Republicans for wanting to turn the clock back to the 1880's and charged various Republican officials with mishandling public funds; retiring Governor Pothier counterclaimed that the Democratic administration in Washington had brought about a business depression in Rhode Island by reducing tariffs, and said that no such party could be trusted to run the government in the state. The *Providence Journal,* decidedly anti-Republican at that time, charged the Republican Party with its "usual practice" of purchasing votes with money and liquor. The paper even posted a $200 reward for information leading to the arrest and conviction of any person paying or accepting money for a vote. The Republicans belittled the liquor issue, and at one point even charged teetotaler Quinn with never having had the distinction of being thrown out of a saloon. Albert B. West was a consistent and effective assailant of the Republicans—indeed, far more challenging than Colonel Quinn himself; but overall, the Republicans did much the better job of publicity. At one stage the perpetual troubles of the New York, New Haven, and Hartford Railroad threatened to enliven the campaign, when twenty present and past directors of the company were indicted for violation of the Sherman Antitrust Law, but the threat did not materialize and the campaign dragged along.[14]

Theodore Francis Green did very little campaigning in 1914, a fact which partially accounted for the dearth of sparkle and wit in Democratic quarters. After serving as chairman of the Democratic State Convention, he made few speeches on behalf of the ticket. On October 23, in Fay's Hall in Providence, he exhorted the voters to judge Beeckman not on the basis of his rise to independent wealth, but on the basis of his present personal qualifications. Green attacked Beeckman for doing nothing as a state senator to further the abolition of property qualifications for voting; indeed, he said, Beeckman had voted against taking the West amendment from committee. A week later Green addressed a Democratic rally in Valley Falls, but he confined himself to the tariff issue and never emphasized either gubernatorial candidate. On the night before the election Green repeated his earlier reference to Beeckman's failure to support the West amendment and closed his address with a tribute to Woodrow Wilson. Clearly, Green's heart was not in the 1914 campaign. Perhaps he was preoccupied with legal matters, perhaps he was disappointed about not being an active candidate himself; then too, perhaps he was not asked to participate more actively because the Democratic Party was also trying to avoid the stigma of his 1912 defeat. But probably the most important factor was that Beeckman was a very good friend, and Green could not bring himself to denounce a man who had gone out of his way to wish Green well in 1912.[15]

The Republicans cut the Democratic majority in Congress in 1914, and in Rhode Island they won a substantial victory. Their state ticket was elected in a veritable landslide; Beeckman defeated Quinn by almost 10,000 votes, and even carried Providence by a slim margin. They won the State Senate, thirty-six seats to three, and more than two-thirds of the lower house. Among the few victorious Democrats was Adamo R. Aiello, who was re-elected to the Assembly. Another Democrat, Mayor Gainer of Providence, was also re-elected, and Congressman O'Shaunessy narrowly defeated Burchard. But Peter Gerry went down to defeat at the hands of Walter R. Stiness, and in the Third District Thomas Haven was smothered by Congressman Kennedy. The only truly bright spot on the Democratic side was the re-election of State Senator Albert B. West from Providence.[16]

Green did not increase his political activity after the election was over. He sent his congratulations and exchanged good wishes with Governor-elect Beeckman, and he reverted to his partisan position by continuing to be instrumental in securing patronage jobs for deserving Democrats—particularly, the appointment of Peter C. Cannon, a Providence attorney, for Assistant United States Attorney for Rhode Island. But otherwise, he largely confined his political activities to rare appearances before gatherings honoring one Democrat or another.[17]

The Democrats' cohesiveness waned apace. The 1915 session of the legislature was as unexciting as the campaign that had produced it; indeed, the Assembly was generally condemned by the Voters' League for its meagre legislation for the general welfare. At the same time, the League went out of its way to commend Republican Lieutenant Governor San Souci for his scrupulously fair method of presiding over the Senate. The state's Democrats were torn by intra-party conflicts, and several times it became obvious that the defeat in 1914 had created bitterness among the professionals. When John B. Sullivan resigned the chairmanship of the Democratic State Central Committee and was replaced by Judge Francis E. Sullivan, the new chairman found that welding the Democrats into a united organization was virtually impossible. Jealousies and rivalries among many Democrats tended to be perpetuated, not glossed over. Disgusted with his failure to elicit support, or rather disgusted with the Democrats who apathetically denied the need for united efforts behind their new leader, Judge Sullivan decided to quit after only a few months in office. Finally prevailed upon not to do so, he scored those Democrats who had resisted reorganization of the party, and set out again to try to effect unification. But the tide of events seemed to be against him. Late in August, 1915, in a speech at a Tilden Club outing, Congressman O'Shaunessy announced to his fellow Democrats that he wanted to head the state's delegation for Wilson at the 1916 national convention, and he asked their support. A few weeks later O'Shaunessy's continuing feud with George W. Greene broke out anew, when the Congressman publicly refused to attend a Democratic outing because he had not been invited to speak. O'Shaunessy resented the fact that George W. Greene was to be one of the speakers; since their clash in 1912, O'Shaunessy had not recognized Greene as national committeeman, despite the decision of the Democratic National Committee. Furthermore, O'Shaunessy believed that in neglecting to ask a speech of him, as Rhode Island's only Democratic Representative in Congress, the party had perpetrated "a maliciously deliberate insult." Meanwhile, ex-Congressman Peter Gerry demonstrated that he was by no means out of the political picture, despite his defeat in 1914. Boomed particularly for the governership and as a prospective challenger of Republican Senator Lippitt—whose seat would, under the Seventeenth Amendment, be filled in 1916 by direct popular election—Gerry declared his intention to remain in politics and spent freely to entertain those Democrats who had to be cultivated.[18]

The infighting so characteristic of the state's Democratic Party continued into 1916.[19] Factions led by O'Shaunessy, Greene, Gerry, and Quinn fought one another: the main bones of contention were the method of choosing delegates to the national convention, the senatorial nomination, and the Greene-O'Shaunessy feud. The latter two issues were resolved by mid-year. First Greene and O'Shaunessy buried the hatchet—at least for the time —when O'Shaunessy withdrew his objections to Greene's being the national committeeman and Greene decided to relinquish the post, which fell to Patrick Quinn. Then the party leaders, hoping to avoid the feuding that had characterized the presidential primary of 1912, decided to select national convention delegates in a special state convention. The State Central Committee drew up a list of delegates and alternates to be submitted to the special convention for its quick approval. The delegates and alternates, including Theodore Francis Green as one of the former, were drawn from both sides of the earlier controversy between O'Shaunessy and Greene.

Those problems being settled at last, the Democrats renewed the struggle over the senatorial nomination. After a long and acrimonious fight—involving, at one time or another, at least six serious candidates—the nomination went to Gerry, and O'Shaunessy settled for renomination to Congress. Addison P. Munroe's desire for statewide nomination was finally gratified when he was chosen as the party's challenger to Governor Beeckman. (Just as the convention was meeting, a German submarine visited New-port and then put to sea, and shortly afterward it sank four Brit-ish and two neutral ships off Nantucket. As a result, the state's Democrats, as well as its Republicans, tied their local campaigns almost exclusively to national concerns, especially the European war.)

The 1916 campaign was the first in which national figures were used extensively in Rhode Island. Charles Evans Hughes, being a graduate of Brown University, was an asset to local Republi-cans. To help counter his influence, Democrats called on Secretary of Commerce William C. Redfield and another energetic and per-sonable young man, Assistant Secretary of the Navy Franklin D. Roosevelt. Roosevelt visited Rhode Island and spoke in defense of Wilson's policies at a Democratic rally in late October. He was introduced by Theodore Francis Green, in the first encounter be-tween two men whose political destinies, at another day, would be intimately linked.[20]

Otherwise, in 1916 Green was so busy helping to reorganize the debt-ridden Rhode Island trolley system that his political ac-tivity had to be severely curtailed. Most of his work was confined to raising money for the Democratic war chests on both the na-tional and the state level. Having been placed on the General Finance Committee of the Democratic National Committee, he was asked by its chairman, Henry Morgenthau, to attempt to so-licit funds from supporters of the national ticket in 1912. Through some error, the Republican National Committee also asked Green to give a financial contribution to the Republican cause, a request he naturally ignored. Green was also made treasurer of the Rhode Island Democratic Party's Ways and Means Committee to raise funds for the state party's purposes. He raised almost $700, mostly from Democratic Party leaders, and contributed fifty dollars him-self. The funds were earmarked for printing circulars, for post-age, and for use in registering voters in Pawtucket, Central Falls, and Woonsocket, where the party had done poorly in 1912. Green handled the donations and directed the payments through Chair-man Sullivan.[21]

From the point of view of Green's personal involvement, the most interesting aspect of the 1916 campaign lay in the interplay between his relationships to Brown University and to the Democratic Party. Charles Evans Hughes' Brown background was used by several Brown alumni as a reason to support him for the presidency. In June, 1916, Hughes came to Brown to take part in the thirty-fifth reunion of his class. It was to be expected that the University would make much of this and, of course, the Providence community was proud of its adopted son. The *Providence Bulletin,* which had supported Wilson in 1912, took this particular opportunity to declare its disappointment in the Wilson administration and now openly supported Hughes. In September a Hughes Businessmen's League was formed and, much to Green's annoyance, Jesse H. Metcalf and Robert H. I. Goddard joined with former Governor Aram Pothier and the President of Brown University, William H. P. Faunce, in this group's backing of Hughes. Describing himself as "just a Brown boy trying to do my duty," Hughes was received on the Brown campus, and in Rhode Island generally, with a great deal of popular enthusiasm. Green might have taken this calmly, but for the fact that a group of Brown alumni sent letters to all Brown graduates asking for ten-dollar contributions to the national Republican ticket, on the ground that Hughes' election would bring great honor to the University. Receiving such a letter so irritated Green that he answered with a fiery protest. The fact that Hughes attended Brown, he said, "should not affect the decision of any loyal American." "A Brown-American," he added with venom, "is little better than the hyphenated German-American." Green sincerely believed that this attitude on the part of Brown alumni would injure the university "in the eyes of the thinking public."[22]

On the other hand, when Green was called upon to defend the integrity of his fellow Brown man, he was unflinchingly prepared to do so. Charles Evans Hughes had been unfairly accused of catering to the so-called German-Americans in 1916, and he had some difficulty denying his alleged anti-British sympathies. A story was about to be circulated in October, averring that Hughes had uttered defamatory remarks about the British and French and, on the same occasion, had declared that the hope of the world lay in the victory of German civilization and ideals. These remarks, which could have been of crucial weight in the election, were supposed to have been made by Hughes at a breakfast given at the home of Theodore Francis Green during the Brown 150th anniversary celebration in June, 1914. Hughes, emphatically denying this allegation, requested President Faunce of Brown University to ask Green for his confidential recollection of the incident. The other gentlemen who were supposedly privy to the 1914 conversation were also brought into the controversy. Green steadfastly asserted his belief that Hughes had never spoken such thoughts, and he was supported in this by another of the participants in the breakfast meeting. There the matter ended, and the would-be accuser kept his silence. That the slur was never made public was in great measure due to Green's part in suppressing the charges.[23]

The results of the election were mixed. Hughes carried the state by about 4,500 votes, but two important Democratic candidates were also elected. Congressman O'Shaunessy was re-elected in the First District, and Peter G. Gerry, in a major upset, defeated incumbent Senator Henry F. Lippitt, thus becoming the first Democratic senator from Rhode Island since 1859. The Democrats gained, but fell short of majorities, in both houses of the Assembly, but they captured no statewide offices and lost the other two congressional contests as well.[24]

Green's personal stake in the outcome—apart from the fact that he could not seriously regret the re-election of his friend Governor Beeckman, an honest and able man, albeit a Republican—was that he again gained by virtue of the national results. The Democratic National Committee, jubilant in their victory, officially recognized Green as "a good Democrat" who could call on the party headquarters in Washington any time for information "properly obtainable." They would aid personally in attending to anything which he "might have up with the Departments." Green would remember this in 1918, when he indeed made use of information supplied him by the Democrats in Washington in his congressional battle with Clark Burdick of Newport.[25]

During most of 1917 Green devoted his time to his law practice, his extensive business interests, and the vexing task of helping direct the affairs of the Rhode Island Company. At a time when local transportation companies were failing all over the nation, he and the four other trustees of the trolley system undertook the formidable job of trying to place the company in a more favorable financial position. The obstacles were huge: the company owed the City of Providence a great deal of money in taxes, the carmen were demanding an increase in wages, and a battle began to shape up over a proposed system of varying the trolley fares according to zones. These activities of the Rhode Island Company, in which Green had already been involved for many months, would suddenly emerge as an important element in the politics of the state in the election in 1918.

Green himself brought the troubles of the trolley system part of the way into politics in 1918. In an interview with a Providence newspaper, he stated that Governor Beeckman should call a special session of the legislature to consider the feasibility of the state's taking over the Rhode Island Company. He suggested that the state establish a board of trustees to oversee the system and run the lines on a service-at-cost basis. Any deficit would be paid by the state, which would then assess the cities and towns served by the line. This, Green argued, was the only sensible thing to do in the interests of the entire public. At almost the same moment, there arose another problem that would soon become a hot political issue. The Federal authorities, attempting to stamp out the widespread vice conditions associated with military areas, declared a radius of ten miles around all military stations to be under the jurisdiction of the Federal government. Newport, long plagued with a vice problem that had grown worse since America's entry into the war, fell in such a jurisdiction.[26]

Meantime, early in 1918 Green had been mentioned as a possible candidate for the Democratic nomination to the United States Senate, despite Congressman O'Shaunessy's well-known hope to follow Gerry into the Senate by unseating the incumbent Republican Senator, LeBaron Colt. In September Lewis McGowan, O'Shaunessy's law partner, tried to smoke out Green's intentions. In a circular sent to each member of the nominating committee of the Democratic State Central Committee, McGowan urged that Green be considered for the Democratic nomination for Congress from the First District, which O'Shaunessy was abandoning in his quest for Senator Colt's seat. Green, vacationing in Maine at the time, was informed of McGowan's action by his own law firm. Not yet wanting to commit himself to any candidacy, Green promptly informed McGowan that he hoped his suggestion would not be "considered lightly nor discarded without consultation" with other prominent members of the Democratic Party.[27]

The nominating committee then strongly recommended O'Shaunessy for the Senate and Green for governor. Just after learning of this action, Green received a letter from Edward M. Sullivan (a law partner of Chairman Francis E. Sullivan) stating his unalterable opposition to Green as the Democratic nominee for governor. Edward M. Sullivan based his position on the grounds that Green's position as a trustee of the Rhode Island Company would make him an extremely poor candidate. He pointed out that Green had publicly favored the zoning system for trolley fares while, in the 1918 session of the state legislature, the Democratic assemblymen were voting against this kind of fare system. This in itself had placed Green on the opposite side in a controversy in which the Democratic Party had been deeply involved and totally committed. Sullivan told Green that he appreciated "the indelicacy of addressing" him in this way, but that he wanted to give Green advance notice of his position. He simply could not support Green, he said, should Green accept the offer of the Democratic nominating committee.[28]

Sullivan's letter was forwarded to Green in Maine by one of the attorneys in his law firm, Frederick W. Tillinghast. Tillinghast believed that under existing conditions the office was at best a powerless one, permitting little opportunity for positive accomplishment; and in view of the tone of Sullivan's letter and the implications of it, he urged Green not to entertain any thought of seeking the gubernatorial nomination. Instead, said Tillinghast, Green should consider trying for Congress. Green pondered the advice, thought out the problem in his own mind, and made his decision.[29]

He then wrote Chairman Francis E. Sullivan telling him that his important war work as Director of War Savings for Rhode Island, combined with his law practice, militated against his accepting the gubernatorial nomination of the party. Careful not to close the door on any other nomination, Green added that there were situations where a nomination to public office took precedence over private concerns, and as such "might assume the nature of a call to duty." But nomination for the governorship, "important as it is," was not such a call. Patrick H. Quinn, the chairman of the nominating committee, was upset by the turn of events and wired Green that his decision not to run, coming under a threat from Edward M. Sullivan, would hurt him as well as the party. On the other hand, he said, Sullivan's opposition to Green would not have hurt him at all. But Green was adamant.[30]

Green then replied to Edward M. Sullivan defending his advocacy of the new zone system, which had been adopted by the legislature over the opposition of the Democrats. Because of inflation, Green said, the new system had already proven inadequate, even if the company did not raise the wages, as the carmen were demanding; there was now a sore need for a fare increase to help the company meet expenses. Certainly no trustee of the line should be attacked for having taken a stand on the question of a zone system. Green then reiterated his firm belief that the best solution to the problem was for the governor to call a special session of the General Assembly and have the state take over control of the trolley line. Even then, there would still be a deficit that would have to be made up by an increase in fares—in itself an unpopular position to take. In view of these facts, Green could not understand Sullivan's reasoning in regard to his possible candidacy for governor. He did not believe that Sullivan's stand would have an "appeal to any considerable number of people," and he explicitly denied that Sullivan's letter had influenced his decision as to whether to become a candidate.[31]

A week later, Green received a telephone call from Secretary of War McAdoo, urging him not to let his job of War Savings Director stand in the way of accepting the nomination for Congress, for now was no time to lose a seat in the House. O'Shaunessy's running for the United States Senate made this a possibility unless there was a strong candidate to take his place. Following this lead the nominating committee, despite Green's rejection of the gubernatorial nomination, now suggested that he be the candidate for Congress from the First District.[32]

On that note, and amidst the first local appearances of the Spanish influenza epidemic, the Democratic State Convention convened in Providence on September 23. The convention promptly nominated O'Shaunessy for the United States Senate and Alberic A. Archambault of West Warwick for governor. Green was the nominee for Congress from the First District, Stephen J. Casey of Richmond from the Second, and William G. Troy of Providence from the Third. The Democratic platform again heaped blame on the Republicans for graft, general corruption, and mismanagement of state affairs, and again it called for extension of the suffrage to women and emphasized a "win the war with Wilson" spirit—to which Green devoted his short acceptance speech. On the next day the Republicans renominated Senator LeBaron Colt, Governor Beeckman, all the incumbent state officers, and incumbent Congressmen Stiness and Kennedy; their only new candidate was Green's opponent, Mayor Clark Burdick of Newport.[33]

In order to devote more of his time to his campaign, Green resigned as State War Savings Director, but he remained a trustee of the Rhode Island Company. So that the status of the other trustees might be completely clear, the board issued a statement asserting that despite Green's candidacy for Congress, the board was "pure and free from all imputations of pernicious activity in partisan politics."[34]

The fall of 1918 was an exciting and at times frightening period. On September 30 Woodrow Wilson drew the first number under the nation's new selective service system, emphasizing in some respects the new role America was to play in the world. Evangelist Billy Sunday came to Rhode Island in an attempt to lead the wayward citizenry back to God. Meanwhile, the Spanish influenza epidemic made new headlines and created more panic as the disease spread from military camps to the civilian population. On October 2 the United States Senate defeated by two votes a proposed constitutional amendment granting women the right to vote. On the same day the Federal War Labor Board approved a long-sought increase in wages for the carmen of the Rhode Island Company, setting a 48¢ per hour maximum and a 43¢ per hour minimum. Green, speaking for himself and not for the board, said that it was impossible to raise the wages of the carmen without some kind of governmental assistance. To meet the approved demands of the carmen the company now sought an even higher increase in fares from the State Public Utilities Commission.[35]

The influenza epidemic became so alarming that in the first week of October the city of Providence clamped assembly restrictions on theatres, schools, and churches, entirely prohibiting indoor political rallies and limiting religious services to once a week. Firebrand Billy Sunday blamed the Germans for the outbreak of the flu and said that prayer was the only way to combat it. Such was the background and mood of the state as the 1918 political campaign began building toward a climax.[36]

In this atmosphere, Green set out to cash in on his political contacts in Washington. On October 2 he wrote to Josephus Daniels, Secretary of the Navy, about his candidacy and pointed out that Mayor Burdick, his opponent, had hampered Federal authorities in their efforts to clean up vice conditions in and around Newport. Green told Daniels that he desired to rest his campaign against Burdick on this issue, as it made "a more direct personal appeal and [was] in itself an object lesson." He asked Daniels' support and requested a compilation of the exact facts as to Burdick's attitudes. Two weeks later Green received an envelope crammed with confidential information about Newport and the conditions that had existed there for some time. Like most navy cities—in wartime or in peacetime—Newport had been plagued by immorality. Newspapers were replete with letters to the editor containing advice about how to handle the hordes of teenagers who prowled the streets. Arguments raged over the causes of juvenile delinquency: parents were blamed, the Navy was excoriated, and government officials at all levels were scorched for permitting flagrant violations of decency.[37]

There was much in Daniels' information that pointed the finger at Burdick, albeit indirectly, for permitting the conditions. Green was informed that Governor Beeckman had written to Assistant Secretary of the Navy Franklin D. Roosevelt in May, 1917, telling him that the naval personnel at Newport were "inadequately taken care of" as far as their living accommodations were concerned. Roosevelt had replied that he was most concerned with the "exceedingly bad" moral conditions in Newport and said that as a result the Navy was being unfairly blamed. He urged the Governor to look into the matter and try to have local conditions improved. Governor Beeckman had forwarded Roosevelt's letter to Mayor Burdick, who then denied that such immoral conditions really existed. On the contrary, he claimed, there was "far less of this than in some years." Burdick further stated that he personally found conditions quite good in the city and felt that Roosevelt's criticism was "not warranted." Furthermore, he believed that "isolated cases may have been cited as custom." The Justice Department had then made an investigation in June, 1917, and found ample evidence of gambling, prostitution, and illegal sale of liquor. Daniels transmitted this evidence to Governor Beeckman and asked him to "take such action to clean up the city of Newport as will make unnecessary any further step by the Government of the United States."[38]

The *Providence Journal* had also entered the fracas in June, when the editor informed Secretary Daniels that the government charges were "absolutely correct." Thereupon Daniels ordered the commandant of the Newport naval station to place military guards wherever necessary to keep naval personnel away from any places which might have a tendency to corrupt the morals of the nation's youth. The language employed was actually a bit stronger than that. Governor Beeckman assured Daniels that he would do his part, but reminded Daniels that the Navy itself had still not supplied the young recruits with proper accommodations at the training station. The Governor added that the citizens of Newport had generously aided these young men and "had done their best in a great emergency." Whether this statement was interpreted by the Secretary to mean that a house of prostitution was a kind of "home away from home" can never be learned. In any event, according to the reports Green had received, conditions did not really improve, and by December, 1917, it had become apparent that the efficiency of the naval training station was being impaired by the bawdy conditions in Newport. At least so wrote the commanding officer of the station.[39]

Green attempted to capitalize on his confidential information. He charged, whenever possible in his campaign, that Mayor Burdick had been responsible for the immoral conditions at Newport. In November, 1918, Secretary Daniels sent to the *Providence Journal* a telegram for publication. The Secretary stressed the necessity of action by the Federal government to protect naval personnel in Newport, saying that this had become clear "after the naval authorities had tried in vain to induce the local authorities to make wholesome conditions for the thousands of young men there under training." Daniels then urged Rhode Island voters to elect Green as congressman, as a man who had helped "while his opponent was hindering through indifference or unwillingness or some other reason which prevented local cooperation in Newport." Whenever possible Green used this argument against Burdick. At a rally in Newport itself he charged Burdick with having permitted vice to continue unabated. Burdick merely ignored the attacks or simply denied the existence of such a state of affairs. In a sense, Burdick was in the more favorable position: the residents of a city rarely like to be told that their community is beset by immoral conditions. Such arguments bring a sense of shame to the citizens, particularly when an outsider casts the judgment, and the citizens are likely to react by resenting the charges and defending their city. Apparently this is the way Newport's voters felt on election day.[40]

A second issue around which Green's campaign turned was that of the trolley system's troubles. Upon receiving the order approving pay raises for the carmen, the Rhode Island Company issued a statement that it could not grant the increase in fact until the fares were also raised. The carmen countered with a threat to

strike; Green now wrote a public letter to the Governor suggesting he call a special session of the General Assembly to consider
state control on a service-at-cost basis. Green asserted that it was
a "case not for the physician with his medicine, but for the sur-
geon with his knife, if the patient is to survive." Governor Beeckman rejected his old friend's advice: two days later he answered
that it would be premature to convene the legislature unless he
were "advised by the public authorities of the cities and towns . . .
especially affected by the present street railway situation that
they desire such action."[41]

The carmen withheld their contemplated strike to see what
would develop. The Providence City Council officially voted to
oppose the granting of fare increases by the Public Utilities Commission. On the other hand, manufacturing and financial interests in the state urged the commission to do anything necessary
to keep the trolley lines running. On October 20 the Public Utilities Commission finally allowed a fare increase. The carmen would
have their wage increase and the strike was averted.

These events boded ill for Theodore Francis Green. Rhode
Island Democrats in general had opposed the fare increase, which
they viewed as added burdens for the workingman. Green was
caught in a squeeze: even though he had stated that he personally stood for state control of the line, in plain fact he was still a
member of the board that had pushed for the increase in fares.
On the one hand, Governor Beeckman attacked Green by charging that state control would lead to state ownership; on the other,
the *Providence Journal* asserted that though Green knew the Republicans were not to blame for the plight of the trolley system,
he had nonetheless gone along with the Democrats in charging
that the Republicans were responsible. Green, then, had been
touched adversely with the trolley issue, just as Edward M. Sullivan had predicted.

A third issue in the 1918 campaign in Rhode Island was the
charge of corruption levelled by the *Providence Journal* at one of
the Democratic candidates for Congress. On the Sunday before
the election the *Journal* broke a story that William G. Troy,
Congressman Ambrose Kennedy's opponent in the Third District,

had been dismissed four years earlier from his job as Deputy Collector of Internal Revenue in Washington for alleged misappropriation of funds. Troy denied that this had been the reason for his having left Federal service, and on the following day Congressman Kennedy denied that he had had anything to do with Troy's exposure. The damage, however, had been done and on election day the *Providence Journal* made a final attack on Troy by printing a front page cartoon depicting Troy, O'Shaunessy, and Theodore Francis Green holding hands. The cartoon was captioned, "What's a Record Among Friends?" The *Journal* had been angered at Green's handling of the issue of vice in Newport: the paper objected to the fact that confidential information "had found its way into the hands of a professional politician" (a description that pleased Green no end) and had been made public by him.

The fourth and major issue of the campaign spelled the end of Green's hopes for victory in 1918. This was Woodrow Wilson's advocacy of a Democratic Congress as necessary to conclude the war and ensure the peace.

In May, 1918, Wilson had told Congress that because of the exigency of war, politics was set aside. As the political campaign was underway several months later, peace feelers were put out by Germany while, at the same time, German submarines continued to sink unarmed liners and merchant ships. Fearing that Wilson would negotiate with the Germans, despite his pledge to the contrary, Henry Cabot Lodge led the cry for our standing for "unconditional surrender" in dealing with the enemy. The next day Theodore Roosevelt, ready at any time to snipe at Woodrow Wilson, joined in Lodge's plea. Wilson vowed that there would be no armistice until the Germans had ceased land operations and sea outrages, the Kaiser had abdicated, and the government of Germany had agreed to Allied terms for evacuation of invaded European territory. Once again Senate Republican leader Henry Cabot Lodge reiterated his demands for unconditional surrender, and the personal battle between Wilson and Lodge was on.[42]

Theodore Francis Green had begun to tie his own campaign with Wilson's leadership. He had regularly associated his name with Wilson's in newspaper advertisements containing a good-sized portrait of himself with the caption "With Wilson"; twice he used Lincoln's argument against swapping horses in midstream; and at a rally before the factory gates of the Brown and Sharpe Company, Green appealed to the workers to vote for the candidate who promises "hearty cooperation with Wilson in his terms of peace and in his plans for reconstruction work after the war."

Then on October 25 Green was caught up in part of a huge public furor, when President Wilson made a bald appeal for all Americans to support him by supporting Democratic congressional candidates. A Republican majority in either the House or the Senate, Wilson said, would surely be "interpreted on the other side of the water as a repudiation" of his leadership in the United States. The return of a Democratic Congress was therefore necessary in the coming election; "the nation should give its undivided support to the government under a unified leadership." Divided counsels, endurable in ordinary times, could not be tolerated now, for the times were not ordinary.

Across the nation, the popular reaction was the opposite of what Wilson hoped for. The country was confused about peace negotiations—which were then going through the labyrinth of international protocol—and many people could not understand why the affair was not quickly at an end. The German armies were in retreat and her allies were seemingly defeated, and yet German submarines were still sinking ships in the Atlantic. Public uneasiness and irritation over these matters was compounded by an unrelated matter, the spread of the Spanish influenza epidemic. In this climate, Theodore Roosevelt and other leading Republicans now began charging Wilson with negotiating instead of demanding unconditional surrender. The result of all this confusion was to make the voters skeptical of, if not hostile to, Wilson's plea.

Locally the newspapers led the attack against Wilson's request for a Democratic Congress. The war, said the *Journal* piously, was the people's war, not a party's war, but it was clear that the paper's judgment varied with the party doing the warring. Sprinkling its editorial pages with rectangular blocks labeled "Unconditional Surrender," the paper suggested that with a Democratic majority in Congress the Germans would be let off with something less. Others followed the same line, and William Howard Taft, Theodore Roosevelt, and several Republican senators seized upon Wilson's statement to intensify their own pleas for a Republican Congress to ensure unconditional surrender. Senator Colt's slogan was, Win the war, dictate the peace. By the end of October it was reported that there was some feeling among Democrats in Washington that Wilson's appeal would result in the election of a Republican Congress.

All this had its effect on the candidacy of Theodore Francis Green. On the evening of the President's message, Green received a telegram from Scott Ferris, chairman of the Democratic National Congressional Committee, advising him of the President's statement "with reference to the necessity of having a Democratic Congress," and suggesting that Green tie his campaign directly to it. If the statement were properly handled, Scott advised, it could "largely take the place of the speaking campaign which [had] been dispensed with due to influenza." On the next day Green received another telegram, advising him that the "correct answer to make to all peace propaganda and queries" was that he would "support the boys at the front and stand by the Commander-in-Chief of our army and navy." A true party man and staunch Wilson supporter, Green followed the advice. That very afternoon, at a rally at Elks Hall (the restrictions on political gatherings having been relaxed) Green equated a Republican Congress with an Allied defeat at the front. Three days later he again placed himself unequivocally behind Wilson.[43]

The campaign soon began to backfire. The *Providence Bulletin* stated that apparently nothing counted with Green "but the ambition to hang the title of Congressman in front of his name." Green, it was charged, had become infected with the disease of demagoguery. Independent voters "who were inclined to support him" would now turn against him "because of their wholesome desire to rebuke the party to which he belongs." On the day before the election, the *Providence Tribune* called for the defeat of Green by name, after having previously called for a Republican

Congress in order to get on "with the stupendous task of recon-struction."[44]

Green's campaign was personally trying for other reasons as well. Following the standard practices of the day, he made street corner speeches every day and evening, racing from one open meeting to another. The timing of campaigns in those early years rivalled in precision the campaigns of the jet age, and they were just as exhausting. By election day, Green was tired and thoroughly discouraged at the outlook. In answer to a pessimistic telegram from Green, the Democratic National Committee tried to cheer him up by wiring assurances that the election was "neither won nor lost until the last vote is counted," but this was whistling in the dark. In his election-eve statement to the press, Green claimed that he was encouraged, but added that a candidate was not the best person to give his impression of the campaign and its possible outcome. The outcome, as it turned out, was dismal.[45]

Despite Wilson's plea for a Democratic Congress, or more likely because of it, 1918 was simply not a Democratic year, and the Republicans took control of both houses of Congress. In Rhode Island, Burdick polled a particularly devastating vote, defeating Green 14,478 to 11,556. As is shown by the table, Green's percentage of the total vote cast in the First District fell far below what O'Shaunessy had won in the two preceding elections. In Newport, the question of vice conditions notwithstanding, Green lost to its mayor by almost seven hundred votes, whereas O'Shaunessy had carried the city in 1916 by almost a thousand votes. Green failed to carry a single town or city, losing even the voting districts in Providence by more than five hundred votes. The rest of the Democratic ticket fared about as badly. Congressmen Stiness and Kennedy thoroughly swamped their Democratic opponents, and Senator Colt defeated O'Shaunessy by almost forty-five-hundred votes.[46]

There was only one exception to the pattern: Governor Beeckman's plurality was cut to half of what it had been in 1916. Alberic A. Archambault of West Warwick lost to Beeckman by 6,651 votes, whereas Beeckman had defeated Munroe by 13,336 votes in 1916; and in 1918 Beeckman ran far behind his ticket. The reason is probably simple. The City of Woonsocket split the ticket, giving victories in the city to the candidates of French extraction, regardless of party. Woonsocket had returned a heavy vote for Beeckman in 1916, when his opponent had been Addison P. Munroe, and it did likewise for Beeckman's running mate, San Souci,

FIRST CONGRESSIONAL DISTRICT
VOTING 1914, 1916, AND 1918

	1914		1916		1918	
	Dem.	Rep.	Dem.	Rep.	Dem.	Rep.
Barrington	125	216	204	277	154	361
Bristol	584	703	626	744	500	728
East Providence	1,279	1,248	1751	1,273	1,267	1,509
Jamestown	95	128	112	176	66	196
Little Compton	31	155	39	185	22	200
Middletown	98	156	113	164	57	163
Newport	2,453	2,046	2,900	1,917	1,988	2,672
New Shorham	194	171	126	237	56	230
Portsmouth	172	172	169	194	65	238
Providence*	7,277	6,122	9,099	7,036	6,713	7,285
Tiverton	270	465	263	394	220	374
Warren	405	498	594	502	448	522
Totals	12,983	12,080	15,996	13,099	11,556	14,478
Total vote cast**	26,072		29,634		26,643	
Percentage of vote	49.4%	45.9%	53.9%	44.2%	42.0%	54.3%
Plurality of victor	903 (Dem)		2,897 (Dem.)		2,922 (Rep.)	

* In 1914, 29 Providence districts were within the First District; in 1916, 30; and in 1918, 31. Basically, the area was composed of the same districts and territory in all three elections.

** The total votes cast take into account those cast for minor party candidates— Progressive, Prohibitionist, and Socialist in 1914; Socialist in 1916 and 1918. The year 1912 was not included as this was the year of the Progressive-Republican split and the figures used would be meaningless for this purpose. 1910 was not included, as Rhode Island then had two not three Congressional Districts and the state was apportioned differently.

against Democrat Arthur P. Johnson. In 1918, however, the Democratic gubernatorial candidate was of French extraction, and Woonsocket gave him a plurality of 386; but in the same election, it gave Republican San Souci a plurality of 380 votes over Jerome M. Fitzgerald of Providence. A similar pattern prevailed in most of the Blackstone Valley. Once again, ethnic considerations had played their part in the state election, though the outcome had not been as appreciably affected as had been the case in 1912.

On the day after the election, the *Providence Journal* wrote an editorial about Theodore Francis Green, attributing his defeat almost solely to the President's plea. "In ordinary circumstances," said the editorial, Green would have been supported by "many independent and Republican voters, but the great majority of these refused to endorse the President's partisan plea. Some of them, in their keen resentment, voted a straight Republican ticket for the first time in their lives." Whatever the cause, the "stupendous task of reconstruction" would be done without Green's help.[47]

Chapter V

The Twenties

Much remains to be done in this state. Deo volente *the liberty of the people and their constitution will yet be established.*
—THEODORE FRANCIS GREEN

A S USUAL, the first work in the wake of defeat was to pay the bills, and as usual, Green was called upon to help wipe out the campaign deficit. The Democratic State Central Committee still owed small sums for furniture, hall rentals, and taxi services, and George F. O'Shaunessy, who never learned to be a graceful loser, refused to help defray these expenses unless all the Democratic state candidates in the previous election would help him with the $2,000 he claimed to have spent for the benefit of all. Ignoring the resentful O'Shaunessy, Green, Patrick H. Quinn, and Alberic A. Archambault each paid a small sum to wipe out the party's debt. Green was also called upon to aid the national party, and later in the year 1919 he made a small contribution to the Democratic National Committee.[1]

As usual, also, Rhode Island Democrats squabbled among themselves until the next election, and then reconciled their differences with compromises between ethnic groups (their three congressional candidates were Pat Boyle, Luigi De Pasquale, and Herve J. Lagace). But for once there was a difference: no one entertained any serious hopes of victory, and everyone settled in for what promised to be a long dry spell.

The 1920 elections were, to Green and most other Democrats, marked by only two points of interest: the first participation of females in a national election, and the first entrance of Franklin Delano Roosevelt into a national campaign.

91

When the Nineteenth Amendment was adopted, women in Rhode Island were quite ready to do battle in political wars. Mindful of the oft-repeated advice that the party which granted women the franchise would be the recipient of their votes, Rhode Island Democrats went even further than might have been expected and nominated two women on their statewide ticket in 1920. Elizabeth Upham Yates, a veteran suffrage worker, and Helen I. Binning, an active participant in women's organizations, were selected as Democratic candidates for lieutenant governor and secretary of state, respectively. Interestingly, among the few speeches Green made in the campaign was an address delivered in October to the Education for Citizenship Committee, a group of women organized by the Local Council of Women. Green gave the ladies the Democratic point of view on the issues of the day, stressing the importance of the League of Nations and Wilsonian principles.

As for Roosevelt, Green met the New Yorker again at the Democratic National Convention in San Francisco, which nominated Roosevelt as the vice-presidential running mate of James W. Cox. Thereafter the two aristocratic liberals began a regular correspondence that would continue many years. During the campaign they exchanged several letters: for example, Roosevelt wrote from California that he was bending every effort "to appeal to the progressive spirit" of the West, and Green applauded him for "emphasizing progress as against reaction." Afterward, Green praised Roosevelt for his forthright and courageous stand in 1920 and told him he had done well under trying circumstances. Roosevelt, he said, was now "higher in the estimation of [his] fellow countrymen even than before," and predicted "great public honors still in store" for the New Yorker. Later, Roosevelt wrote asking Green to head the Rhode Island committee to project plans for a memorial to Wilson, as "there was no one in the State of Rhode Island who could so worthily represent the movement there." Throughout the twenties the two men corresponded, and as they did Roosevelt drew Green's personal support ever closer and became, as well, ever more obligated to Green for that support.[2]

The vote in 1920 was swelled by the large numbers of women

who voted for the first time. It would be an understatement to say that the Republicans swept to victory. They gave Democrats a sound thrashing almost everywhere. In Rhode Island, the entire Republican slate, from gubernatorial nominee Emery San Souci and the three incumbent congressmen on down, won handily, Miss Yates and Miss Binning notwithstanding. The Republicans improved their already strong position in the legislature; the Democrats won only twenty-two seats in the lower house and five in the Senate. Even the city of Providence returned a Republican as its state senator. Only Joseph H. Gainer, perennial Mayor of Providence, survived the onslaught; the popular Democrat was elected for his fifth consecutive term.[3]

The *Providence Journal,* like most other newspapers in the country, rejoiced at the outcome of the election. Theodore Francis Green was one of the most eloquent dissenters. In a moving tribute to Woodrow Wilson, he deplored the refusal of the nation to accept Wilsonian principles. "It is difficult for us Yankees to express our deepest emotions," he wrote the ailing President, but "it has made me indignant to see men put party above country and humanity. It has made me ashamed to hear their false appeals. . . . I am both indignant and ashamed to realize that temporarily they have by these means and by facing both ways achieved their purpose. But I am not depressed. . . . I am convinced that the great mass of the people want [the League of Nations], that some way they are going to get it, and that if they do, they will come to a realization of what you have done for them, and of what you have given of yourself in the doing."[4]

On reflection, Green said later that he had concluded that many who had voted for Harding and the Republicans had done so on the assumption that "the best way to secure entrance of America into the League was to elect a Republican Administration." The wish, however, was clearly father to the thought, for the country was decidedly in a mood to return to its isolationist traditions.[5]

As the nation turned inward, so did Rhode Island, and throughout the decade state issues dominated state politics. Barely five months after the 1920 election, Democratic Senator Lucius F. C. Garvin of Cumberland raised what was to be the most persistent reform issue of the period. He asked that the question of calling a constitutional convention be submitted to the people of the state for their approval. The issue was fundamentally partisan, for one of the main purposes of a new state constitution would be to redistrict Rhode Island, without which the State Senate seemed destined forever to be a rotten-borough stronghold of the Republican Party. Naturally enough, Garvin's measure was never accepted in the Senate. Garvin himself, a stalwart advocate of political reform to the very end, died in October of the following year. Zechariah Chafee, Jr., writing from Harvard shortly after Garvin's death, suggested to Green that Green write a series of articles, resembling in some ways the *Federalist Papers,* emphasizing the need for a constitutional convention in Rhode Island. By this time, however, Green was thoroughly discouraged, for not only had Garvin's proposal failed in the legislature, but even the state Democratic platform for 1922 barely mentioned the issue. But the discouragement was misplaced, for events were brewing that would, in the 1922 elections, give Democratic reformers an opportunity to turn the question of a constitutional convention into one of the most spectacular issues since Dorr's Rebellion.[6]

At first, the election might have seemed routine enough. For governor, the Rhode Island Democrats nominated William S. Flynn, a popular representative from Providence and the Democratic floor leader in the lower house; for the lieutenant-governorship, they nominated Felix A. Toupin, a little-known Franco-American from Lincoln. They also nominated a woman, Mrs. Susan Sharp Adams, for secretary of state, renominated Senator Peter G. Gerry, and nominated O'Shaunessy to seek his old seat in Congress. In every respect save one, the party's platform was a most dry document (even literally, in that it called for rigid enforcement of prohibition laws). The exception was the issue that would bring victory: the Republicans' handling of some serious textile strikes that had erupted during the year.[7]

Republican Governor San Souci was in trouble, for when the textile strikes had broken out early in the year, he had called out troops as strike-breakers, and the popular outcry against his action was furious. After much manipulation and trading, the Republicans decided to nominate Lieutenant Governor Harold J. Gross for governor and to retire San Souci to pasture as the collector of customs. Then they renominated the other incumbent state officers and unanimously chose ex-Governor Beeckman to oppose Senator Gerry, whose senatorial seat Beeckman had long coveted.[8]

Theodore Francis Green himself set the pace for the campaign: as chairman and keynote speaker at the Democratic Ratification Rally in October, he attacked the Republicans in his most biting manner and aroused the partisan audience to a high pitch. The ensuing campaign was particularly bitter, and when the votes were counted, the results were mixed. Gerry had been returned to the Senate by almost 14,000 votes, O'Shaunessy had been defeated, and one Democrat, Jeremiah E. O'Connell, had been elected to the House of Representatives.[9]

But the important results were in the elections for state offices. Flynn and Toupin won by decisive margins, thus giving the Democrats the governorship for the first time in fifteen years and, what was even more important, the presiding officer of the State Senate would also be a Democrat. The only Democrat who failed to win a statewide office was Mrs. Adams, and she lost only by a tiny margin. In the General Assembly, too, the Democrats made meaningful gains. Only twenty Republicans were elected to the State Senate, as against sixteen Democrats and three Democrat-Independents; in the lower house, the Republicans won just half the seats, the Democrats forty-eight, and Democrat-Independents two. The Grand Committee, then, had seventy Republicans, sixty-four Democrats, and five Independents.

In the debacle that was about to ensue, the details of the distribution of power were crucial.[10] For organizational purposes, the Republicans found themselves in a majority in the lower house when the Independents aligned themselves on their side. The State Senate was also Republican, but it was presided over by Democratic Lieutenant Governor Felix A. Toupin. Possession and control of the records of the Senate was in the hands of the Secretary of State—a Republican, J. Fred Parker, who had barely managed to win over Mrs. Adams. The sheriffs, whose function it was to carry out the orders of the presiding officer in preserving the decorum of the upper house, were also Republicans, having been appointed by the High Sheriff, who in turn was elected by the Republican-controlled Grand Committee.

Early in 1923 the Democratic legislators decided to assert their power. Despite being in the minority they could, because a Democratic lieutenant governor presided over the Senate, employ delaying tactics, including the filibuster, to wear down the Republican senators. The lieutenant governor and the Democratic senators, led by Robert E. ("Fighting Bob") Quinn of West Warwick, the nephew of Patrick H. Quinn, organized a veritable Weber and Field routine in the upper house. Essentially what the Democratic senators did in 1923 was to adopt the methods Theodore Francis Green and his colleagues had used in 1907, adding only the weapon of the filibuster. They were effective: it took the Senate a month merely to adopt rules and select committees. The purpose of these maneuvers was to show up the Republicans for what Democrats believed they were, a reactionary group of protectors of the vested interests in the state.

Finally, in May, the Democratic senators won their victory when the Republicans agreed not to hold back in Republican-dominated committees three Democratic bills which had stemmed from many Democratic platforms of the past. Proposals for calling a constitutional convention, for abolishing property qualifications for voting, and for redistricting the state were all reported to the floor of the Senate. As expected, once they were on the floor the measures were rejected by the Republican majority, but that was not the point. The Democratic strategy had its hoped-for effect: the Democrats had held up the normal business of the state until they could force the Republicans into openly rejecting three reform measures which Democrats had repeatedly advocated. In a sense, they had exposed the reactionary Republicans in all their iniquity. What had been a wild time for several months, however, would seem like an East Side tea party compared to what was in store in the 1924 session.

Theodore Francis Green had no part in these doings. In 1923 he tended to business and legal affairs and took a trip to Japan, after which he conferred with his old friend, Secretary of State Charles Evans Hughes, about Japanese-American relations.[11] But by year's end he was conferring with Toupin, Quinn, and other Democratic senators, laying plans for the second session of the legislature which had been elected in 1922. The fruit of these plans would be a legislative gathering, the likes of which Rhode Island had never seen.

In January, 1924, Green and several other Democratic lawyers started the operation in motion by making public statements that the people of the state could call a constitutional convention even without legislative approval. A few days later Senator Robert E. Quinn, assuming more and more of the leadership of the Senate Democrats, followed by introducing a bill proposing a popular referendum on the question of calling a constitutional convention. Green and others then spoke on behalf of the bill at a hearing of the Senate Committee on Special Legislation. But then the Republican-controlled committee pigeon-holed Quinn's bill, deciding to kill it in committee. That set the stage for a filibuster to end all filibusters.[12]

Under Quinn's and Toupin's leadership, the Senate Democrats determined to stop all normal business, including the annual appropriations bill, until the Republicans assented to a vote on Quinn's proposal. To enable the state to meet its monthly payroll, the Democrats did offer to pass monthly appropriations in piecemeal fashion, but the Republicans, wanting to blame the Democrats for any delays caused in payments of bills and salaries of state employees, rejected the proposal. Thus legislation reached an absolute impasse, and the strain soon began to show on everyone. The Republicans had to be in their places on the Senate floor at all times to answer to quorum calls requested by Democrats, lest the Democrats could vote the bill out of committee with their temporary majority. Lieutenant Governor Toupin also found the situation trying, for the strategy called for his continued presence as presiding officer. If he failed to occupy the Senate chair, even for a moment, the Republican President pro tempore could seize the gavel and bring about adjournment at will.

Day after day, week after week, the filibuster dragged on. In the face of mounting popular pressure, Theodore Francis Green was the principal defender of the senators' action. "We shall never be able to assert the rights of the majority of the people of this State," he said, "by simply being mild-mannered and saying 'please' to the Republican machine. . . . Pressure will have to be brought to bear, and pressure which will hurt someone." This is not, he continued, "an instance of forcing men to act against their conscience. It is an instance of forcing men to . . . restore to the people the right to which all the best constitutional authorities say they are entitled."[13]

Later, when Democrats began to be blamed for stopping the workings of the state government, Green advocated emergency appropriations, to which the Democrats again said they would agree. Heaping verbal abuse on the heads of the Republicans, he asserted that "the responsibility for any suffering [is] fixed on the Republican Senators." William C. Pelkey, chairman of the Republican State Central Committee, countercharged that the whole operation was a crass political maneuver. Toupin's sole motive in keeping the prolonged filibuster going, he said, was to advance the cause of Theodore Francis Green for the United States Senate in 1924. That, in turn, said Pelkey, was designed to get Green out of the way so as to clear the road for Toupin himself to win the nomination for governor. But despite all charges, the filibuster went on.[14]

The Republicans were now finding it difficult to keep all their members on hand. Once, when a Republican senator failed to appear, he explained to the anxious Republican leaders that there was really no danger because he had two Democrats in tow with him. Other senators took the hint, and pairing now began to take place regularly.

On Friday, June 13, 1924, with the filibuster in its sixth month, the State Senate began what turned out to be the first of a series of sensational sessions. All that day and all that night Democratic senators, in two-hour relays, read from books or just rambled on about nothing in particular. The next afternoon, the Senate having been in continuous session, Lieutenant Governor Toupin rapped his gavel for attention and ordered the sheriffs to round up all the senators and keep them in the chamber. Upon counting heads, Toupin noticed that there was one Republican missing and declared the Senate "at ease" until the absent senator appeared. At this point the Republican President pro tempore, standing at his own chair on the floor, stood up and claimed the right to preside. He immediately moved for an adjournment, and in one of the fastest roll call votes ever recorded, the Senate stood at adjournment until the next legislative day on June 17.

On the 17th, the Lieutenant Governor of the state of Rhode Island found that Republicans had physically blocked his way to the Senate chamber. Inside the chamber the Republican President pro tempore again called the Senate to order. Immediately "Fighting Bob" Quinn rushed up to the Reading Clerk and tried to pull the roll from his grasp. A riot, involving senators, spectators, and sightseers then ensued. During the melee, Toupin finally managed to enter the chamber, but he could not restore order. In came Governor Flynn himself, to find that the sheriffs, all Republicans, were siding with their party cohorts against Democratic senators. While Flynn contemplated what to do next, the Providence chief of police, in response to a hurried call from someone, arrived on the scene with more than a dozen officers. Eventually, the police restored a semblance of peace. For three more days Providence police remained in the chamber, and the Democratic filibuster droned on.

On Thursday morning, June 19th, the climax came. A thug, allegedly hired by Republican chairman Pelkey, exploded a bromine gas bomb in the Senate chamber, and pandemonium broke loose. The bomb was not very powerful, but it was enough to set off fits of coughing and gagging, and senators scattered out of the chamber in complete disorder. Two hours later Toupin called the Senate back to order, only to find that the Republicans had disappeared. No Republicans, no quorum, no filibuster, no legislative business. The next day, the Republican senators sent word that they had taken refuge in a hotel in friendly Rutland, Massachusetts, outside the jurisdiction of the state of Rhode Island. There they would stay, they said, until constitutional government had been restored in Rhode Island. And so they remained through the summer in Massachusetts—faring much better than had the Dorr insurrectionists who, almost a hundred years earlier, had been arrested in Massachusetts by the Rhode Island militia.[15]

Just after the bomb had been exploded, a letter was prepared from Toupin to Governor Flynn. The Lieutenant Governor stated that the sheriffs had failed to produce the Republican senators, who had left the chamber after bromine gas had filled it. He therefore was calling on the Governor to provide the necessary assistance to force the Republican senators back to the capitol. Flynn then had a proclamation drawn up, stating that under his prerogative as governor he was going to appoint a sergeant-at-arms of the State Senate to enable the Senate to carry on its business. Instructions were also drawn up ordering Mayor Gainer to withdraw the Providence police from the Senate chamber, ordering Sheriff Andrews of Providence County to assist the new sergeant-at-arms, and informing the State Police commissioners of the powers of the new officer. The orders were all for naught: all these letters and proclamations were dated June 20, and because the Republican senators had left the state while the correspondence was being drafted, the several orders were not put into effect.

The interesting thing about the matter is that Toupin's letter, the Governor's proclamation, and the orders to Gainer, Andrews, and the police commissioners were all written by Theodore Francis Green. He even prepared the references to the state constitution which supposedly gave the Governor the power to do all this. Toupin, Flynn, and Green sincerely believed that right was on their side but the flight of the Republican senators to Massachusetts made the orders useless.[16]

Pelkey had been at least partially right in charging that Green's ambition to be a United States senator lay at the root of the filibuster. Green received encouragement from some who thought he deserved the nomination because of his consistent support of the Democratic Party through lean years. He carefully and privately canvassed the state's key Democratic leaders in an effort to sound out his chances for the nomination. Much to his disappointment, he found that he was running a rather poor fourth behind Mayor Gainer, O'Shaunessy, and Governor Flynn, who also had his eye on Senator Colt's seat. Undaunted by the evidence, Green tried to convert more sentiment to his favor. In April he had given a ringing keynote address to the state convention which chose delegates (of whom he was one) to the national convention, and in June he requested Senator Copeland in Washington to have the address inserted in the *Congressional Record.* He offered to pay for the printing expenses if Copeland would send copies to people in Rhode Island. His request arrived too late, for Congress had just adjourned for the summer's political festivities. Green also distributed several hundred statements over the signatures of a few citizens of Rhode Island, none of whom, however, was particularly important or influential in Democratic Party circles. Stress was placed on his past labors for the party, his ability to attract independents in the election, and his "stature" as a native Rhode Islander.[17]

Green kept careful track of the various delegates selected in town and city caucuses for the coming state convention. As each slate was chosen, he solicited its support either by letter or personal call. But in late September he was for all practical purposes eliminated from the running when Mayor Gainer received the pledges of forty of Providence's fifty delegates. In East Providence four of the five delegates were also pledged to Gainer, and Newport's unpledged slate leaned towards O'Shaunessy. Governor Flynn seemed just ahead of Gainer in the Pawtucket delegation as well. Nevertheless, if the battle between Flynn, Gainer, and O'Shaunessy developed into a deadlock, Green could well be the dark horse candidate. At least, so he hoped.[18]

The hope and all Green's efforts were in vain. An apathetic state convention, meeting at the end of September, proved to be in no mood to duplicate the long-drawn-out national convention that had been held in New York two months earlier. Furthermore, because the Rhode Island Senate was still in a state of limbo (all the Republican senators except one, who stayed around to challenge the existence of a quorum at every legislative meeting, were yet living in communal bliss in Massachusetts), the Demo-

crats were not anxious to add to their image as the party of dila-
toriness. Accordingly, they made quick work of the business.
O'Shaunessy threw his support to Flynn to prevent Green from
becoming a compromise candidate, and Flynn defeated Gainer
for the nomination, with most of Green's backing eventually going to the Governor as well. The Democrats went on to nominate
Toupin for governor and Quinn as his running mate.[19]

On the next day the Republicans held their convention and
quickly chose Jesse H. Metcalf for the United States Senate to replace Senator Colt, who had died unexpectedly during August.
Metcalf, Green's old colleague on the Lincoln Party ticket in 1907,
had since cast his lot with the Republican Party. Ambrose Kennedy was again shunted aside, as the party called on former Governor Aram Pothier to recapture the governorship.[20]

The election was a disaster for the Democrats. As some Democrats had feared, the filibuster ran high against their candidates.
Republicans successfully blamed the Democrats for the turmoil
at the State House and the resulting disrepute in the eyes of the
nation. Democrats went down to defeat under a mass of protest
votes. Coolidge and Dawes won the state's electoral votes, carrying every town and city save three; Metcalf was elected to fill both
the remaining lame-duck term of the late Senator Colt as well as
the full term; and Republican Congressmen Burdick and Aldrich
were both returned to Washington by pluralities nine times
greater than O'Connell's, who as the sole Democratic survivor
was re-elected by a scant 2,271 votes. The entire Republican
statewide ticket was also elected, by a plurality of more than
30,000 votes. The Republicans won two-thirds of the seats in the
lower house and all but six in the State Senate. Even Mayor
Gainer had a close call, winning re-election by a mere 2,535 votes.
The self-exiled Republican senators who had been re-elected in
November, 1924, fifteen in number, triumphantly trooped back
to their home state in January.[21]

For Green, the end results turned out to be fortunate. Had he
been nominated, he would have suffered just as serious a defeat
at the polls as had Flynn. As it was, he could afford to consolidate
his own position without having the stigma of a defeat on his
record in that disastrous year.

In 1925 the state Democrats reorganized their leadership in an attempt to stage a comeback in 1926. The chairmanship of the Democratic State Central Committee went to Luigi De Pasquale, who then tried to reshape the party. His efforts bore little fruit, but they did succeed in beginning to point the party in a new direction. Under De Pasquale, the Democrats replaced Mrs. Adams, the vice-chairman of the state committee, with Adelard J. Fortier, a Pawtucket Democrat of French extraction. That action—as well as the selection of De Pasquale himself—attested that the Democratic Party was now beginning to pay increasing attention to ethnic groups other than the Irish. More Italian and French names, particularly, were appearing on the roster of the Central Committee than ever before.

For the moment, the overhaul of the party stopped there, and as far as the Democrats were concerned, the 1926 elections could have been omitted, for they failed to win a single important office. Their campaign oratory that year sounded tired, even when Green (who was not a candidate) invoked the name of Thomas W. Dorr. And on the surface, it might have seemed that the Democrats were tilting at windmills; after all, it was no longer the 1890's, and at least some of the reforms of the Progressive Movement had rubbed off on Rhode Island. The state had established public utility and insurance commissions, it had built some modern highways, and at least two of its Republican governors—Beeckman and Pothier—seemed honest and able.

But when, as chairman of the state convention in October, 1926, Green blasted the Republicans for corruption and oligarchic misrule, he knew whereof he spoke. Under a surface of improvement lay one of the most blatantly corrupt political systems in the nation. Republican dominance rested on their exploitation of three features of the state government: the Brayton Law, the rotten-borough system, and the fact that sheriffs were not accountable to anyone for the fines and fees they collected. The Brayton Law (stipulating that if gubernatorial appointees were not confirmed by the Senate within three days, the power of filling the office fell to the Senate itself), effectively placed the power of appointment in the hands of the Senate. The rotten-borough system placed control of the Senate in the hands of a majority of the towns but a small minority of the population. The non-account-ability feature provided the oil for the machine. Most Democrats knew—though none could document—what the sheriffs (all of whom were Republicans, being appointed by the Grand Com-mittee-appointed High Sheriff) did with the huge amounts of fines and fees they collected. They pocketed enough to make themselves rich, kicked back enough to the rotten-borough sena-tors to perpetuate themselves in office, and contributed enough to the party organization to finance its campaigns. Even without the corporate wealth and bribery that Democrats assumed also fed its coffers, the Republican machine was self-perpetuating.

But out of the 1928 campaign—even though the Democrats lost again—would come a single action that would spell the begin-ning of the end for the Republicans: Theodore Francis Green be-came Democratic State Chairman.

The background of this turn of events was the presidential election and a hotly-contested race for governor. Rhode Island Democrats convened in April to select delegates to the forthcom-ing national convention in Houston. So many of the state's Demo-cratic politicians wanted to make the trip to Texas that the dele-gation was doubled in size by giving each delegate a half vote. Led by Patrick H. Quinn, the state was represented by twenty delegates, including Green, and twenty alternates. Throughout the trying convention, the Rhode Island delegates fought for Governor Al Smith of New York—and not for altruistic reasons. It was generally felt that if Smith, a Roman Catholic, became the Democratic candidate for President, the state party's chances in the election were much improved over 1924, for Rhode Island's population was heavily Catholic. When Smith won the presiden-tial nomination, Rhode Island Democrats began scrambling for the gubernatorial nomination.[22]

There was another reason for their eagerness: Republican Gov-ernor Aram Pothier, whose popularity was enough to discourage most candidates from challenging him in any political contest, had died suddenly in February, 1928, and the race was wide open. There ensued indeed a plethora of Democratic candidates for governor. Joseph Gainer, who had run and lost in 1926, was anx-ious to try again, and he had the support of the Providence wing of the party. Alberic Archambault, with strong backing in the Blackstone Valley, also entered the picture, as did former Lieutenant Governor Felix A. Toupin and former State Senator Albert West. Theodore Francis Green, too, wanted the nomination.

In July James H. Kiernan, a rising young Democrat from Providence, began to ascertain for Green the sentiment of the party leaders. Green wanted to refrain from announcing his candidacy until he felt the time was right, because he was particularly anxious to avoid a damaging intra-party feud. Kiernan concluded that Green did have a fighting chance to secure the nomination, and during Green's absence on a long trip in the West, Kiernan was busy keeping Green's name before the public, inserting newspaper stories about his trip, and laying the foundation for a "Green for Governor" club.[23]

In the late summer and early September, after Green returned to Rhode Island, the Democrats held several rallies, ostensibly designed to show their wholehearted support for Al Smith but actually to serve as forums for the major candidates for the gubernatorial nomination. On September 13, Green formally announced for the governorship, after Archambault and Toupin had already declared their candidacy. Ex-Mayor Gainer decided to withdraw. The Democratic National Committeeman, Patrick H. Quinn, declared his intention of remaining neutral in the coming contest.[24]

The Republicans, meeting first in 1928, nominated Felix Hebert over Ambrose Kennedy as their senatorial challenger to Peter Gerry. Norman S. Case, who had succeeded to the governorship upon Pothier's death, was renominated, as were all three congressmen: Burdick, Richard S. Aldrich, and Monast.

Six days later, on October 9, the fight for the Democratic nomination for governor was carried to the floor of the Democratic State Convention. Gainer, now openly supporting Green, seconded his nomination. Archambault led Green in the first two ballots and Toupin was a close third. Deciding that he was out of the running, Toupin finally threw his weight on the side of Archambault, who was nominated on the fifth ballot. Gerry was renominated by acclamation for the United States Senate, and the three congressional nominees were John J. Cooney, Sumner Mowry,

and ex-Congressman Jeremiah O'Connell. The Democratic platform praised Al Smith and, as usual, condemned all Republicans.[25]

During the 1928 campaign Green did little work on behalf of
the Democratic ticket, though through no fault of his own. On
the contrary, Green claimed that the state Democrats, in their
allocation of speaking engagements, were ignoring him and his
supporters. He was the chairman of one rally in November, but
he made it clear that he was standing for Al Smith and not bother-
ing with the rest of the ticket.[26]

The results of the election were a grave disappointment. Smith
became the first Democratic presidential candidate since the Civil
War to carry the state without benefit of third-party influence,
but he won by only 1,451 votes out of 236,000 cast. Although the
Democrats improved their standing in the General Assembly, the
rest of the results made it clear that the Democratic Party badly
needed overhauling, for despite Smith's victory, the entire statewide Democratic slate lost to their Republican opponents by substantial margins. Peter G. Gerry, taking a particularly bad beating in Central Falls and Lincoln, was surprisingly defeated by
Felix Hebert by a plurality of almost three thousand votes.
O'Connell managed to retrieve his former congressional seat in
the Third District, but Republicans Burdick and Aldrich were easy
victors in the other two districts.[27]

After a defeat that should have been a victory, the Democratic
state committeemen waged a bitter intra-party fight. The follow-
ers of ex-Congressman O'Shaunessy battled those of ex-Senator
Gerry, until Gerry suddenly threw his support to a third faction.
Thereby Theodore Francis Green unexpectedly emerged as the
State Chairman of the Democratic Party.

Green went about his task systematically and carefully. He
brought in J. Howard McGrath, head of the new Young Democrats League, as vice-chairman of the State Committee. Feeling
himself the only person having the will and the strength to bring
about the changes the state party urgently needed, Green began
to reshape and recast the party machinery in his own fashion. He
sought and received advice from a number of persons, the most
notable of whom were Franklin D. Roosevelt and Louis Howe,

Roosevelt's political advisor. On the advice of former Brown Professor J. Q. Dealey, Green began to enlist young college men on
the party's behalf. Dealey also pointed out to Green the advisa-
bility of appealing to the various religious groups in the state, although he also warned Green not to align himself too closely with
any single one. Finally, he suggested that Green push the constitutional convention argument into the background and dedicate
the party to reform and economy. This, he believed, would have
an appeal to the growing electorate.[28]

It soon became clear that Green had great organizational ability, which he tempered with humor and wisdom. To increase his
knowledge of the state legislators and to aid them in legal matters, as well as to co-ordinate their work with that of other Democrats, he established a Law Committee. He organized a Women's
Organization Committee, a Legislation Committee to guide assemblymen on matters before the legislature, a Finance Committee to raise money for the party, a Speakers' Committee, a Nat-
uralization Committee, and a Registration Committee. With
Dealey's advice in mind, Green carefully distributed the membership of each of these committees among all the ethnic and
religious groups of the state. Many declined to serve on the committees because of the press of their own affairs, but, at the same
time, they were flattered at having been singled out for one honor
or another.

At the Jefferson Day Dinner, always a grand affair, Green gave
ample recognition to many groups in the state on the party list,
at the head table, and on the distinguished guest list. Italian
names in particular began to appear in greater quantities. He himself delivered a magnificent address in which he stressed an emphasis on youth and vigor in the party. In brief, as chairman during
the year 1929, Green began to turn the Democratic Party of Rhode
Island into an effective working coalition of ethnic and religious
groups. Indeed, he preceded Franklin D. Roosevelt in recognizing
the necessity of such a coalition. With Roosevelt, it was an uncon-
scious result; it just happened that way. With Theodore Francis
Green, it was planned. On this basis would rest the Rhode Island
Democratic Party for years to come.

Chapter VI

The Political Campaign of 1930

The Governor's office is a political office. Its occupant should deal with political questions. He should take action in such political matters on his own initiative. He should lead and not wait until he is driven into action by an aroused public opinion. —THEODORE FRANCIS GREEN

SHORTLY after the turn of the year 1930, William C. Pelkey, Green's counterpart in the Rhode Island Republican Party, attacked him for using his party position to further his personal ambition to be governor. Green denied the charge, but only halfheartedly. It was not true, as Pelkey charged, that Green had made a deal with Gerry, whereby Green would have the chairmanship and the gubernatorial nomination and Gerry would get the senatorial nomination. Indeed, Green was not sure of Gerry's support until late in July, 1930, when Gerry, who longed to be returned to the Senate, indicated that he not only would not stand in Green's way, but he might also contribute a sizeable sum for purposes of "increasing the numbers of registered voters"—a prevailing euphemism for less savory electioneering practices. But in fact Green had by then been running hard for eight months.[1]

In December, 1929, after a long conference with J. Howard McGrath, Jeremiah O'Connell, and Gerry's man Henry D. Hamilton, Green had decided he would make a concerted effort to secure the nomination for governor in 1930. In the ensuing six months, Green left scarcely a stone unturned. He purchased dance tickets for more social and religious organizations than he could hope to use. In his official role of state chairman, he attended banquets of local town and city committees, keeping in close touch with political events through the town and city chairmen as well.

108

He became ever available for brief talks before ladies' groups or for appearances at church whist parties, and he spoke before such varied organizations as the American-Polish Club, the Sophocles Chapter #106 of the Order of Ahepa, and the Providence Chapter of the Zionists of America. At each affair he praised the aims of the particular group, singing the virtues of Pulaski to Rhode Islanders of Polish extraction, describing Greece's magnificent fight for independence to those whose heritage was Greek, and recounting the glories of ancient Israel to those of the Jewish faith. He appeared before such lodges as the Woonsocket Chapter of the Fraternal Order of Eagles and even donated money, voluntarily, for prizes offered at the American Legion state convention. Few citizens of Rhode Island failed to see and hear Green somewhere, sometime during 1930. Theodore Francis Green was in his social as well as political glory.[2]

Meantime, Green worked on a document in which he hoped to set forth in precise terms a set of principles the state's Democrats would be able to support. This was not to be a party platform in the strict sense of the word, but a declaration of principles around which all Democrats could rally. The final draft was finished and polished by the end of February and released for publication on March 4. The Declaration of Principles called for strengthening the power of the governor in administration and appointments, extending the period of registration of voters through September instead of having it end on June 30 as was then the case, making the distribution of Senate and House seats more equitable for the more populous areas of the state, granting more home rule to the cities and towns, and making sheriffs and clerks accountable for fines and fees.[3]

Besides calling for a sweeping reorganization of the administrative machinery of the state, the Declaration also urged the repeal of the state law for the enforcement of the Federal prohibition amendment. Rhode Island had never ratified the Eighteenth Amendment and the Democratic "wets" thought it thoroughly inconsistent that a state law should have been enacted to enforce it. The law was particularly abhorrent to these "wets" who claimed, and with some justice, that the Republican administration enforced it strictly when offenders were Democrats and loosely or not at all when they were Republicans.

Green received a great deal of publicity from the publication of the Declaration. To carry out the various pledges many measures were introduced into the state legislature by Democratic minority leaders Representative Thomas P. McCoy of Pawtucket and Senator Robert E. Quinn of West Warwick. These proposals never came close to passage in the Republican-controlled Assembly, but Green obtained considerable personal mileage from their mere introduction.

In 1930 the legislature did pass several bills which appeared on the surface to be reform measures, but which were actually attempts by the Republicans to ensure their continued control. A year earlier, it might have seemed that such ruses would never become necessary. "Boss" Pelkey and his cohort, Frederick S. Peck, State Finance Commissioner and former State Representative from Barrington (known to their Democratic detractors as the "firm of Peck and Pelkey") had ruled supreme. Both had managed to survive unscathed the notoriety caused by the bombing in the State Senate in 1924. Pelkey was never prosecuted for his alleged part in the legislative gas attack, and few people were aware of Peck's involvement in the financial arrangements which had kept the refugee Republican senators in unaccustomed splendor in Rutland, Massachusetts. But the stock market crash in 1929 and the deepening depression in 1930 created a new and restless popular mood, and the uneasy Republicans began to prepare for a possible storm.

Under the authority of three recent amendments to the state constitution, the legislature redistricted the city of Providence, reshuffled six seats in the lower house, and realigned two of the three congressional districts. The eighteenth amendment to the state constitution had provided for biennial registration of voters, though the period of registration was not extended through the summer months. The nineteenth amendment had provided for future redistricting of cities to create more representation in the State Senate. Any city with more than 25,000 qualified electors was to be allowed one senator for each additional 25,000, but no city could have more than six senators. Furthermore, the amendment put the legslature in charge of any redistricting necessitated by an increase in the Senate. By the twentieth amendment, the property qualification for voting for city and town councils had finally been dropped, although the qualification was continued on votes concerning tax propositions in towns, as distinguised from cities.[4]

With this as background, the 1930 session of the General Assembly was the scene of several new electoral laws, implementing in particular the nineteenth amendment. The 1928 election had shown that Providence would continue to return Democrats to the State Senate. The Republicans therefore decided to add three more senatorial seats in Providence, on a district basis, hoping thereby to ensure that one or two Republicans would be elected from that city at all times A bill was introduced into the lower house whereby Providence was divided into four well-gerrymandered senatorial districts. Another provision of the bill, applying to the lower house, took one seat each from Newport, Central Falls, and Burrillville, which usually elected at least two Democratic representatives, and gave the seats to Cranston, East Providence, and Warwick, which invariably returned Republicans. A second bill introduced by the Republicans divided Providence into thirteen new wards, subdivided into voting districts with new boundary lines. A third proposal provided for a shifting of the boundaries of two of the three congressional districts in hopes of reducing Democratic strength in the Third District. The three bills passed the House of Representatives on March 21, 1930, by an almost straight party vote; only six Republicans bolted their side and cast their ballots with the Democrats. The Senate passed the bills in April and they were signed into law by Governor Case.[5]

When the bills had been voted upon in the lower house, six Democrats had been absent from the chamber. At a North Providence Democratic Club meeting that evening, state vice-chairman J. Howard McGrath called the six absentee Democrats traitors, intimating that they had sold out to Pelkey who, knowing that some Republican legislators might desert the party on the final vote, wanted to ensure passage of the bills. McGrath's open charges profoundly irritated several Democrats, and Green, who had witnessed the debate and vote, was called upon to calm many ruffled feelings. Mrs. J. Frank Sullivan of Providence, the wife of one of the absentees, called Green after McGrath's speech and denounced McGrath in extremely vituperative language. Green calmed her as best he could. This incident pointed up one of the advantages of having someone like McGrath as the vice-chairman of the State Committee. McGrath had a great deal of political knowledge and, along with James H. Kiernan, a bright representative from Providence, managed many of Green's sorties into the forests of Rhode Island's Democratic politics. But McGrath not only advised Green, he also served as a protective screen for him: often, by his outspoken ways, he diverted to himself animosity that otherwise would have been directed at Green.[6]

Although the redistricting boded ill for the Democratic Party, it helped Green politically, for it necessitated a reorganization of the district committees in the city of Providence. Furthermore, an earlier act had modified the caucus system itself to permit the state chairman, if he desired, to take an active hand in organizing town and city caucus meetings, which selected delegates to state conventions. Green so desired and worked closely with all the chairmen, in particular William A. Shawcross, chairman of the Providence City Committee. Green thereby became an even more important cog in the Democratic machinery. True enough, some of the town and city committees resented his activities, but on balance he gained vastly in personal influence.

The Democrats' registration drive was another asset working for Green. The combination of Gerry and Green helped a great deal. Gerry wanted no obstacle to his bid for the nomination to the United States Senate. From his desk at the *News-Tribune*, which he ran as his official press, Gerry sent a number of checks to the Democratic organization, ostensibly to help the party registration drives in the various towns and cities. Indeed, Peter G. Gerry contributed over $13,000 to the party for the "work of registration." How much of this was used for registration and how much found its way into the pockets of various key personnel of the party one never knows. At least expenses were paid, one way or another. In addition, Gerry sent a $1,000 check which he earmarked especially for the town of Warren.

Green continued to urge the town and city chairmen to press for increased registration, handling each instance with adeptness and skill. It is quite remarkable that he stirred up so little resentment while pushing so many of the thirty-nine town and city chairmen. And along the way, Green encountered a man who would become almost his right arm. In March the Democrats had swept the local elections in Warren, and Green personally congratulated Edward J. Higgins, one of the chief campaign managers of the party there, and Edward Bullock, the town chairman. Under Bullock and Higgins the Warren Democratic organization grew in strength, in large measure due to the efforts of the young Higgins, whom Bullock called "a genius for getting out the votes." Higgins was an energetic politician with whom Green was beginning to form a friendship destined to evolve into one of the most efficiently working combinations in politics. Already Higgins was marked out for a long political career.[8]

But not everything was smooth; in North Providence, discontent continued to fester. In January, 1930, Charles M. Hall, chairman of the Democratic Town Committee, resigned both his chairmanship and his membership on the committee because the expected candidacy of Peter G. Gerry for the United States Senate had become "increasingly abhorrent" to him. In charging that Gerry had a "shifty will to self aggrandisement," Hall was probably referring to Gerry's distribution of monetary donations. Hall also had other complaints. North Providence contained a sizeable number of Italo-Americans, and Hall was concerned that the Democratic Party might not give proper recognition to them. In February Hall wrote Green that Gerry did not deserve the nomination for the Senate but that Green did. Furthermore, he argued, Gerry would lose in 1930 just as he had done in 1928, whereas Green could win. He insisted that the Democratic ticket in 1930 be balanced ethnically, with Toupin and De Pasquale near the top of the slate. Indeed, failure to nominate De Pasquale would be political folly. Hall pointed out that McGrath had "bitterly antagonized North Providence Italians" and unless this problem were settled, there was "potential dynamite" imbedded in the coming election. Continuing his attack on Gerry, Hall publicly charged that Gerry was contributing heavily to the registration drives in the cities while neglecting the towns. Gerry hoped to win the nomination and election as United States senator by concentrating on the cities. Hall felt that Gerry had decided that the towns would vote Republican anyway and was thus slighting them in giving money for "registration." Gerry's neglect of the towns, he said, would doom the state to more Peck-Pelkey exploitation. Gerry's newspaper promptly castigated Hall as a traitor to the party and even charged that Hall was in the pay of the Republican Party to foment trouble within Democratic ranks.[9]

In answer to this claim, Hall angrily demanded that Green call a meeting of the State Executive Committee to air the issue and prove whether he or "do-nothing" Gerry was the honest man. Hall made the letter public and Green, not wishing to keep the feud before the public scrutiny, denied Hall's request and admonished him that charges such as these are to be expected in politics and that the party's energies should be "directed principally to building up the Democratic Party," not tearing it apart. Hall was scarcely placated.[10]

To complicate matters even further, Joseph Maresca, Treasurer of the North Providence Town Committee, took exception to the way McGrath was handling political relations between the State Committee and the North Providence Town Committee. McGrath, he charged, was bypassing him in allocation of registration funds (which Hall had said were insufficient anyway). Maresca took this as a slur on his honor. Charging that both McGrath and Gerry's man Henry D. Hamilton were "enemies of the Italian people," Maresca told Green it was in his power as chairman of the State Committee to "remove the blot" on his name. Maresca did not charge Green with any nefarious tactics. Hall, of course, supported Maresca. Green had to call on the best of his persuasive powers to soothe Maresca's feelings. He wrote him that registration money had been paid directly to the chairman of the North Providence Town Committee in order to avoid splitting the party any further. As Maresca was involved in an altercation with McGrath and Gerry, it was felt that the town chairman, rather than the town treasurer, would be in a more favorable position to "handle the finances." He urged Maresca to continue to support the party and closed his letter with a reference to their mutual friend, Theodore Roosevelt.[11]

Meanwhile Green had launched a private survey among important state Democrats to ascertain his own chances in the coming convention and election. Not only did he want the nomination for governor, but he felt that McGrath ought to succeed him as state chairman. When Green sounded out Patrick H. Quinn, still the Democratic National Committeeman from Rhode Island and a power to be reckoned with, Quinn was noncommittal on both accounts. A poll of various town and city committeemen was also quietly undertaken. From the results of this poll, Green decided that his candidacy looked favorable. After conferring with James H. Kiernan and Patrick Curran, his legal associate, Green concluded that the best method to announce his candidacy would be to draw up a petition, signed by the town and city chairmen, requesting him to be a candidate for governor. He continued to receive private pledges of support from several persons, including Edward J. Higgins.[12]

On August 6 Green formally received a brief petition from thirty-seven of the thirty-nine town and city chairmen, asking permission to place his name in nomination for governor at the state convention. The petition, presented to Green by Patrick Curran, received wide publicity in Rhode Island newspapers, and Green seemed to have the field to himself. Former Governor William S. Flynn stated clearly that he was not a candidate and it was generally held that Toupin, with Gerry's backing, wanted the nomination for mayor of Woonsocket. When the petition was made public, Charles M. Hall declared that Luigi De Pasquale would be a candidate for lieutenant governor, a strategy Hall claimed to be absolutely necessary if the Democrats were to win the statewide elections.[13]

The two signatures missing on the petition were those of William A. Shawcross of Providence, who had declined to sign the document after having conferred with former Governor Flynn, and the chairman of the West Warwick Town Committee, who had decided to remain uncommitted until Patrick H. Quinn made his move.[14]

Until the formal receipt of the petition, Green had refused to discuss publicly the problem of political candidacy, always claiming that the registration of voters, which had ended June 30, was his primary concern. He now answered the petition in a public letter, approved by McGrath and Hamilton, in which he stated that the request had come "almost as a command." He realized that no one could speak for the convention but as far as any group could represent the party in August, the thirty-seven chairmen certainly composed such a body. Green was now in the open.[15]

The future became less bright, however, when in late August, at a banquet given by North Providence Democrats in honor of Peter Gerry's enemy, Luigi De Pasquale, Charles M. Hall boosted De Pasquale for the nomination for lieutenant governor. Speaking in both English and Italian, De Pasquale stated he would accept but would not seek the nomination. Joseph Maresca followed by declaring that Theodore Francis Green would be an excellent man for governor, particularly with De Pasquale as his running mate. Then, after Hall boomed De Pasquale and Maresca backed Green, Placido Caranci, another prominent Italo-American Democratic member of the Town Committee and of the State Central Committee as well, urged the selection of Peter G. Gerry for the United States Senate. The situation was confusing enough when Patrick H. Quinn stood up and delivered a long speech, charging that Gerry had already denied De Pasquale a place on the ticket. Quinn gave reserved praise to Green, but added that though his associations with Green had been pleasant, De Pasquale had been treated badly by the Gerry-Green combination. De Pasquale was "popular not only with the Italian people, but with all classes," said Quinn, and he was a tireless worker who could not be ignored by the Democratic Party.[16]

Furthermore, Quinn added, unless the candidates for United States senator, governor, and lieutenant governor were drawn from the French, the Italians, and the Irish, the ticket could not

win. "It is a fact that the so-called Yankee Democrats are not suf-
ficient in number to turn this State one way or another," he said.
"Both Mr. Gerry and Mr. Green," he continued, "have been
greatly honored by the Democratic Party. The party is not indebted to them. They are indebted to their party and they would
probably readily acknowledge this." Quinn also warned Green
and Gerry that they could not push aside the majority of the
Democrats, "in whose veins run foreign bloods." After criticizing
the interference in North Providence by the Democratic State
Central Committee—for which he blamed Gerry more than
Green—he closed his frank speech with these words: "A man need
not be a tramp to qualify for membership in the Democratic
Party but neither need he be an extremely high-hat variety of
citizen."

On the following day Alberic A. Archambault, the 1928 Democratic candidate for governor, endorsed Quinn's opposition to
Gerry and Green. Thus once again ethnic and religious considerations had arisen to plague Green. In 1912 the French vote had
hurt him badly, and now it looked as if it might be the turn of
the Irish, aided by a few dissident Italians and French. He was
not discouraged, however; ignoring Quinn's outburst, he pressed
on with his campaign.[17]

Democratic political activity moved into high gear in September. Still upset by the probability of Gerry's being the Democratic
senatorial nominee, Quinn charged that Gerry had encouraged
McGrath and Hamilton to write a series of letters that had been
sent to certain town and city chairmen and committeemen, telling
them to take charge of pre-convention work in their localities.
These tactics angered some of the local organizations, which felt
that Gerry was attempting to use his heavy contributions as an
excuse to dictate to them. The Woonsocket City Committee, for
example, went so far as to denounce the candidacy of Felix A.
Toupin for mayor solely as a rebuke to Gerry, who was obviously
supporting Toupin. Somehow, Green was able to vindicate Hamilton and McGrath by saying that the letters had been properly
authorized by the Democratic State Committee, and yet escape
adverse criticism himself. But Gerry continued to be a ticklish

ally to handle: he refused Green's suggestion that he attend a
harmony meeting with Quinn.[18]

The campaign for the Gerry-Green slate was launched early in
September at the annual Democratic outing at Rocky Point. Patrick H. Quinn, for the first time in many years, was not invited to
speak at the gathering. Former Governor Flynn sat in the rear of
the audience, refusing Green's invitation to sit on the speakers'
platform. Toupin, still smarting from his rebuke by the Woonsocket City Committee, intimated in his speech that many "Pel-
key-Democrats" would disrupt the party because of personal
grudges. But when Green lashed out at disgruntled party members who would stir up talk regarding "Irish-Americans, French-
Americans, Italo-Americans, and Anglo-Americans or Yankees," it
was clear where the power lay. By virtue of it, a semblance of
unity began to take shape in the party. Within a few days Quinn
came around. Saying that he was a Democrat above all, but actually just recognizing that he was on the losing side in the feud,
Quinn declared that he would support the Democratic nominees,
whoever they might be.[19]

The rest of the month was a busy time for Green. He had to
convince a union that the men employed by him for some renova-
tion work on his home in Providence were not non-union laborers. He held daily conferences with many Democratic politicians,
particularly McGrath, Kiernan, and Curran. He persuaded Vernon C. Norton of the *Pawtucket Times,* an influential political
writer, to write human interest stories during the campaign, and
to do it without compensation. He achieved the extremely difficult task of convincing both Hall and Maresca to support Gerry
for the senatorial nomination. And slowly, carefully, skillfully, he
patched the political fences that had been dented or ripped down
by Quinn and Hall. As the state convention approached, it was
obvious that the Democratic ticket was going to be a Gerry-Green
combination after all.[20]

Two hundred Democratic delegates crowded into Elks Hall
in Providence on October 1 to nominate their candidates and
adopt a state platform. The assembled Democrats sat in stunned
disbelief when the temporary chairman delivered an hour-and-a-

half keynote speech in which he raised the religious issue again. John J. Cooney, known to his enemies as "Jackass Cooney," was a Providence attorney whose choice as temporary chairman had been approved by Peter Gerry, who did not want O'Shaunessy to preside at all. In his extended oration Cooney charged that the Republican Party had purposely set about to pit the Irish against the Italians while, at the same time, denying representation to "foreigners" in the top echelons of the Republican Party. Furthermore, Cooney accused the Republicans of discriminating against Catholics in appointments to public office. Cooney then claimed that Catholics would undoubtedly vote for two Protestants, Gerry and Green, in the Democratic Party because "Mr. Gerry had consistently supported Catholics for public office . . . [and] Mr. Green, since his entry into public life in 1906, has been a thorough, steadfast, and loyal supporter of every Catholic that ran on the Democratic ticket."[21]

After Cooney's speech, a sense of uneasiness pervaded the hall as the Mayor of Newport, Mortimer A. Sullivan, nominated Gerry for the Senate. Sullivan went out of his way to say that he did so as an American and was nominating Gerry as an American also. Gerry was quickly chosen, without opposition, and Green was nominated and speedily accepted by acclamation.

Luigi De Pasquale was most unhappy. His desire for the party's nomination for the lieutenant-governorship was thwarted by Gerry's personal opposition, and just before the convention began he withdrew from consideration, assailing the "Gerry money-machine." It had been decided that Thomas P. McCoy of Pawtucket, the minority leader in the lower house, would make a good Irish contribution to the ticket, and he was nominated for lieutenant governor, also without opposition. Green wanted an Italian as secretary of state and personally chose Louis Cappelli, a Brown University and Harvard Law School graduate, and a practicing attorney in Providence with no known political enemies. His name was proposed not as an Italian but as the son of an American citizen. The delegates, preferring to show their more liberal sides, greeted this declaration with thunderous applause. Then they proceeded to give the ticket additional ethnic balance by nominating a Franco-American, Louis T. Rocheleau, for general treasurer, and an Irish-American, John P. Hartigan, for attorney general.

Patrick H. Quinn, who had so vehemently denounced the Gerry-Green combination a few weeks earlier, now mounted the platform to announce his unqualified support of the ticket. He told the assembled Democrats that he would "wither" his right hand before he would say "a word intentionally that would disturb the harmony of a Democratic convention." Just after the convention, Green had his way in another important respect: McGrath succeeded him as state chairman.

The platform adopted by the Democrats was based primarily on the Declaration of Principles written by Green earlier in the year. It called, as well, for the outright repeal of the prohibition amendment to the Federal Constitution, as a violation of "the basic principles upon which this government was founded." So stated Rhode Island's Democrats.

As the convention adjourned, many delegates were still a bit shaken by Cooney's speech. They all wondered who, if any, of the principal nominees knew beforehand what he was going to say. The *Providence Journal* called Cooney's speech a deplorable "appeal to religious prejudice" and stated that the soil of Rhode Island "would not nourish such seeds of intolerance." Green told reporters that although he was touched by the personal tribute Cooney had paid him, he had had no idea what Cooney had intended to say.

John J. Cooney asked Green to make no further statement until he had had a chance to talk with him. After conferring with Cooney, Green issued a statement contending that Cooney had only sought to "refute the proposition that the nomination of two Protestants at the head of the Democratic ticket would result in the bolting of the ticket by many Catholic Democrats." Cooney's argument was "not in favor of religious prejudice but against it—an argument not for introducing religion into politics, but for keeping it out." Cooney's appeal, said Green, had been misconstrued. Henry D. Hamilton would say no more than that he had been unaware of Cooney's topic before the speech was made.

Peter G. Gerry joined with Green in defense of Cooney and said religious tolerance was a "tradition" in his own family. He castigated the *Journal* for having labeled Cooney intolerant and charged that the paper's backhanded attempt to inject religion into politics was "one of the oldest and most contemptible of political tricks."[22]

The fact is that Green had been genuinely unaware of the contents of Cooney's speech before it was made. Presumably only one member of the Gerry organization—and no one knows who that was—had glanced at it quickly just before Cooney spoke. It is also doubtful that Gerry knew the exact wording beforehand. Had he been aware of it, he would more than likely have kept Cooney from using it, for the speech would scarcely serve to unify the party at a state convention. In any event, the incident soon blew over.[23]

The Republicans, as expected, renominated Senator Metcalf, Governor Case, and the state officers, and adopted a platform lauding President Hoover's and Governor Case's administrations. The two parties now began their biennial struggle for control of the state. One aspect of the struggle looked bad for the Democrats; despite all their efforts to increase the numbers of registered voters, there had actually been a loss of more than 2,000 since 1928. It was possible that registered Democrats had increased and registered Republicans had decreased, but there was no way of knowing, and on the surface the Democrats had no cause for rejoicing.[24]

The campaign was expensive for Green personally. He contributed $3,500 to the State Committee for general political expenses and gave Patrick P. Curran, his campaign manager, more than $4,500 to pay for expenses of his own campaign. He also spent some $700 for thousands of green match books and mirrors which were distributed throughout the state as an advertising stunt. (Green was quite specific about the exact shade of green to be used. The companies supplying the material were also specific about payment, demanding a check before any shipments were made.) In addition, the State Committee spent a great deal of money, the largest portion of which came from the Gerry family.

Besides the large amounts of "registration" money Gerry had distributed before the state convention, the family contributed more than $50,000. De Pasquale had not been wrong when he said the Democratic Party was indebted to the "Gerry money-machine."[25]

The 1930 state campaign was, in one respect, unlike any yet held. A new era had been ushered in a few years ealier with the arrival of the radio, and Green was one of the first to make use of it in political campaigns. He told radio audiences that a vote for him was a vote for a party that would resist, as the Republicans had not, the efforts of powerful and selfish interests to fasten themselves on men elected to public office. The Rhode Island branch of the League of Women Voters arranged for Governor Case and Green to speak on a joint radio broadcast. When the Governor backed out, pleading "the shortness of the campaign," Green spoke alone under the League's auspices. To the ladies and the radio audience, Green challenged Governor Case to make known his stand on prohibition and to stop straddling the issue. As for himself, Green said he stood for repeal of the Eighteenth Amendment, for giving the governor a real power of appointment, and for repealing the state law that permitted the "rotten-borough State Senate" to upset gubernatorial appointments by the simple device of delaying their confirmations for three days. The Democratic Party, Green said, stood for tariffs that had a public not a private purpose, for honest administration of government, adoption of fair workmen's compensation laws, and the destruction of the Republican machine. On another broadcast, paid for by the Democratic State Committee, Green hammered at the growing unemployment problem brought about in the aftermath of the stock market crash in 1929. He accused Governor Case of doing nothing to alleviate the serious conditions in the state. A few days later he asserted that Governor Case had no convictions on the question of prohibition and was a helpless tool of the Republican machine. He further attacked the Republican state organization as a survival of Braytonism and charged that the "machine" was holding back the economic development of Rhode Island. Green was rapidly learning a new technique of reaching the electorate. Later, he would become a master at it.[26]

Green had campaign help from other unusual sources in 1930. Always known as an athlete himself, despite his small size—Green was a more than adequate wrestler and tennis player—he was endorsed for governor by a host of Rhode Island athletes who formed an "Athletes' Green for Governor Club," and Vernon Norton publicized the many names of the club members, handling the releases and following through on publicity articles in several newspapers. Eddie Dowling, a Rhode Island boy who had gone off to make good in the world of entertainment, wired Green from New York that he would be happy to tour his native state on behalf of the Democratic ticket. Dowling, one of the best name-droppers in show business or politics, also wrote Green that he would do his utmost to influence Al Smith, who was due to make a campaign trip to Rhode Island in late October, to give a good speech on behalf of Gerry and Green. In one letter Dowling managed to convey the idea that he personally was running the Roosevelt and Lehman campaigns in New York, as well as playing cards daily with Al Smith. He even offered to bring the Grand Exalted Ruler of the Elks of America if Green wanted. In fact, he did just that.[27]

Ever the artist, Dowling did not want to follow too closely on the heels of Al Smith, and he wrote Green that the last few days in October and the first few in November would be proper for his appearance in Rhode Island. Making certain that the home folks knew he had postponed a trip to Hollywood and delayed plans for a new Broadway play in order to do his bit "to elect Theodore Francis Green and Peter G. Gerry," the "Cumberland minstrel boy" roared into Rhode Island on October 29.[26]

One of those showmen who cannot resist the temptation to combine show business with politics, Dowling delivered a maudlin speech in his hometown of Cumberland, telling seven hundred spellbound persons that he had been a success because he had a heart. At several rallies in the state, Dowling invoked the name of his idol Al Smith, always telling the assembled throng to vote for Gerry and Green because Al Smith "loved 'em, and I, his little boy Friday, I had to love 'em too!" Competing with Senator David I. Walsh of Massachusetts at a tremendous rally in Providence just before the election, Dowling entertained with a number of songs and then made a speech in which he "revealed a personal knowledge of political conditions" in Rhode Island, which indeed he did have.[29]

The biggest campaign splash of all took place in October when Al Smith himself journeyed to Rhode Island to make his first major political appearance outside New York in a long while. Smith was a personal friend of Peter Gerry, whose family had extensive holdings in New York State, and while in Rhode Island he stayed at Gerry's home. Wherever the "happy warrior" went huge crowds always gathered, and Rhode Island was no exception. Sixteen thousand people crowded Rhode Island Auditorium in Providence—and another ten thousand waited outside—as Smith tore into President Hoover and the national Republican Party for having promised a false prosperity in the 1928 campaign. Smith passed out appropriate accolades for Rhode Island Democratic candidates, paying particular attention to Peter Gerry. More than likely, Smith was in Rhode Island for two major reasons: he was pushing his own candidacy for the presidential nomination in 1932, and he was personally obligated to Gerry.[30]

Senator David I. Walsh of Massachusetts came into his neighboring state to help out, too. He pleaded for the election of Gerry as "a man who stood with the common people." On the same program, Green told a crowd of eight thousand that Case was "padlocked by Pelkey," and State Senator Robert E. Quinn attacked the Republican Party as the "tool of the interests." He charged that banks and utility companies in Rhode Island had contributed large sums to the Republican Party in exchange for legislative favors from the Republican-controlled legislature. Quinn also took Rhode Island mill owners to task for not having reinvested their profits in new machinery instead of hoarding their dividends or investing them in the South. Had they done so, Quinn rightly charged, "they would not be in the position of raising the cry of competition from labor in the South as a means of reducing wages in mills of the North."[31]

Green focussed his personal campaign on three major points: unemployment, prohibition, and the existence of the Republican machine. On October 18 he sent Governor Case a long letter pointing out that the coming winter would add further suffering to the "very large number of unemployed in Rhode Island." Citing President Hoover's statement that the alleviation of suffering in the forthcoming winter was the responsibility of the states, Green asked Case what steps he was planning to take. Green advised the Governor to follow the example of the Governor of Illinois and immediately call a conference of the state's leading citizens to discuss the unemployment situation. Green blamed the Governor for not having taken any steps to relieve unemployment in Rhode Island, and told Case that he could not

evade a reply by stating that this is not a political question. It certainly is a political question in the highest sense of the word. The Governor's office is a political office. Its occupant should deal with political questions. He should take action in such political matters on his own initiative. He should lead and not wait until he is driven into action by an aroused public opinion.[32]

Case responded angrily: he wrote Green that industry in Rhode Island was doing its utmost to provide for those out of work and to keep from reducing the wages of workers still employed. He hoped that the financial activities with which Green was personally connected and identified were fully co-operating along those lines. He deplored Green's introduction of problems of unemployment into the "field of partisan politics and political campaigning." He further implied that Green was one of those who President Hoover had said resented "the notion that things will ever get better and who wish to enjoy our temporary misery."[33]

Green came back with the accusation that Case was dodging the real issues in the campaign and telling the people "bedtime stories." He suggested that the Governor thoroughly investigate the unemployment problem brought about by the depression, which would lead him to the conclusion Green had already reached— that the state government had to do something positive to relieve the plight of the people. Green charged the Governor with attempting nothing and proposing nothing, and of following Republican Party bosses who had ordered him "not to discuss a single issue."[34]

Case still refused to "drag our temporary misfortunes into the field of partisan politics." He challenged Green to show any real evidence of genuine concern for the welfare of Rhode Island workingmen. Claiming that Green neither mixed with his fellow citizens nor was really known by them except impersonally and by reputation, Governor Case called Green "the Machiavelli of the Toupin Administration."[35]

Green assailed the Governor's silence on prohibition, charging that he had evaded the issue completely. Case, according to Green, had neither convictions nor opinions on the matter, and his evasion of a discussion on prohibition was "politically nothing short of cowardice." He also challenged Case to prove that he had not catered to the vested interests when he had refused to veto a bill leasing Rhode Island oyster grounds to private concerns. Green further claimed that State Police boats were protecting the interests of "those fishermen protected by the Republican machine." Case's concurrence with a law that left selection of the Providence city treasurer, harbor master, and director of public aid with the City Council was a "manifestation of the Republican machine's effort to interfere with Providence."[36]

Case wound up his campaign by telling a Republican audience at a Providence rally that Green was an "arch traitor to Rhode Island's tradition and government."[37]

On election day, Green ran a good deal better against Case than Archambault had in 1928, but he still lost the election by 3,512 votes. That was the pattern throughout the state: Democrats made sizeable gains but the entire Republican statewide slate was again elected. Gerry was also unsuccessful, losing his bid for the United States Senate by 2,515 votes, about the same as his margin of defeat in 1928. Only one Democratic candidate, Francis B. Condon of the Third Congressional District, won a major office. The Republican Party won absolute control of both houses of the state legislature, with majorities of roughly three to two in the House and three to one in the Senate.[38]

Although Green had lost another election, he could not be counted out for the future. He had run only a thousand votes behind Gerry throughout the state and had been strong in Providence, Woonsocket, and West Warwick. An elaborate analysis of the outcome of the election was prepared for him by James H. Kiernan, who found by comparing the results with 1928 that Green had actually been defeated by "dissatisfied Italian Democrats" in such key places as Bristol, Johnston, North Providence, Tiverton, Warren, and the Federal Hill section of Providence. In each of these areas there was a strong Italian population which appeared to be voting against the Democratic ticket. Vernon Norton of the *Pawtucket Times* was convinced that Gerry had caused Green's defeat. Had Gerry not been the candidate for the Senate, Norton claimed, the Italian vote would have been the decisive factor in swinging the election to Green. With only an 1,800-vote turnover, Green would have been elected. Norton was certain that in bypassing Maresca and ignoring De Pasquale, Gerry had alienated the Italians.[39]

But Italian dissatisfaction had not been the sole cause of Green's defeat. True enough, North Providence returned a substantial plurality for Case in 1930, whereas it had given a victory to Archambault in 1928, and Democratic pluralities had also been cut in the key Italian districts. Nevertheless, it can be maintained that many votes had simply been hired away from the Democrats. Ten days before the election, Edward J. Higgins presented a memorandum to Green stating that he understood that a great deal of Republican money had recently been freely distributed to several Democratic committeemen. He was certain that neither Gerry nor Green would win the election, and was convinced that the poor registration in 1930 would hurt Green's chances. Gerry and Green were being "crossed" in several places. Another careful study after the election confirmed Higgins' opinions.

Franklin D. Roosevelt had won a great victory as governor of New York, and after conferring with Louis Howe, Higgins decided that Green's chances in 1932 would be more favorable with Roosevelt as the presidential candidate. Even so, the tasks ahead —increasing voter registration in 1932, and securing the gubernatorial nomination again—were formidable. Realizing that a tighter organization would be needed next time, Green asked Higgins to become his permanent campaign manager and personal secretary. McGrath and Hamilton both approved, and Higgins accepted Green's offer. McGrath was re-elected as chairman of the State Committee, and Green was placed on its Executive Committee. Thus Green's group of Democratic leaders began preparations for the 1932 campaign.[40]

Chapter VII

Mr. Green Wins the Governorship

The test of true success isn't accomplishment but endeavor.
———Theodore Francis Green

I
N 1931 the nationwide depression was the most serious problem facing America, and many proposed solutions were
bandied about in Rhode Island as elsewhere. The central issue in
Rhode Island was whether the state or the local communities
should be responsible for administering relief to the distressed.
In November, taking a political page from President Hoover's
book of traditional and conservative rules, Governor Case stated
that it was "the duty of the local committees, chiefly, to care for
their own unemployed and needy." "The primary obligation,"
Case argued, "rests on the city and town"; he would have them
spend money for relief and then have the state reimburse them
by *lending* them money at 3 per cent interest.[1]

Theodore Francis Green did not agree with Case's approach to
the problem. Three weeks after Case's appeal to a special session
of the General Assembly for legislation to implement his proposal, Green (calling himself the "present head of the Democratic
Party by virtue of his candidacy for governor in 1930") issued a
nine-point statement taking Case to task. Case's approach, he
charged, would result in dealing with the relief program in a
"strictly partisan manner," through a Republican-appointed commission of overseers. Furthermore, Green argued, if Case's plan
were followed, it would only mean an eventual increase in taxes
on the local level to pay the principal and interest of the state
loans. More important, Green believed that Case's approach was
fundamentally unsound. To Green, the cause of unemployment

was the inequitable distribution of wealth, and the only way the economy could be revitalized was by an increase in consumer purchasing power. That could be done in part by raising minimum wages. Additionally, he believed, state money should be given to localities as outright grants with no restrictions on them by outside groups, and the cities and towns should spend the funds, not as relief, but as payment for work rendered by the people. The people, he said, did not want charity; they wanted work, and the state ought to supply them with jobs. Finally, the solution rested, in part, on the enlightenment of the owners of industry and others who could afford to carry the burdens of the poor. Calling for a luxury tax as one way to raise money, Green urged that as long as the state had emergency funds, it should levy no other extra taxes.[2]

The General Assembly, however, passed a bill putting into effect the Governor's version of relief. The Democrats attempted to amend the measure by striking out the need for repayment of loans to the state, but they were voted down by the Republican majority. Thereupon, rather than risk being accused of hamstringing relief, the Democrats went along with Governor Case's bill. It passed the lower house unanimously and was quickly approved by the Senate, and thus one-and-a-half million dollars were appropriated and a commission was appointed by the Governor to distribute state funds to the towns and cities. On the commission were State Banking Commissioner Latimer C. Ballou, General Treasurer George C. Clark, and chairman of the State Tax Commission Zenas W. Bliss, Green's old political antagonist in the 1907 legislature. Naturally, all the commissioners were Republicans.[3]

Meantime, Green was diligently working on the upcoming campaign. Much of the work was simply keeping abreast of developments inside the party. For one thing, as late as the end of 1931 Green was still not certain what Peter Gerry intended to do about his political career. In June James Kiernan had told him that Gerry was seriously thinking of becoming a candidate for governor, thus hoping to keep his political chances alive for the 1934 senatorial race against Republican Senator Felix Hebert. In December Kiernan told Green that Gerry was an "active but not avowed candidate for Governor." Green continued to have state Democrats sounded out as to their feelings towards himself. Edward J. Higgins conducted an informal confidential poll, from which Green concluded that there was more sentiment for him for governor than there was for Gerry. Furthermore, South County Democrats seemed anxious to support Green, and there were indications that if the towns in that section of the state were well organized behind him, Green had an excellent chance to win in 1932. Nevertheless, Higgins warned, an ethnically balanced ticket was more of a requirement than ever.[4]

Green closely followed political trends in Rhode Island. In January, 1932, Luigi De Pasquale told him he wanted to return to party work, intimating that he would like to be Green's running mate the following November. De Pasquale informed Green that his interest in being lieutenant governor was more in gaining recognition for Italo-Americans than in any personal success. Remaining temporarily noncommittal on this issue, Green attempted to keep in friendly contact with all leading Democrats in the state. To this end, in February he gave a private dinner party for all former Democratic gubernatorial candidates, and he regularly attended State Executive Committee meetings, where personalities were avoided and the main emphasis was placed on increasing voter registration.[5]

On one matter, however, personalities were unavoidable. Given the nature of politics in Rhode Island, Al Smith's political fortunes were a key factor in Democratic politics in the state. Early in February Smith released a public statement saying that although he would make no pre-convention campaign for the Democratic presidential nomination, he would definitely be willing to run if nominated. Staunch Smith supporters in Rhode Island, led by J. Howard McGrath, Mayor James Dunne of Providence, and Providence City Chairman William A. Shawcross, thereupon urged the activation of Smith Clubs in Rhode Island. National Committeeman Patrick H. Quinn, however, mindful of the tie between Gerry and Smith, thought that Smith's nomination would be unwise. He also believed that Smith could not be elected even if he did win the nomination. Quinn was joined in this opinion by Alberic A. Archambault and Luigi De Pasquale. Green sided with the anti-Gerry Democrats on the ground that it was doubtful that Smith would be stronger in 1932 than he had been in 1928. Though he fully realized how important it could be for Rhode Island if Smith headed the national ticket, Green nevertheless warned that "Democrats anxious for success in the next campaign should not let their enthusiasm run away with their judgment." Aligned against Green in these sentiments were Party Treasurer Joseph Broderick; former Governor William S. Flynn; and the 1930 candidate for attorney general, the popular John Hartigan. Peter Gerry himself publicly endorsed Smith for President.[6]

Though it might appear that Green was risking his gubernatorial chances by taking a stand in opposition to Gerry, in reality he was not. By the time Smith had made his statement, Green had decided to declare his independence from Gerry, who had caused so much resentment among Democrats in the 1930 election. In that election, Green had gone down in defeat with Gerry, despite the facts that both of them had had Smith's personal support, that he had campaigned for them in Rhode Island, and that he had himself carried the state's electoral vote. Green therefore decided to sever his public connection with Gerry. He would, of course, back Smith if the national convention selected him, and he would go to Chicago pledged to him as a member of the state delegation; but his judgment was that Franklin D. Roosevelt now looked like too formidable a candidate.[7]

Green was praised by many people for his stand. A few days later, he had occasion to elaborate his position privately. Frederick H. Allen, a New York attorney and early backer of Roosevelt, asked Green for his opinion about Rhode Island and the coming presidential race. Green answered that he felt Roosevelt would be by far the strongest candidate the Democrats could nominate. He also said that though many Rhode Island Democrats had expressed strong Smith sentiment, their private feelings were that Smith could not win if nominated. Green believed that they spoke in support of Smith "for public consumption only and because they think that Smith, the most popular candidate here, would help the Rhode Island situation the most."[8]

Despite this problem, Green managed to remain on fairly close terms with most state Democrats. To accomplish this, he spent most of his time in conferences with his manager Higgins and in negotiations with other political leaders. In the main, he was successful: National Committeeman Patrick H. Quinn, for example, even gave Green his proxy to represent Rhode Island at the national committee meeting in Washington. Quinn also urged him to have another meeting of former Democratic gubernatorial candidates, to try to induce them to press harder for increased voter registration. He reminded Green that Gerry was not now, as he had been in 1930, disposed to furnish funds for this purpose. Green, however, wanted to delay any such meeting until late spring. Meanwhile he took to radio to urge his fellow citizens to register for the coming election.[9]

Green's caution stemmed from the fact that though he was the front-runner, he was not the only aspirant for the governor's chair. Felix A. Toupin, Mayor of Woonsocket and still beholden to Gerry, was one threat to Green. Another was John J. Cooney, the grandiose keynoter of the 1930 state convention, who announced his candidacy for the gubernatorial nomination in 1932. Cooney quickly had such "surprising success" among potential delegates to the 1932 convention that James Kiernan, after a careful study, admonished Green that unless he soon announced his own candidacy, Cooney might well have the nomination "sewed up" in a short time. Kiernan was for Green, but he warned him that if by convention time Cooney had gathered enough strength to win the nomination, Kiernan would then have to "face conditions as they are." Many people thought that Green was still "largely in the hands of the enemy," meaning Gerry, and Kiernan himself would have to take care lest his own connection with Green hurt him in the party. Louis Cappelli, whom Green had picked for secretary of state in 1930, joined the Cooney forces as vice-president of the Cooney for Governor Club. Peculiarly enough, however, he told

Green that he was still for him for governor and would resign his position anytime Green asked him to. Green advised him to make up his own mind; he would not do it for him.[10]

In mid-April Green met with the Democratic members of the legislature at their customary banquet after the adjournment for the year. He held several conferences with leading Democrats of the House and Senate, sounding them out about his and Cooney's chances. Higgins prepared another summary for Green after having conducted a poll among various town and city committeemen. Contrary to what Green had been told about Toupin's candidacy, Toupin himself assured Higgins that he was going to run for re-election for mayor of Woonsocket and had even refused a spot on the Cooney ticket. Antonio Prince, Woonsocket City Auditor and of French extraction, convinced Higgins that Toupin would never be able to obtain Woonsocket support for the gubernatorial nomination at the convention. Higgins then concluded that Green was still the leading contender, in that political leaders in the state refused to take seriously "Jackass" Cooney's candidacy.[11]

Early in May Green received a temporary setback in his hopes for the national ticket. Frederick H. Allen had informed Green confidentially that he had tried to persuade J. Howard McGrath not to tie the Rhode Island delegation to Al Smith in the coming national convention. McGrath expressed to Allen the hope that Roosevelt would stay out of the fight in 1932, as his nomination would not be good for Rhode Island Democrats. After talking with Peter Gerry as well, Allen concluded that McGrath and Gerry were pushing Smith's candidacy solely because they thought that by so doing they could make their control of the state organization more secure. Allen had advised Roosevelt to stay out of the Rhode Island feud and allow the local people to work out the problem themselves. He knew full well that Green was personally for Roosevelt, and he had hopes that the Rhode Island delegation would at least go to the national convention unpledged. Allen's optimism proved unfounded, however, for the Democratic State Convention instructed the Rhode Island delegates to the national convention, including Green, to vote for Al Smith. At the Democratic National Convention in Chicago in late June, some Rhode

Island delegates did not favor Smith, but they all obeyed their instructions and stood by him. Even after Roosevelt was assured of the nomination on the fourth ballot, Rhode Island held firm to the "happy warrior." That did not, however, prevent some of them from working in other directions behind the scenes. Green, despite his official commitments to Smith, made several contacts at the convention with James A. Farley, and thus began an association that would bear fruit in campaigns to come in Rhode Island.[12]

Although Louis Cappelli, working both sides of the political fence, had told Green in June that he thought that he could see the Cooney boom bursting before long, Cooney continued his efforts to secure the gubernatorial nomination. And even after as few as 125 people showed up at a grand campaign ball he staged late in July, Cooney would not abandon hope. Meantime, Green had continued to remain noncommittal, issuing a statement in mid-May that he was not declaring any unwillingness to be a candidate, but that for now all political efforts should be directed toward increasing voter registration. After that had been completed there would be plenty of time for candidates' statements. Indeed, Democratic efforts, thanks particularly to Edward J. Higgins, eventually did bring about substantial increases in the voter registration. A net gain of 15.5 per cent over 1928 was reported; 306,281 people, nearly 44 per cent of the total population, registered to vote in 1932.[13]

On his return from the national convention, Green was greeted by a form letter from the Cooney forces, attempting to prove that Cooney was the party's best prospective candidate. Green then decided it was time for him to issue his own public statement, and he accordingly announced on July 7 that he was available for the Democratic nomination for governor. Green immediately began campaigning openly by attacking Governor Case for his "lackadaisical" attitudes toward the unemployed workingman. When Henry T. Samson, chairman of the Governor's Conference on Unemployment and Relief, criticized Green for injecting partisan politics into the unemployment picture, Green retorted that unemployment was a political matter and that he would continue to press his point.[14]

In his campaign for the nomination, Green chose to disregard all other Democratic hopefuls and concentrate on attacking Case. He gave little weight to Cooney's chances, and Gerry had removed himself from all political activity in the selection of the state ticket. Or, so he said. Gerry would not seek the nomination for himself, but he might well try to select the nominee from behind the scenes. Gerry had rankled at Green's open challenge to him in refusing to endorse Smith before the national convention. In Chicago, Gerry had been a delegate too, and word had reached him of Green's confidential chats with James A. Farley. Furthermore, Green had been the first of the state delegation to support Roosevelt publicly after the convention. After these events, Gerry had been especially cool to Green.[15]

In keeping with Higgins' well-planned strategy, South County Democrats endorsed Green for governor two weeks after the announcement of his availability. Cooney remained unmoved, declaring such support negligible, and it began to be reported that former Mayor Gainer of Providence, expecting that a Green-Cooney deadlock might develop, hoped to bring about his own selection as a compromise candidate. But Higgins pressed on, systematically and effectively. Inducing Green, Mayor Dunne of Providence, and J. Howard McGrath to plea publicly for party unity, he privately went to work on the delegates from Newport County. In late August Green gave a quiet dinner for the eighteen key committeemen from that area. (Indeed, it was so quiet that extensive directions were required to enable the guests to find the secluded inn, far from the main road, at which it was held.) His purpose was accomplished when, after the dinner meeting, he was endorsed by Democratic leaders from Jamestown, Little Compton, Middletown, Portsmouth, and Tiverton. Only one important figure balked. Mayor Mortimer Sullivan of Newport, who controlled his city's committee and who, some felt, was Gerry's secret candidate, refused Green his endorsement and stated that Green had by no means secured the nomination. Even so, as summer moved into September, Green was the leading candidate for the nomination. He was followed by a fading Cooney, a hopeful Gainer, and an opportunistic Sullivan. The lieutenant-governership was wide open. James Kiernan told Green he would like to be his running mate, but Green preferred State Senator Robert E. Quinn, the minority leader in the upper house.[16]

By the third week of September, despite the usual rash of protestations that it was anybody's race—and despite a rumor published in the *Newport Daily News* that the Gerry faction was organizing behind Gainer to head off Green—a Green-Quinn slate seemed assured. Higgins claimed Green had between 120 and 135 delegates pledged to him, more than enough to give him the nomination on the first ballot.[17]

Rhode Island Democrats met in state convention on October 7. Only two outbursts of friction disrupted its otherwise harmonious proceedings. Pawtucket boss Thomas P. McCoy, irritated by McGrath's continued interference in Pawtucket politics and unwilling to share the proceeds of his position with anyone, succeeded in working into the party platform an indirect rebuke of McGrath. At his instance, the platform pointedly reiterated an old Democratic principle, that of the importance of home rule; and though McGrath was not mentioned by name, he was obviously the target of McCoy's motion. The other discord was a contest over credentials between two factions from South Kingstown, which was quickly settled in favor of the slate of delegates that opposed Green.[18]

The convention speedily adopted a platform—calling for outright grants to towns and cities, for the cancellation of the unemployment relief loans, for increasing the powers of the governor, for repealing the Eighteenth Amendment, and for reorganizing the state's administrative system—and then it turned to the business of nominations. Theodore Francis Green was nominated by none other than the sister-in-law of Peter Gerry, Mrs. John Nicholas Brown, an act of which Gerry hardly approved. The only other name placed in nomination was that of John J. Cooney. In a speech seconding Cooney's nomination, his cousin Thomas F. Cooney attempted to kindle enthusiasm for his candidate by reminding the delegates of Green's record as a loser in the elections of 1912, 1918, and 1930. Unimpressed, the delegates gave Green an easy victory—127 to 51—on the first ballot, as Higgins had predicted; and when the count was announced, the convention voted Green their nominee by acclamation. Even so, the vote was by no means a runaway; Green actually had no really solid support from any substantial bloc of delegates. Providence, like most other towns and cities, split its votes, giving Green a slight majority. Adding these votes to those of the handful of solid Green towns gave him a healthy majority in the final analysis, but McCoy received thirteen votes and Mayor Sullivan four, even though neither had been nominated. And it was obvious that Peter Gerry was not on Green's side when his man Friday Hamilton, himself a delegate, cast his ballot for Cooney.

After selecting Green, the convention turned to the business of choosing the rest of the slate. Robert E. Quinn was nominated for the lieutenant-governorship without opposition after Kiernan and McCoy withdrew, and the candidates for secretary of state and attorney general, Louis Cappelli and John Hartigan, were also unopposed. Antonio Prince secured the nomination for general treasurer by defeating Clarence Palmer, 134 to 40. In the speech nominating Prince, the delegates were reminded that without him on the ticket, the northern tier of the state—that is, the French—would have no representation. Most of the delegates wisely realized that this was to be avoided, and Prince had little difficulty in fighting off Palmer. Congressman Francis B. Condon was renominated, and for the other district—representation having been cut to two as a result of reapportionment after the census of 1930—the convention nominated Dr. John W. O'Connell, a state senator from Westerly.

In their convention a few days later, the Republicans renominated Governor Case and endorsed his relief program, though not without some opposition. They nominated former Congressman Ambrose Kennedy for lieutenant governor and renominated, without opposition, the rest of the state officials. Congressman Burdick was selected to do battle with Condon, and State Senator Thomas P. Hazard was chosen to vie with O'Connell.

The 1932 gubernatorial contest was sharp and bitter. Green opened his bid for the governorship at a rally in Newport, where he emphasized that unemployment would be a major issue in his campaign. He did not hold Hoover and the Republican Party directly responsible for the depression, but he charged that they had been wrongheaded and lax in doing something constructive about it. On the ground that the replacement of men by machinery had been a contributing factor to rising unemployment, Green denounced Republican proposals to encourage an increase in production. The solution, he said, was in providing a more "equitable distribution of wealth and machine production." His own slogan for Rhode Island, he concluded, was "humanity first." (That was the fundamental difference between the two parties. At a rally of the Rhode Island Republican League of Colored Voters, a speaker attacked Green's approach to unemployment as being dictated by his heart and not his head; there was, said this Republican, "no place in statecraft for the man who would be swayed by sympathy rather than by his own reasoned judgment as to the policy which would best serve the interests of all the people.")[19]

Green attacked Case as a man who had "refused to recognize, or perhaps did not understand, the necessity of such social measures as old age pensions and unemployment insurance." He berated Case for inaction in alleviating the evils of the depression in Rhode Island and blasted the Republican machine for jamming Case's ill-advised loan-relief program through a special session of the legislature. Calling the Republican record in the state destructive instead of constructive, Green charged that the Pelkey-led machine was "sucking the lifeblood" out of its own party. Green appealed to all Republicans who believed that a political party was "a means to an end and not an end in itself" to cast their votes for him. He claimed that national and state aspects of the economic plight of the people were closely related, and said that a vote against Hoover should also mean a vote against Case. Case remained aloof at first and refrained from answering Green's attacks. When Green challenged him to a debate, Case merely ignored the invitation.[20]

In Newport, at a rally of the Colored Unit of the Young Men's Democratic Club, Green explained his own sincere interest in the Negroes of the state. Shrewdly, he began by mentioning that he had recently entertained in his own home a leading colored poet who was giving a series of lectures at Brown University. Then he reminded the Negro voters that they had often "voted Republican not because the Republican Party is doing anything for the colored people . . . but merely for the traditional gratitude for what the great Republican President Abraham Lincoln did for the race in freeing the slaves." The true interest of the Negro, he said, was as workingmen, and as such they should not vote "to maintain in power a party machine which legislates and administers the laws in the interest of a small group of the very rich."[21]

At Woonsocket Green turned to an attack on the machine of Peck and Pelkey. Speaking in French to a predominately French audience, he said that although he himself was a real estate taxpayer in Woonsocket, he, unlike Republican Pelkey, still believed in humanitarianism above financial profits. At this same rally he also assailed Case. For once, Green was on fortunate footing in the Blackstone Valley: he had no French opponent, he had in Antonio Prince a French running mate, and the Democratic mayor of Woonsocket was Felix A. Toupin. Too, Green's subscriptions to such newspapers as *Le Jean-Baptiste* began to return a profit to him; both Green and Prince were able to bring "le message de la democratie aux Franco-Americains dans leur propre language." Indeed, the French press in the Blackstone Valley was solidly behind Green. The French vote was now his and his alone.[22]

At a rally in West Warwick, Green declared that just as the people of the nation were turning to Franklin D. Roosevelt, the people of Rhode Island were turning to him and the Democratic Party to rid the state of "autocratic, selfish, materialistic, and inefficient rule." In River Point he again excoriated the state's Republicans for not contributing money for unemployment relief but only lending it to the cities and towns. At Portsmouth and Middletown—that latter having its first Democratic rally since 1912—Green promised a "square deal for the fishermen" of Rhode Island. He would, he said, protect the "constitutional rights" of all the state's fishermen to take fish from any of the state's waters and stop the Republican practice of granting the best fishing locations to friends of the Republican machine. To lure the Irish voters to hear him denounce Case's lack of leadership, Green imported the former Mayor of Boston, John Fitzgerald, to serenade his Rhode Island neighbors with his famous rendition of "Sweet Adeline."[23]

Before the Colored Women's Non-Partisan Political and Civic League, Green answered four questions the League had posed. He endorsed repeal of the Eighteenth Amendment, though repeal should be accompanied by state legislation making impossible the return of the saloon. Second, he was for more home rule in the towns and cities; particularly, he opposed legislative interference in the matter of police boards and commissions. He was, third, in favor of old age pensions and, fourth, he believed that all citizens should be treated alike without regard to race, color, or religion. Because of this and his many other addresses to Negro audiences, it began to appear that Green was making heavy gains with Negro as well as French voters.[24]

In late October, finally realizing that Green was making an impact on the electorate, Governor Case began to accept Green's challenge instead of ignoring him. The Governor demanded to know what Green would do specifically to improve the financial condition of the state if he were elected. Green was bristling with answers. He would, he said, reorganize and consolidate eighty overlapping boards and commissions into a few executive departments, thereby saving the taxpayers' money and improving the credit standing of the state. He would clean out all the political appointees on the commissions and boards—many of whom were also state legislators—who had been given useless jobs by Republican administrations and Republican legislatures. He would prevent such political subterfuges as the Republicans' plans for a five million dollar bond issue to erect a bridge over Narragansett Bay, which he charged was a scheme cooked up by Boss Pelkey and only ostensibly a means of putting men to work. Finally, he threw the ball back to Case by advising the Governor to start talking "about appropriating the money for the relief of suffering humanity in Rhode Island." A week later, Green said that instead of constructing a bridge over the bay, the state should erect a bridge "to cross over the chasm of despair."[25]

Congress' refusal to grant immediate payment of the veterans' bonus in 1932 had created another large bloc of dissatisfied people, readily accessible to the politician's appeal for votes. At a rally well attended by unemployed ex-soldiers in late October, Green depicted the Democratic Party as the real friend of the veterans. The Republicans could hardly be looked upon as friends of the veterans, he said, in view of the way Hoover had used the army, three months earlier, to rout out veterans encamped on the mudflats of Anacostia. Unlike Hoover, said Green, Woodrow Wilson had always approved every measure of benefit to veterans, and Roosevelt would do even more. The assembled ex-soldiers cheered, stomped their feet, and demanded a bonus all over again.[26]

Late in October Al Smith addressed an enthusiastic audience in Providence, delivering a brief speech on behalf of the state Democratic ticket, and a few days later the Democratic candidate for President, Franklin D. Roosevelt, visited the state in search of its four electoral votes. Accompanied by Theodore Francis Green, Roosevelt motorcaded through Pawtucket, East Providence, and Providence on his way north to Boston. Rhode Islanders were not yet as enamored of the New Yorker as they were to become; he simply could not warm the crowd the way Al Smith had done. Only in Woonsocket did Roosevelt receive what could be called a zealous reception.[27]

The last week of the campaign was particularly trying and frantic. While Case and Green continued to swap insults and charges, the Republican candidate for secretary of state, incumbent Ernest L. Sprague, revived an issue that had hurt Green in 1930: the filibuster of 1924. He accused Green of having been the chief adviser of Democratic policy on that infamous occasion, and another Republican, State Senator Sidney Clifford of Providence, charged that Robert E. Quinn had had an all-important hand in the affair. Green and Quinn wisely ignored the charges, directing their fire instead at Republicans for past ballot manipulation and urging careful watch over the vote count on election day. Green said that his ambition to be governor was an ambition to serve the people of the state, not merely to warm the chair as Case was doing. That was an unethical statement, said the Governor, and it only proved that Green was unstable, immature, unsound, and incapable of employing constructive ability.[28]

To answer whispered allegations that his bachelorhood was indicative of an effeminate tendency, Green published a full page advertisement in the rotogravure section of the *Sunday Journal.* Several pictures showed him in various stances chosen to amplify Green's obviously muscular physique. One picture displayed him, stripped to the waist, wielding an axe on a sturdy tree; another showed him carrying a huge boulder while building a wall; and still another pictured him as a wrestler applying a wristlock to an unfortunate opponent, possibly a Republican, writhing in apparent agony. Green was also shown in poses as a lawyer, businessman, and soldier, each time dressed accordingly. The advertisement made a strong impression and even evoked nationwide interest: *Time* magazine deemed it appropriate to take note of Rhode Island's latest political innovation in handling a smear campaign.[29]

Under Higgins' skillful direction, Green had waged a good campaign, and on election day he had his reward. After twenty-six disheartening years in Rhode Island politics, he was finally, on November 7, 1932, elected governor of the state. The *Providence Journal* called his victory "the greatest upset in history," but it was by no means a fluke. He had beaten Case by a plurality of 31,036 votes, running ahead of all his fellow Democrats in the state, though all statewide candidates and both congressional candidates won handily. Only Franklin D. Roosevelt ran ahead of Green, and he did so by a mere two hundred votes. Green almost had an Assembly of his own party: the Democrats fell just two delegates short of a majority in the House of Representatives, and just six short of a majority in the rotten-borough State Senate. Green lost only the cities of Cranston and Warwick, and he piled up great majorities in Providence, Woonsocket, Central Falls, Pawtucket, and Newport. He made large gains in the ordinarily Republican towns, carried the French areas by almost three to one, increased the Democratic vote among the Italians on Federal Hill in Providence, and carried North Providence by more than seven hundred votes, whereas he had lost it in 1930 by two hundred.[30]

Higgins had done a brilliant job in getting out the voters, and the Democrats obviously gained by the increased registration. Indeed, their gains clearly came not from Republicans who voted for Democrats, but from the vastly greater number of registered Democratic voters. Case, in fact, actually received three thousand more votes in losing in 1932 than he had in winning in 1930. But Green gained 38,000 votes in 1932, and this was the difference between the parties.

In accounting for Green's victory, however, a single fact was perhaps more important than all the detailed considerations: the economic depression that had engulfed the nation since 1930. Voters blamed the Republicans for the depression and swept Democrats into office to do something about it—a familiar phenomenon in American history. The main significance of Green's and Higgins' careful work was that it laid the foundations for successful campaigns in the future.

The shrewder Republicans quickly grasped the implications of their defeat. Two days after the election, State Chairman William C. Pelkey said that "Republicans in Rhode Island never are discouraged by temporary setbacks," but within a month he saw fit to resign. An era was coming to an end.

Chapter VIII

Governor Green's First Term: 1933–35

> *We meet here under unusual conditions. The people of this State of different party affiliations have expressed emphatically their desire for a change in administration. The conditions which in part created that desire are such as to call for all wise counsel and all the patriotic devotion of which we are capable. We must remedy those conditions.* ——THEODORE FRANCIS GREEN

THE firing of a seventeen-gun salute on the grounds of the Capitol in Providence, a quaint Rhode Island custom announcing that the governor of the state has been duly sworn into office, was unexpectedly delayed for several hours on inauguration day, January 3, 1933. Theodore Francis Green had arrived at the State House at the proper hour, only to be kept waiting while the Republicans in the House of Representatives fought over the choice of Speaker. As it turned out, the delay was beneficial. The new governor profited considerably from the intra-party feud, which was based on one of Rhode Island's most common causes of friction, ethnic considerations.[1]

The Democrats had won forty-nine seats in the House, two short of a majority, and thus the Republicans should have been able to select one of their own as Speaker. But Benjamin Cianciarulo of Providence, twice Republican floor leader, believed himself eminently deserving of a higher position, namely the speakership, but few of his colleagues agreed. Cianciarulo charged that there was a conspiracy among Republican legislators to deny him his rightful place simply because he was of Italian lineage.

He asserted that Republicans should recognize the Italo-Americans of the state by making him Speaker, and he threatened to bolt the party ranks unless he were chosen over Roy Rawlings of Richmond. On the first ballot, Cianciarulo received only one vote, but that was enough to keep Rawlings from winning; he received only forty-nine votes to Democrat William E. Reddy's fifty. A majority of the hundred representatives was necessary to win and obviously one other Republican had voted in the secret ballot for Reddy. A second secret ballot resulted in a fifty-fifty tie between Rawlings and Reddy—thus Cianciarulo or the other Republican had again voted for Reddy. Six more ballots were taken, with the same result each time. Between ballots, while Green was waiting for a decision, Republicans tried in vain to convince Cianciarulo that his best interests lay in backing Rawlings. Then on the ninth ballot Cianciarulo and his unknown Republican collaborator teamed up and William E. Reddy of West Warwick, a Democratic veteran of the House for twenty-two years, received fifty-one votes and became Speaker.[2]

Under House Rules the Speaker still selected the membership of the committees and had unchecked power of recognition. Immediately, the Democrats began to use these weapons to give House Republicans a taste of their own tactical medicine. On the second day of the session the Democrats, with Reddy presiding and Cianciarulo leading their strategy, passed the old House Rules by voice vote. This meant that Reddy would continue to determine the composition of the permanent committees and thus that they would have Democratic majorities. Several Republicans, furious that Reddy had ruled the adoption of the Rules by voice vote, arose to demand a roll call. Reddy merely ignored their demands and refused to recognize any of them. He appointed James H. Kiernan as the Deputy Speaker, and Democrat Edmund W. Flynn found himself ostensibly House majority leader instead of minority leader.

The Republicans in the State Senate, with a narrow but safe majority of six seats, selected Harry T. Bodwell of Cranston their majority leader while the Democrats chose William G. Troy of Providence as their minority leader. Naturally, Lieutenant Governor Quinn was the presiding officer.

This was the state of affairs in the Assembly as Green took the oath of office and then delivered his inaugural address. The address, a relatively short one, was an appeal for the legislature to pass good laws and not to be concerned with who got credit for their introduction. He recommended several specific measures, some political, some humanitarian. To ensure accurate counts in future elections, Green asked the legislature to consider the purchase of voting machines and the reorganization of the State Returning Board in a nonpartisan manner. He also urged a constitutional amendment abolishing the inequities in the distribution of Senate seats. Among the welfare measures Green recommended were an old-age pension law, the extension of mothers' aid to include all families where children were in need of milk and food, and the reorganization of the system of factory inspection to make working conditions safer in the state's mills. The Governor also called for public works projects, particularly to improve the state's water and air transportation facilities, which would ultimately attract new industry and immediately create jobs for the unemployed. At the same time, the several departments and commissions of the state administration should be overhauled in the interests of efficiency.

By far the most important part of the Governor's message was that dealing with relief for the unemployed. In Providence alone between four and five thousand families were on welfare rolls, and relief money was fast running out in ten cities and towns that were equally hard-hit by unemployment. To rectify the problem Green asked first that the legislature appropriate for immediate relief the sum of $3 million in the form of outright grants to the cities and towns. He further requested that the legislature return the repayments of all loans, which totalled $2.5 million, made thus far by the localities under the 1931 law. To make money available for immediate relief, Green recommended that previously-collected gasoline taxes be diverted from the control of the State Board of Public Roads to the general treasury. He also urged all future gasoline taxes be employed for general purposes instead of just for roads. To raise additional quick income, Green asked for a 1 per cent income tax on public utilities. Finally, Green suggested that the state help local communities find funds for relief by endorsing all town and city bond and note issues. The Governor's program was indeed formidable.

Despite the urgency of the situation, however, Green's plans for obtaining funds ran into huge obstacles. His plan of transferring gasoline taxes was attacked by the State Board of Public Roads, and the state's contractors were equally upset. Even the Automobile Club of Rhode Island joined in denouncing the Governor's plan: an organization calling itself the Rhode Island Highway Taxpayers' Association was quickly formed to combat the proposal. As expected, the public utilities also protested the Governor's plan, claiming they were unable to absorb the extra tax on their income. But unexpectedly, Henry T. Samson, secretary of the Governor's Conference on Unemployment and Relief, called together by Governor Case in August, 1932, complimented Green on his program, calling it courageous and daring.[3]

Meantime, House Democrats went to work on the composition of the permanent House committees. Governor Green, floor leader Flynn, Speaker Reddy, his deputy Kiernan, and the ubiquitous J. Howard McGrath held several meetings to select the Democratic steering committee which would actually choose the committees Reddy would announce from the rostrum. An outbreak of the old McCoy-McGrath feud delayed the proceedings until McGrath agreed to place two pro-Gerry and pro-McCoy Democrats, Pawtucket's Harry F. Curvin and Patrick B. McCaughey, on the steering committee, which then went to work. By the third week in January the assignments were ready. All the committees were Democratically controlled. Republican Cianciarulo was rewarded for his defection by several choice assignments, and eight Italo-American Democrats, who had earlier agitated for recognition of Italians on the committees, were also happy with their assignments. This treatment of Cianciarulo and the Italian Democrats gave the Rhode Island Republican Party considerable cause for concern, and to rub salt into their wounds Governor Green, at a testimonial dinner in honor of Louis Cappelli, called his election as secretary of state "a triumph for persons of Italian extraction." Luigi De Pasquale's people had at last attained the political status for which they had so long fought.[4]

The House was one thing, the Senate another. More than twenty years had elapsed since Charles R. Brayton's death, but his ghost still haunted the state. The infamous Brayton Law, enacted in 1901, still controlled the power of appointment, effectively lodging it with the Senate instead of the governor. As long as twenty-seven Republicans held together in the upper house, Governor Green's major appointments were destined to be unconfirmed. In January Green decided to test their solidarity by nominating Thomas D. Higgins, brother of the ex-governor, as Insurance Commissioner, and nominating several other Democrats for state positions. The Republican-dominated Senate promptly rejected Higgins and after waiting three days, as required under the Brayton Law, appointed a Republican to the post. Likewise, the Senate rejected virtually all the Governor's other appointees.

Yet another obstacle barred Green's way. The office of State Finance Commissioner, established during Republican times and occupied by Frederick S. Peck, had the power to review all bills affecting expenditures that were presented in the legislature. Because he also prepared the annual budget for the state, the commissioner had great influence in the administration, and because Fred Peck was a skillful veteran of Rhode Island Republican politics , he was the crucial cog in the political works. Democratic leaders in the House tried unsuccessfully to destroy both these barriers: they passed a law repealing the Brayton Law, only to see it die in the Senate, and they failed by three votes to steer through the House a bill abolishing Peck's office and giving his power to the governor and a deputy finance commissioner.

These various barriers effectively prevented the Democrats from implementing much of the Governor's program. Representative Bernard J. McElroy of Providence introduced a bill giving a dollar a day to all persons over sixty-five. McElroy's measure was referred to Finance Commissioner Peck, who disapproved it, then to the Finance Committee, which approved it, and then back to the House, which passed it in April. The House also passed a bill introduced by Democrat Anna D. Hewett of North Providence, the only woman member of the House, that would have extended mothers' aid to more children. Both these measures died in Senate committees. The Senate also killed a bill designed to implement Green's recommendations for improving working conditions in Rhode Island mills. Bills permitting biennial registration of voters and extending the period of registration from June to September were also defeated, as was a proposal to float a bond issue to purchase voting machines. Green's recommendations for reorganizing the state administration fared scarcely better, though it appeared for a time that a reorganization bill would pass through the co-operation of Republican Senator William H. Vanderbilt of Portsmouth.

A more involved struggle developed over the pending repeal of prohibition. Prohibition legislation had brought about the marriage of many an underworld figure to many a politician, and the pending changes in the law meant that illegal operators could now come out into the open. Green wanted to establish an unpaid, five-man bipartisan commission to study legislation for controlling the problem. Over the protests of William G. Troy, the Senate minority leader, Green negotiated with Harry Bodwell, the Senate majority leader, and in late January the Senate and House passed the resolution establishing the study commission. The Governor described this as the "first important constructive bill" of his administration, and he appointed five commissioners, three Democrats and two Republicans—J. Howard McGrath, Patrick P. Curran, Mrs. John Nicholas Brown, Charles P. Sisson, and Frank Mauran, Jr.—to the board.[5]

In April the commission recommended passing a beer act and establishing an Alcoholic Beverage Commission. For once, bipartisan co-operation was seen in Rhode Island. The Federal anti-beer law having been repealed, the state could legally permit the sale of beer on April 7. At 3:50 A.M. on that day the House passed a bill legalizing the sale of beer, at 4:05 the Senate concurred, and at 4:17 Governor Green signed the measure into law. Minutes later beer flowed freely, albeit expensively, in Rhode Island. A new five-man commission was established to regulate the dispensing of licenses and to supervise the conduct of their recipients. Towns were given a share of a state beer tax and the right to restrict beer permits. (This was old-fashioned "Home Rule," for it gave towns power over permits. It was also practical local politics, for it enabled town politicians to enforce a "kickback" system between purveyors of 3.2 beer and the town fathers.) In mid-April the Governor named five people to the new commission, at an annual salary of $3,000 per commissioner, and asked the Senate for their confirmation. The Brayton Law was waived in this instance and Democratic Senator William G. Troy, already angered because of other disagreements with Green, was personally affronted that Green had not named him to one of the posts. To placate Troy, he was promised a position as legal advisor to the ABC, and on April 13 the Senate confirmed the Governor's appointees: Patrick P. Curran, Frank Mauran, Jr., Edouard S. Lafayette, James S. Daneker, and Michael F. Costello—an ethnically well balanced group. In a special election held two weeks later, Rhode Islanders voted by a majority of seven to one in favor of repeal, and a state ratifying convention approved the Twenty-first Amendment, repealing prohibition.[6]

The most important aspects of the Governor's legislative program in 1933 were his recommendations for the economic relief of the state's destitute. On the last day of January Green went before the Grand Committee and delivered a ringing message calling for laws to implement this program. Proclaiming an unemployment emergency in Rhode Island and urging immediate action, the Governor asked the lawmakers to remember that "the state exists for the people, not the people for the state. Humanity comes first." In response, the chairman of the Republican State Committee, Charles P. Sisson, promised that his party would treat Green's proposals fairly, and Democratic Representative Flynn introduced the previously prepared "Emergency Unemployment Relief Act of 1933," incorporating the Governor's recommendations. The House and Senate decided to have their respective finance committees hold joint hearings on Flynn's bill. As they did so, Green himself delivered a radio speech appealing to the residents of the state to pressure their senators and representatives on behalf of the bill. "Speak, write, or telephone," he told the citizens, "but make sure the legislators know what you want."[7]

In an attempt to press for legislation of their own, Republicans introduced a series of bills onto the Senate floor the day before the scheduled hearing on Flynn's measure, but they hastily retreated when Green and Lieutenant Governor Quinn threatened a filibuster like the one in 1924. When the finance committees met jointly on February 8, more than 700 people crowded the State House, and at one point a large and loud group invaded the governor's chambers to demand immediate economic relief and jobs. At the hearings, representatives of the Providence Gas Company and the New England Telephone and Telegraph Company appeared to oppose the proposed public utilities tax, the Rhode Island Highway Taxpayers' Association opposed the gasoline tax-diversion plan, and the State Grange opposed both. Green was supported by the Rhode Island League of Women Voters, several unemployed persons who were permitted to air their views in impromptu speeches, and even a representative of the Women's Republican Club of Rhode Island.[8]

But whatever the pleas of special groups, the mood of the mass of the people was clearly impatience and anger; and whatever the predilections of politicians, it was clear that the two parties had to come to a common understanding, and quickly. On Sunday afternoon, February 12, a four-hour conference was held between Democratic and Republican legislative leaders, Governor Green, and the Republican and Democratic State Chairmen, Sisson and McGrath. The outcome of the meetings was a compromise on the relief plans. By the agreement Governor Green was to attempt to obtain a Reconstruction Finance Corporation loan of $3 million from the Federal government and the state would float a $3 million bond issue to back it up. (Under Federal law, RFC funds were given only to those states which had made provisions to help themselves. There was, however, no Federal requirement of state legislation beyond proof that the state had passed appropriate relief measures. Furthermore, RFC money was lent directly to the governor of the state, on his mere pledge that his state would repay it, and repayment could be made in the form of the state's refusal to accept Federal rebates coming to it under Federal grants-in-aid in highway construction. Rhode Island had such rebates coming.)

Another feature of the Democratic-Republican compromise was that the state bond issue would be paid for by amortizing the loan over a period of five years out of funds raised from gasoline taxes during the same period. Immediate diversion of gasoline taxes was dropped. A third aspect of the compromise was the acceptance of Senator Vanderbilt's suggestion to rebate immediately $611,774.10 of the $2.5 million the towns and cities owed the state, and later the whole amount. Fourth, the towns and cities would have to match state funds, but only by showing that they had made preparations for appropriating money. Fifth, Green agreed to abandon his request for the utilities tax. Finally, the program would be administered by a four-man Unemployment Relief Commission, consisting of the Governor, Finance Commissioner Peck, and the chairmen of the House and Senate finance committees, Edward C. Brown and William H. Vanderbilt—two Democrats and two Republicans. In return for Green's backing down on several points, the Republicans promised to pass the bill at once.[9]

A few rural Republican legislators balked at the deal, but Sisson whipped them into line with Green's threat of a filibuster, which this time would hurt the Republicans. On February 15 the compromise plan passed both houses without a single dissenting vote and the Governor immediately signed the bill.[10]

William H. Moss, First Assistant to Attorney General John Hartigan, was dispatched to Washington as the Governor's emissary to obtain an RFC loan to cover the $611,774.10 due the towns and cities. A week later Green announced that the RFC had lent him $896,000 for the months of March and April, and that the money would be repaid from Federal highway funds. He also announced a bold plan for administering the funds. He had borrowed the money himself, he said, and he and he alone would superintend the parceling of the money to the various towns and cities. He would not release RFC funds to localities that did not meet the standards he set for them, nor would he tolerate mismanagement of funds or any kind of "politics" in handing out relief; local governments could engage only trained social workers hired by the state. When the *Providence Journal* and some politicians protested, RFC officials supported Green's stand.[11]

Soon thereafter the Governor flew to Washington to attend the inauguration of Franklin D. Roosevelt, leaving Robert E. Quinn as acting governor. The economic plight of the nations' banks had reached alarming proportions by this time and on Saturday, March 4, while Green was in Washington, Quinn declared a bank holiday in Rhode Island. Green notified him of his approval and Quinn stated that he would order the banks to remain closed on Monday unless President Roosevelt did something positive to guide the states. The President declared a nationwide bank holiday on Monday morning, and on the same day the Rhode Island General Assembly made ready to pass legislation, as was being done in several other states, authorizing the use of scrip as a currency substitute.[12]

Green returned to Rhode Island after the Governors' Conference with the President, and on Tuesday the state legislature hurriedly passed an emergency banking law. The measure—which gave the banking commissioner (Lattimer W. Ballou) "power to regulate the extent to which banks may open, to regulate the issuance of scrip as a currency substitute, and to limit withdrawals, but always subject to approval by the Governor"—was presented to the House at 6 P.M. by Democrat Flynn and Republican Walter Curry. Green spoke from the rostrum of the House on its behalf, urging immediate adoption on a nonpartisan basis. The bill unanimously passed the House at 7:12 P.M., the Senate at 7:31 P.M., and the Governor affixed his signature at 7:35 P.M. Under the authority of the act, Green authorized the issuance of scrip, limiting the amount distributed to $10 per week in salaries and $10 for bank withdrawals. By March 16 the bank holiday had virtually ended in Rhode Island and the scrip was returned to the banks. Except for a small amount kept as souvenirs, all of the $1,750,000 in scrip was given back by April 4.

In the meantime, Governor Green had been carefully parceling out RFC funds. In March he authorized a total of $227,859 to Providence, Warwick, West Warwick, Central Falls, and Johnston. He informed officials in Woonsocket, hinting at "dirty work afoot there," that he would not permit its own Welfare Board to distribute RFC funds, but reserved that right to himself. Henry T. Samson lauded Governor Green for "separating politics from the administration of relief funds." Before Green would approve granting RFC money to towns and cities, they had to show him they were going to use the money to supply work for the unemployed. Under these conditions he gave money to Newport and North Providence but refused it to Warren, Edward J. Higgins' hometown.[13]

Samson, whom Green made secretary of the Unemployment Relief Commission, soon ran into trouble with Democrats who were not so anxious to separate politics from the relief program. Ostensibly because he had hired a handful of out-of-state social workers, but actually because they wanted the patronage, Democratic Senators Troy of Providence, Cullen of Cumberland, and Kiernan of North Providence began to grumble. Working with several Republicans, they created a special five-man investigating committee, headed by Troy, to investigate Samson's operations. The rest of the committee consisted of Republican Senator Harry T. Bodwell, who had wanted Samson's job in the first place; Luke Callan, an Independent from Bristol and who in 1934 was to be the Republican candidate for governor (Green had also suspended payment of funds to Bristol because of irregularities and incompetence on the part of officials there); Democratic Senator Paul J. Robin of Providence; and Republican Senator Alfred G. Chaffee of Scituate. Governor Green said that he was delighted to have the Senate "shed light" on the matter, but in a speech to 500 members of the Rhode Island Social Workers' Institute, he defended his and Samson's actions, saying that money was being spent "humanely, efficiently, and wisely."[14]

The Troy committee conducted an investigation that Green likened to the "Tennessee monkey trial." After about a week of charges and counter-charges before the committee, a bill restricting the social worker jobs to Rhode Island citizens, was introduced and speedily passed; Green let it become law without his signature.[15]

Meantime, as the investigation proceeded, Green angered some more Democrats by withholding RFC funds from Pawtucket, on the ground that the city should use the Community Chest files for listing their welfare cases instead of their own inadequate city files. The Governor insisted that he did so on the advice of RFC officials who had been in the state; until Pawtucket met his demand and had its revised lists verified by professional social workers, the city would have to do without the state's help in supporting its 2,500-family relief roll. After one day, the Pawtucket Director of Public Aid, Dr. Robert E. Kelley, agreed to have the city file system reorganized and Green promised to release the funds.[16]

The legislative session ended late in April, after the Assembly passed a joint resolution continuing the Troy investigating committee beyond adjournment. Thereupon, for the first time in many years, a governor of the state exercised his right of veto. Because the legislature had adjourned it had no opportunity to override the veto, and the Troy committee was perfunctorily ended. In vetoing the resolution Green denounced the Troy committee for having been engaged not in investigation but in prosecution.[17]

Green followed this veto with several others. He killed a bill that would have added some town roads to the jurisdiction of the State Board of Public Roads, and another that would have permitted assistant pharmacists to be registered as full-fledged pharmacists without having to attend an accredited school of pharmacy. The Governor also vetoed a bill abolishing the State Board of Chiropody, which the General Assembly had passed as a rebuke to the head of the board. Two bills were vetoed as wastes of money—one appropriating $52,000 for killing diseased cattle and one appropriating $10,000 for a state representation at the Century of Progress Exposition in Chicago—and two more, one concerning fire insurance and the other concerning the advertisement of tax sales of real estate, were vetoed because they were loosely or improperly drawn.[18]

The most significant veto of all related to horse racing. This bill had an involved and controversial background. Republican Herbert Bliss had prepared a race track bill in the lower house. It was generally understood that Bliss' bill would legalize race tracks in the state and permit pari-mutuel betting. (When asked who, in a time of such serious economic troubles, would be interested in putting up the large amounts of money necessary to build a track, Bliss refused to comment. Several clergymen, notably the Reverend James V. Claypool of East Providence, answered for him: it was the "underworld influence" seeking to invade the state.) Before Bliss could bring his bill to the floor, Democrat James Kiernan also proposed a bill to legalize race tracks. Kiernan's bill, which would have established a racing commission, charged the owners of the tracks a fee of $1,000 per day of racing and levied a 20¢ tax on all admission tickets. Kiernan's bill was read and referred to the Committee on Corporations which Kiernan himself chaired. A few days later Bliss presented his bill, which would have legalized race tracks without providing a racing commission to regulate them and collect fees for the state. The potential owners of the tracks, whoever they might have been, naturally preferred the Bliss bill. It is to be noted that neither bill made provision for dog racing; both were concerned solely with horses. After a skirmish over a motion by Providence Democrat Edward C. Brown to refer it to the Finance Committee, which Brown chaired, the Bliss bill was committed to the Corporations Committee, to be judged alongside Kiernan's.[19]

The Corporations Committee worked out a bill it called, in a fit of bipartisanship, the Bliss-Kiernan Bill. The new bill provided for a state charge of $1,000 per racing day for regular horse racing, $25 per day for harness racing, and a 20¢ tax on every admissions ticket, but did not establish a racing commission. Nor did it provide for a statewide referendum on the whole subject; instead, it required a referendum in the town or city, but not in the county where the potential track was to be located. Naturally enough, prospective owners would prefer that system to a statewide referendum. On April 11 the Corporations Committee reported the new bill favorably. Over Edward C. Brown's charges of graft, the House passed the bill on a voice vote. The Senate concurred on the last day of the session by a vote of thirty to nine, with no Democrats voting against it.[20]

When the bill reached the Governor's desk, Green vetoed it "for the best interests of the citizens of the state." The Governor claimed that race tracks would produce no net revenue, for they would bring undesirables into the state, necessitating more extra police than could be paid for by license fees. Furthermore, legalization of race track gambling might encourage unemployed people to waste their meagre funds betting on horses in hopes of making easy money. Most important, Green said, the public had not asked for race tracks and a law legalizing them "would be justified only in response to a public demand." In short, if there were to be race tracks in Rhode Island, legislation permitting them would have to be approved by a referendum of the people.[21]

A few days after the legislature adjourned, the voters of Rhode Island approved the $3 million bond issue by a seven to one majority. Green then travelled to Washington to confer with RFC officials and Secretary of Labor Perkins. (On his return the Governor took time out to engage in a publicity stunt, taking a nineteen-minute airplane ride, stopping in all five counties of the state to advertise the need for improvement of air facilities. Many unemployed men, paid out of RFC funds by the local communities, had been put to work grading and repairing the state airport at Hillsgrove. Later, an extension of that airport would bear Theodore Francis Green's name.) At the end of May Green's trip to Washington bore fruit as Rhode Island received from the Federal government another $229,292 to tide it over until the bond issue could be sold. This proved not at all difficult; a brokerage firm bought the entire bond issue early in June at a slight premium.[22]

Meantime, President Roosevelt was pressing the Congress for approval of his industrial recovery and public works bill. Expecting this to materialize, Green called a conference of Rhode Island mayors and town clerks and urged them to prepare public works projects in order to be ready for a windfall of new Federal money. Providence was already prepared with an ambitious $4 million plan for highway, school, and storm sewer construction as well as a sewage disposal plant, and other places began similar plans. State reimbursements, using RFC funds, continued to flow very smoothly as another $380,282 was filtered through Governor Green to the towns and cities. In mid-June Samson and Green conferred with President Roosevelt about the pending public works appropriations, and when they returned Green immediately called a special session of the General Assembly to enact legislation required to qualify, under the National Industrial Recovery Act that Congress passed on June 16, for $12 million of Federal aid allotted to Rhode Island. Under the new Federal law the state had to show its willingness to have the Federal government pay 70 per cent of the cost of reconstruction loans and highway grants. Governor Green called for the special session of the state legislature to meet on June 27.

Green asked that the Assembly limit itself to a consideration of unemployment relief and economy measures. He urged the legislature to pass laws cutting the pay of state employees, including the judges of the Superior and District Courts, and to reconsider Vanderbilt's administrative reorganization proposal. He argued that decreasing the salaries of the state judges (except for those of the Supreme Court, which were protected by the state constitution) would not impair their independence. Besides, he asserted, since all judges were subject to recall by the General Assembly—a fact he said he deplored—the judges were not really independent anyway. The Rhode Island Bar Association took Green to task for this statement, claiming that judges were subject to recall only for misbehavior in office. This apparently minor byplay between the Bar Association and the Governor would prove important for political events to come eighteen months later.[23]

Governor Green delivered a personal message to the Assembly when it convened on June 27. He urged legislation accomplishing seven objectives. First, he wanted permission to borrow the $12 million assigned to the state under the NIRA, to administer it through the Unemployment Relief Commission, and to repay it by diverting taxes and through local taxation; the State Board of Public Roads, having received a huge sum in a separate Federal bestowal, had withdrawn its earlier objections. Second, the governor asked for a 10 per cent cut in the pay of all state employees earning over $1,500 a year, including Superior and District Court judges. Third, he requested the creation of a commission to study governmental reorganization along the lines of the defunct Vanderbilt bill. Fourth, he sought the establishment of another commission to study wages, hours, and labor conditions in the state. Fifth, the Governor wanted an act to permit Rhode Island banks to borrow money from the Federal Home Loan Banks so that they could extend home mortgages. Sixth, he requested the Assembly to set up a study of real estate taxation in Rhode Island with a view to surveying the possibility of obtaining more revenue from property owners. Finally, Green asked the legislature to create a joint Federal-state unemployment agency to give free service to people in search of jobs.

The Republicans were willing to go along with the first request provided that Green would agree to add Tax Commissioner Zenas W. Bliss to the four-man Unemployment Relief Commission, thus giving the Republicans control of the commission. Green asked in return to be given a veto power over any proposed public works program in the state, regardless of the opinions of the rest of the Unemployment Relief Commission. Republicans and Democrats compromised the two points by the simple expedient of dropping both requests. The bill, introduced by Flynn in the House and implementing the first proposal of the Governor, passed the legislature. Otherwise, however, only the fifth proposal, enabling the state banks to borrow money from the Federal Home Loan Banks, was passed by the General Assembly.

But Rhode Island had its $12 million in Federal aid for reconstruction work, and many Rhode Islanders could now be put to work. Thanks partly to the million dollars the RFC had lent the state, unemployment had already declined from 19,650 in April to 17,739 in June, and there was now increased reason for optimism. Throughout the rest of 1933 Rhode Island used Federal funds to launch highway and public works construction programs, and in addition Federal funds flowed in to supplement the welfare and relief programs of the most depressed towns and cities. Civilian Conservation Corps camps were also established in the state, and gradually the numbers of idle in Rhode Island decreased.[24]

Popular morale rose apace. Many parades were held in Rhode Island in September and October, symbolizing fraternal co-operation to help one another rather than to destroy "inferior people," as was being urged in Germany. Governor Theodore Francis Green himself, dressed impeccably in his morning suit, marched two miles in a gigantic parade of 70,000 people one cool October day, rallying Rhode Islanders around the New Deal. Similar parades of smaller size took place in Rhode Island's towns and cities that month. However, not all was tranquil on the Rhode Island industrial front. A particularly bitter and prolonged strike of rayon and silk workers in the Blackstone Valley erupted into violence more than once. On the whole, however, the administration of Governor Green appeared to be bringing the economic problems of the state under control.[25]

Political drums continued to beat in Rhode Island. Rumor had it that J. Howard McGrath wanted the Federal post of United States Attorney for Rhode Island, then held by Henry M. Boss, Jr., whose term was due to end in December. Governor Green urged Roosevelt to appoint McGrath, and Roosevelt did so the following January. Indications of increased Democratic strength in Rhode Island were manifested by the sweep of the town elections by Democrats in South Kingstown in early June. In fact, Senator Vanderbilt stated that the Republicans had become the minority party in the state and they might well have to learn to play their political cards quite differently. In December Charles P. Sisson resigned as chairman of the Republican State Committee and was replaced by former Secretary of State Ernest L. Sprague. Democratic Representative Edward C. Brown resigned his seat to become Deputy Collector of Internal Revenue for Rhode Island and Democratic State Senator O'Neill resigned to accept a Federal job. On December 21 a special election was held to fill the vacancies, and Democrats held on to both seats. In short, Democrats had reason to look forward to the 1934 campaign with optimism.[26]

Toward the end of 1933 Green found that he would have fifty-five appointments to fill on the various commissions and boards during the second session of the legislature due to meet in January. One such vacancy set off a long and rancorous dispute: the position of Superintendent of State Police, which Everitte St. John Chaffee had held since the State Police had been estab-

lished in 1925. Pressure had been brought to bear on the Governor
to reappoint Chaffee as early as September, on the ground that
if Chaffee were reappointed, his office would be saved from politics.[27]

The act that had created the State Police Department had ex-
empted the office of Superintendent from the Brayton Law. Instead, the governor's choice had to be approved by the Senate
within seven legislative days after his name was submitted; if the
Senate rejected the appointee, the governor merely offered another. On the very first legislative day of the second session in
1934, Green nominated Edward J. Kelly, Superintendent of the
Providence Police Department, to replace Chaffee, whose term
expired on January 31. Even Democratic senators were unpre-
pared for such quick action, and when Republicans objected to
immediate consideration, the nomination was laid on the table.

Chaffee had much to recommend him for reappointment, and
he had many friends. He had headed the State Police relatively
well for eight years and had whipped the small nucleus of state
officers into an efficient organization. As soon as Green's move to
replace him was made, the *Providence Journal* began to circulate
a petition urging Green to change his mind, and by the end of
January the signatures totalled almost 13,000. But Governor
Green wrote Chaffee that he had not been giving enough time to
crime prevention and detection, and said he had decided to replace Chaffee with a man who could devote his time to all the
problems of the office. At a caucus, Republican senators decided
to delay action on Green's appointment of Kelly for a few days to
see if Green would withdraw his name. Republicans were divided
in their support of Chaffee, however. Senators Handy of Lincoln
and Toomey of Johnston voiced their admiration of Kelly, while
the Women's Republican Club, the Federation of Women's Clubs,
the State Grange, and others urged Governor Green to change his
mind. While the debate boiled, Green calmly insisted that the issue was not Chaffee's qualifications but Kelly's.[28]

The Governor received word that the Republicans intended to
vote Kelly's name down and then pass a resolution seeking a
State Supreme Court advisory opinion as to whether Chaffee

would continue as Superintendent if, when his term was up, no one had been confirmed to replace him. The Republicans could not themselves nominate Chaffee, but with a Republican Supreme Court it was conceivable that Chaffee could thus be continued in office. Green contended that Chaffee's continuance in office would be illegal under those circumstances, but he decided to take no chances.

On January 9 Republican Bodwell moved that Kelly's nomination be taken from the table and disapproved. Lieutenant Governor Quinn, presiding over the Senate, was ready for the maneuver and adopted the simple device of not recognizing any Republican who rose to second Bodwell's motion. Instead Quinn recognized Democratic Senator Troy, who moved that Kelly's name be taken from the table and approved. This was quickly seconded by Edward Dwyer, Democrat of Woonsocket, and the Lieutenant Governor, keeping his head down at all times so as not to see Republicans who tried to attract his attention, called for a voice vote. The Democrats cried "aye," the Republicans "no," and Quinn declared Kelly elected on the strength of the lungs of thirteen Democrats as opposed to twenty-seven Republicans. Bodwell immediately rose to demand a reconsideration on a roll call vote but Quinn refused to recognize him. While the Republicans fumed, Green's secretary, Edward J. Higgins, went for Kelly in the governor's official car and brought him to the State House, where Secretary of State Cappelli, with the Governor happily looking on, immediately swore in the new Superintendent even before the term of the outgoing one had expired.

The Republicans claimed that they had at least twenty-four votes against Kelly, had Quinn permitted a roll call. Furthermore, they claimed that Rule 3 of the Senate Rules made it mandatory for the presiding officer to order a roll call vote when requested. In this assertion they were quite correct. Possibly this was the subject of the conversation the evening of the vote when Senator Bodwell and Lieutenant Governor Quinn dined together.

To forestall any Republican attempts to declare the vote illegal or to vote against approval of the minutes of the January 9 session, Quinn adjourned the Senate on a voice vote immediately

after opening the session on the following day. He refused to recognize any Republican who rose to demand a roll call vote on the
question of adjournment. The Democratic purpose was to conclude seven legislative days so that Kelly would have been elected
within the prescribed legal period. Had Quinn permitted Republican activity within that time, it was quite possible the Republicans could have resolved Kelly right out of the appointment. On the seventh legislative day several Democrats alter-
nated sitting on the presiding officer's chair even after the adjournment to keep the Republicans from occupying the chair and
declaring a "rump" session in order.

Much of the citizenry, particularly members of upper socio-
economic groups, were not happy at the legislative maneuverings
of Governor Green and Lieutenant Governor Quinn. (Indeed,
the treatment of Chaffee remains to this day a source of irritation with many of Rhode Island's aristocracy.) The Governor
took to radio on January 17 to show that he had replaced Chaffee
with a well-qualified officer. The *Providence Journal,* which had
attacked Green and the Democrats for the procedure in the Senate, did not print the speech or even mention it. Even so,
Green received many congratulatory letters on the speech and
sent a copy of it to every person who wrote him. The dispute
raged on all through January, until the Republicans finally decided to concede defeat and drop the whole matter.[29]

The Democrats could not, of course, employ such practices all
the time, and most of the Governor's appointees, subject to the
1901 Brayton Law, were not approved by the Republican majority in the Senate. In particular, two important appointments went
against Green when he tried to place Mayor Dunne of Providence
on the Providence Board of Safety, which ran the police and fire
departments of the city, and George B. Clegg, a prominent member of the Knights of Columbus, as Finance Commissioner. The
Senate rejected Dunne and re-elected George T. Marsh and joy-
fully re-elected Frederick Peck instead of Clegg.

The composition of the State Senate changed slightly in January, when Democrats won a special election necessitated by the
death of a Republican senator from Smithfield. The Democrats

also added another representative when in February Harold Burdick defeated Frederick Smith in a special election in Richmond
caused by the elevation of Roy Rawlings, by the Senate, to the
State Public Utilities Commission. Burdick was the first Democrat elected from Richmond since 1909, and the House was now
evenly divided.[30]

The politics of the regular session in 1934 was much the same
as in the previous year. An old-age pension bill was passed by the
House but killed in the Senate. A Democratic bill calling for a
constitutional convention was defeated in the House by a tie vote.
Senator Vanderbilt's attempt to establish a study commission to
reorganize the administrative machinery of the state was again
buried in a Senate committee, and Governor Green's renewed
requests for the utilities income tax bill and his bill to extend
voter registration from June to September were smothered by the
Senate Judiciary Committee. The Republicans also kept from the
Senate floor bills regulating the hours of employment of women
and children, one calling for the popular election of sheriffs, and
another which sought to legalize a state lottery as a method to
help balance the state budget.

Three major legislative matters in 1934 deserve particular attention. The first of these was the race track controversy. Republican Bliss and Democrat Kiernan again introduced their joint
bill to permit racing. The measure would have established a three-
man racing commission, appointed by the Governor but subject
to the Brayton Law, so that the Senate would really control the
selection of the commissioners. The bill also provided for a daily
fee of $1,000, an annual limit of 100 days of racing per track, and
a percentage of the total bets to go to the state. Again, the measure was referred to Kiernan's Corporations Committee. Much
factional strife ensued among the Democrats. Green's request
that Kiernan provide for statewide referendum on the question
of horse racing bordered on a demand when the Governor threatened to veto the bill again unless this were done. Kiernan reluctantly agreed and after only one day the Corporations Committee
reported the bill out favorably. Democratic Representative Flynn
then moved the bill be sent to the Judiciary Committee, which

was also done. Green was still angry about the bill and in an attempt to placate him the Corporations Committee wrote a brand new bill providing for the selection of the Racing Commission solely by the governor without the necessity of Senate approval. The new bill also required local permission for the establishment of a track, but did not require statewide referendum. Green reiterated that he would veto the bill unless this were added again, and with minor exceptions they finally let the Governor have his way. Both a statewide and a local referendum were required and the three-man Racing Commission was to be appointed by the governor with the consent of the Senate. The commission was to consist of one Democrat, one Republican, and one "neutral" who had knowledge of the horse-racing business. The Senate could not substitute its own nominees for those of the governor. The state would receive 3½ per cent of the total bets made, the owners of the track 6½ per cent, and the revenues then split between the state and local municipality. The bill, calling for horse racing and pari-mutuel betting, was then sent to the Senate.[31]

At this point an interesting side issue arose. Representative Frank X. Shunney, Democrat of Woonsocket, had introduced a bill which would have legalized dog racing as well as horse racing. He accomplished this by simply providing for a racing commission without mentioning the word "horse." The bill went to Finance Commissioner Peck and then to the House Finance Committee, which pigeon-holed it when Governor Green declared that he would veto any dog-racing bill under any conditions. Shunney then made several attempts to have the word "horse" eliminated from the Bliss-Kiernan bill everywhere the word occurred. He was unsuccessful, and in April the final bill was sent to the Senate after having passed the House. Chairman Vanderbilt of the Senate Finance Committee, to which the bill had been referred, then noticed that the word "horse" had been crossed out with a green pencil every time it appeared on the typed copy of the bill. He called the committee's attention to this and the matter was corrected. The bill was passed by the Senate and signed by Green on April 26. A special election was set for May

18 to decide, among other things, whether or not the people of the state approved race tracks operating in Rhode Island.[32]

At the referendum only 75,000 of the 300,000 eligible voters went to the polls; they approved of the track measure by a four to one majority. The following day, it was announced that a group headed by James E. Dooley and Walter F. O'Hara was ready to purchase the What Cheer Airport in Pawtucket from John F. Letendre of Woonsocket, who held the option on the land. Governor Green appointed to the Racing Commission Democratic State Central Committeeman Thomas F. Kane, Republican Senator Russell H. Handy of Lincoln, and as the "neutral" George W. Rooks of Warwick, who was made chairman. James C. Thornton of West Warwick, Lieutenant Governor Quinn's brother-in-law, was made secretary of the commission. Green admonished the new commissioners "to see that the law is administered fairly and honestly."[33]

There was much resentment on the part of those who had labored long and hard to persuade the legislature of Rhode Island, behind the scenes, to legalize dog racing as well as horse racing. The Governor's opposition had been reported in Chicago to several influential people, but it proved unnecessary for them to press their point when, not long afterwards, a dog track was opened in neighboring and friendly Massachusetts. Rhode Island would have its Narragansett Park and Massachusetts would have its Taunton Track, only a few miles from the border of Rhode Island.

The second major legislative difficulty in the regular session of 1934 was over the problem of liquor. To put the matter briefly, the liquor interests, ostensibly legitimized by the repeal of prohibition, wanted to sell hard liquor as well as 3.2 beer, anywhere in the state. Some of the more cautious citizens feared that unless strict controls were enacted, the old open saloon would return. The battle was fought out behind the closed doors of committees as well as in the governor's office. Finally a liquor bill was passed by the legislature which permitted the sale of hard liquor in clubs, saloons, and restaurants. In the long run it was futile to try to exclude saloons, for a saloon could always masquerade as a restaurant by listing a couple of sandwiches on a whiskey-stained menu and maintaining a small sink in the back of the establishment. When Green reluctantly signed the bill, prohibition was gone for good—if indeed it had ever really existed in Rhode Island.

Money was the third major problem in 1934. Finance Commissioner Peck had predicted a million dollar deficit in the state budget. To balance the budget Green sought to cut the appropriations of the various state departments, particularly the State Board of Public Roads. This proposal engendered a dispute with Peck and the Republican senators, with the result that the matter was put off until a special session in June. In the meantime, preparing for such a session, the General Assembly passed three resolutions putting it to the people whether the state should borrow $1 million to offset the expected deficit, borrow $1 million for more unemployment relief, and engage in twenty-eight Federally-backed public works projects which would cost the state $2.5 million as its share. These three questions were approved at the same referendum that endorsed horse racing, and early in June the Governor called for a special session of the legislature.[34]

The special session of the General Assembly met on June 14 "to enact necessary legislation to carry into effect" the approved measures, and also to pass the annual appropriations bill which had been left over from the regular session. The first purpose was quickly accomplished by both houses but no agreement was ever reached on the appropriations bill, and the state government was forced to run on a deficit basis for the rest of the year. Although many attempts were made to write a bill acceptable to all sides, the Democrats and the Republicans could never get together. Finance Commissioner Peck and most Democrats thought the remedy lay in cutting the amounts allotted to the various departments and commissions of the state. To make the Republicans even more obdurate, the Narragansett Race Track opened, enticing huge crowds, and by the end of September the track had paid into the state treasury several hundred thousand dollars. An absolute impasse developed, and the special session dragged on officially until December without accomplishing anything; the House and Senate actually met for only a few minutes a day.[35]

For most of the year economic and social conditions in Rhode Island were relatively good and the state was spared the labor violence that plagued much of the nation. In September, how-ever, everything suddenly changed. At that time the United Tex-tile Union, following a breakdown in negotiations with manage-ment, called a nationwide strike. The strike began in the South, where trouble had been festering for months, and rapidly spread northward. At first, most Rhode Island rayon, cotton, and woolen mills tried to remain open, but in the second week of the month many non-striking workers throughout the state found their ac-cess to the mills blocked by active pickets. After a minor clash be-tween strikers and State Troopers at a mill in Saylesville, Green again resorted to radio in an attempt to clarify his own position. Urging all sides to remain calm, he said that his duty was to see that the laws of the state were observed and that order was "maintained in the interest of both employer and employees, and more especially in the interest of the general public." The manu-facturer, he said, had the right to run his mill and hire whom he pleased, just as the worker had the right to work where he pleased and try to persuade his fellow worker to do the same, but lawless-ness by either could not be condoned. He also stated that the State Police force would restore order any time violence broke out, but that the force was too small to police all mills to prevent violence. He assured the people, however, that he had brought labor leaders and sheriffs into an agreement that would prevent future violence.[36]

The agreement proved to be most tenuous, and riots soon erupted anew in Saylesville. Stones and a few rifle shots were aimed at the steel-helmeted State Police, who retaliated with tear gas bombs and clubs. Again Green went on the radio to announce that he was calling out the National Guard on a standby basis. While he was at it he praised the State Police and denounced the

Sheriff of Providence County and his deputies for having pro-
voked the strikers into violence. The Governor charged that the
mill owners were the actual employers of the deputies, who were
hired by the Sheriff but paid by the manufacturers. Green also
asked the legislature to authorize the hiring of war veterans as
temporary State Police, to empower him to remove any deputy
sheriff in time of strikes or riots, and to authorize him to close the
mills to prevent further violence. The legislature refused.[37]

The day after Green's radio address, violence in Saylesville became worse and when deputy sheriffs fired into the assembled
crowd of strikers, Governor Green ordered the National Guard
to enter the area and restore order. Tear gas routed the strikers
and pickets. Fighting rapidly spread to Central Falls and Woonsocket. Several people were wounded by rifle fire, and two were
killed. Governor Green then appealed to the people to stay away
from the area and issued a proclamation relieving all state officers
from civil action for damages resulting from the quelling of riots.
Charges were hurled recklessly: Attorney General Hartigan
scored the deputy sheriffs for having touched off the violence by
unnecessary shooting, Senator Bodwell defended them, and
Quinn reiterated the Governor's statement that the National
Guard was being used to keep the peace and not to break the
strike. Green rightly charged that Communist agitators had also
instigated the pickets into violence at Saylesville and indeed several Communists, not all from Rhode Island, were arrested by the
police under Green's direct orders. By September 19 the National
Guard had the violence well under control, and three days later
the United Textile Union, pressured from Washington, called
off the nationwide strike.[38]

Senator Bodwell repeatedly accused Green of having used the
strike to play politics. He charged that the Governor had purposely delayed calling out the National Guard in hopes that violence would bring public wrath on the mill owners. Actually,
Green had been reluctant to call out the Guard. In 1922 Governor San Souci had done just that, and doing so had cost him the
nomination in the fall of that year. Indeed, Green barely man-

aged to escape the ire of the Rhode Island branch of the American Federation of Labor, which in state convention in October, nearly voted a strong rebuke to Green for having called the Guard out. No doubt the presence of Communists among the strikers helped take some of the pressure off Green. San Souci had not been so fortunate. Green had also ordered the arrest of the Communists, but not the bona fide strikers, and this too helped thwart the possibility of labor taking out its vengeance on him.[39]

In short, Theodore Francis Green's first term had brought about a shift in the location of governmental power in Rhode Island. Because of the close division of the House and its resulting tension, the Democrats did not deluge the House with bills, as had been their custom in the past, but had them first cleared by party leadership and Governor Green. This policy was designed to effect a smoother relationship between the legislature and the Governor, and also to present to the public the picture of a united party effort, but the substantive result was to place additional power in the governor's office during Green's first term. The economic facts of life in Rhode Island during the depression also facilitated a shift of power from the legislature to the executive. Governor Green took over the administration of RFC funds, by-passed the state legislature, and used the funds as a weapon to force local communities to do his bidding. Too, Green's power was enhanced by the fact that Franklin Roosevelt, in the absence of Democratic senators from Rhode Island, pointedly channeled Federal patronage through Green. Finally, Green's skill in dealing with legislative leaders of both parties and his use of the veto, particularly at the end of the 1933 session, were additional reasons for the growing importance of the governor in Rhode Island politics.[40]

The fortunate end of the textile workers' strike also worked to Green's advantage. He emerged from a situation which, handled badly, would have spelled the end of his political career. The Governor, however, was berated not by the workers for having called out the Guard, but by the Republicans and many, although not all, of the mill owners. After the strike was over, Green used it to turn the minds of most of Rhode Island's citizens against the Republicans. Once more he used radio to tell the people that the forward-looking legislation in the Democratic Platform of 1932 had not been acted upon by the General Assembly because of Republican intransigence. It was now time, he said, to pay attention "to laws promoting social justice." So began Theodore Francis Green's campaign for re-election in 1934.[41]

Chapter IX

Governor Green's Second Term: 1935–37

Let us hope that the New Year may resurrect much delayed legislation of benefit to the State as a whole.

——THEODORE FRANCIS GREEN

DESPITE grumblings by various Democratic legislators over the increasing concentration of power in the executive branch, Green faced only one serious challenge in his party leadership in 1934. Pawtucket boss Thomas McCoy (who aspired to become State Chairman) attempted to form a coalition with Lieutenant Governor Quinn (who aspired to become governor) and Congressman Condon (who aspired to become United States senator) to wrest control from Green, Gerry, and McGrath; but apart from sound and fury the effort accomplished nothing. The McCoy coalition was defeated, 68 to 25, when it forced a vote on the chairmanship at a special meeting of the State Central Committee. The state convention went smoothly, all incumbent state officers and incumbent Congressmen O'Connell and Condon being renominated, and Peter Gerry being chosen as the opponent to Republican Senator Felix Hebert.[1]

For Green's opponent the Republicans chose Luke Callan, a popular Bristol contractor and war hero who in 1932 had been elected to the State Senate as an independent. Senator Herbert was renominated, and the rest of the slate reflected an effort to effect some balance of ethnic groups in the Republican ticket.

Callan conducted a vigorous, somewhat demagogic campaign. He referred to his own war record and pointed out that, while he was fighting in France, Green was "engaged in selling war stamps

in Rhode Island." He sought favor with the workers by charging
Green with cowardice in having called out the National Guard,
and sought favor in the rural districts by asserting that the Democrats planned to gerrymander the small towns out of their Senate
seats. One sequence of exchanges on this matter probably planted
the seed of a revolution that was about to come. Democratic State
Senator Troy, talking on the issue of representation in the Senate,
casually remarked that "some skunkhunter from West Greenwich"
had as much power in the State Senate "as a good citizen" from a
larger community. In response, Callan and the Republicans promoted a series of "Skunkhunters' Rallies" at which they accused
the Democrats of seeking to "steal our birthright through a Constitutional Convention." In a moment of enthusiasm at one such
rally, Callan claimed that if the Democrats won control of both
houses of the General Assembly, they planned to oust the State
Supreme Court justices. This was a coincidental reference to what
actually did happen, for the Democratic leaders had not yet con-
ceived the idea. Quite possibly, it was Callan who gave it to them.[2]

The Democrats geared their efforts to two things. On the general level, Green led a campaign identifying the Democrat's state
program with the New Deal. Defending his own record in the
relief program in Rhode Island, Green heaped lavish praise on
President Roosevelt and the national administration, which he
said had sought "to lift us out of our difficulties along the American road of intelligent self-help." The New Deal had pointed the
way towards social security and insurance against unemployment,
rendered bank deposits secure, repealed prohibition, ended manipulation of the stock market, and brought the re-employment of
nearly four million people throughout the nation. Above all, the
Governor asserted, the New Deal had "recreated hope and confidence in the hearts of men." Rhode Island Democrats had co-
operated in these achievements, said Green, but a new political
deal was also badly needed in the state, and Green told his radio
audiences that the election of a Democratic legislature would do
just that.[3]

On the more specific level Green, Quinn, Senator Kiernan,
Edward J. Higgins, and a handful of other Assembly leaders de-

cided to concentrate a great deal of effort in an attempt to win the State Senate seats in several key towns. Quinn was made chairman of this inner group in charge of operations, and even before the Democratic State Convention, efforts had been made to convince the Town Committees of Coventry, Johnston, North Smithfield, Portsmouth, South Kingstown, Tiverton, and Westerly to select competent Democrats as nominees for the Senate. Republicans had been elected from these towns in 1932, but the Democrats felt that they stood an excellent chance of winning them all in 1934. Green himself supplied most of the money for expenses in the town campaigns. Senator Metcalf had not been as free as usual with his "registration" money, and this had caused some resentment on the part of Republican powers in the towns. Making a determined bid to wage strong fights in these communities, Democratic state headquarters supplied a great deal of printed matter and physical aid and several automobiles for the use of Town Committees and the candidates who had been selected by them.[4]

In general, there was never any real doubt of the outcome of the state election in 1934. Gerry, riding for the most part on the magic of Roosevelt's name, more than made up for the beating Hebert had given him in 1928 by carrying every city but Cranston and Warwick as he swept to victory. Green was re-elected governor by a plurality 4,000 votes greater than his margin in 1932. The entire Democratic ticket, including O'Connell and Condon for Congress, was easily elected. The real interest in 1934 centered on the General Assembly. The Democrats won the normally Republican House seats in Cumberland, East Providence, Lincoln, Newport, Pawtucket, and Tiverton, carried twenty of the twenty-five Representative districts in Providence, and emerged with a comfortable margin of eight seats in the lower house. Democratic candidates for the Senate scored upset victories in four of the seven key towns—Johnston, North Smithfield, Tiverton, and Westerly. In addition, Bristol had also elected a Democratic senator, even though the town had voted for Callan in the gubernatorial contest. In Coventry a very distressing thing had occurred on the night of the election. Lieutenant Governor Quinn had been informed by a Democratic watcher that about a hundred Democratic ballots had been literally destroyed so as to give the Republican candidate, Edwin H. Arnold, Jr., the Senate victory over Democrat J. W. Butler, by a plurality of only twenty-three votes. Coventry was at least temporarily Republican. In Portsmouth and South Kingstown the news was bad for the Democrats. On the night of the election, for a short while, the *Providence Journal*'s count had Democrats ahead in both towns. The returns in the morning, however, showed that in Portsmouth, Republican B. Earl Anthony had defeated Democrat Joseph P. Dunn 535 to 496, a plurality of thirty-nine. In South Kingstown, the same thing had happened, as Republican Wallace Campbell edged out Democrat Charles A. White, Sr., 1377 to 1321, a plurality of fifty-six. Democratic watchers told Quinn that the Republican town wardens had merely thrown out enough Democratic ballots, on the claim that they were defectively marked, to give the Republicans the victory.[5]

With these three towns—Coventry, Portsmouth, and South Kingstown—in the Republican column, the State Senate apparently stood at twenty-three Republicans and nineteen Democrats. Quinn and the Democrats raised a clamor about Coventry, and two days after the election the Republican-dominated State Returning Board, with all of the Democratic state officers except Green looking on, recounted the ballots and declared Democrat Butler the victor 1490 to 1476. The vote in South Kingstown was also recounted later, but the board ruled that Republican Campbell had gained a net increase of five votes, and the count now stood Campbell 1369 and Democrat White 1308. Portsmouth was unchanged and since there was no reversals anywhere else, the State Senate stood at twenty-two Republicans and twenty Democrats.

Prospects for the passage of Democratic legislation now appeared dim. Democratic leaders held a series of meetings with Governor Green at his home in Providence, trying to find a way to reverse the decisions in Portsmouth and South Kingstown. Thirty-nine votes in the former town and sixty-one in the latter separated the Governor and the Democratic Party from control of the legislature. The combined houses, in Grand Committee, had a slight edge in favor of the Democrats, and in the event of a vacancy on the State Supreme Court, the Democrats would have the advantage. Nevertheless, without a majority in the Senate itself, the Democrats would be unable to pass any kind of reform legislation.

Attending the meetings with the Governor were Quinn; Attorney General Hartigan; his first assistant William W. Moss; Senators Troy and Kiernan; House Speaker Reddy; his deputy James Kiernan; chairman of the State Committee Kennelly; House leader Flynn; Higgins; and McGrath, who, despite his Federal position as United States Attorney, continued to mastermind many of the Democratic moves in 1934. The meetings were held in such secrecy that even the *Providence Journal* was taken completely by surprise at the events which transpired on New Year's Day, 1935.[6]

Lieutenant Governor Quinn, convinced that the Republicans had won their elections in Portsmouth and South Kingstown by fraud, suggested that the State Senate itself had the constitutional right to recount the ballots cast in those towns. He based his opinion on Article IV, Section 6 of the State Constitution, which made each house "the judge of the elections and qualifications of its members." Although the Senate had never recounted ballots cast in any other election—there never had been any occasion to—there was no reason it could not invoke the power now. Quinn suggested that the ballots, which were deposited in the vault at the State House, be ordered out and given to a special Senate committee for scrutiny. The Lieutenant Governor was certain that if a senatorial recount were made, Democrats would be found elected to the Senate from Portsmouth and South Kingstown. After considerable discussion the Democratic leaders hit upon a plan to catch the Republicans by surprise. They decided to appoint a three-man Senate committee on the first day of the new session to examine and count the ballots of those towns. Wanting a trustworthy Republican on the committee, they settled on Archibald B. Kenyon of Richmond. The Democratic Senators were to be Francis J. Kiernan of North Providence and Edward F. Dwyer of Woonsocket. Confident they would win, but mindful of the need for discretion, they decided to withhold their plans from the rest of the Democrats in the legislature until the very last moment. The Governor expressed his approval of the plan.

One of the first things the inner group of Democrats agreed they would do after obtaining control of the Senate would be to pass a resolution declaring the State Supreme Court offices vacant. To do this, as with any bill, they needed approval of both houses. The Grand Committee would then replace the five Republican Supreme Court justices with three Democrats and two other Republicans. Some of the inner group wanted to have Democrats in all five judgeships, but Green insisted that if this were done the Democratic Party would be accused of doing just what it had been berating the Republicans for over the years. The two Republicans decided upon were Hugh B. Baker, a Yankee Protestant, and Antonio A. Capotosto, an Italo-American, two capable Superior Court justices. One of the Democrats was to be Congressman Francis B. Condon, upon whom almost all agreed. Green and Higgins particularly wanted Condon on the court in order to remove him as a threat for the United States Senate in 1936. For a Yankee Democrat the group selected William W. Moss, who had conducted much of Green's negotiations with the Federal government regarding RFC funds. Pawtucket's McCoy urged that the third Democrat be Edmund W. Flynn, the House Leader. Flynn urged it, too. Nevertheless, former Mayor of Providence Joseph Gainer was selected as the third Democratic judge. The ethnic balance had been well kept: two Irish Democrats, one Yankee Democrat, one Yankee Republican, and an Italian Republican.

Moss was assigned the job of preparing a series of bills which would be rapidly introduced into the Senate and then the House. The bills were to declare vacant the Supreme Court judgeships and the office of High Sheriff of Providence County, abolish the office of Finance Commissioner, remove the Providence Safety Board from state control, and provide for the administrative reorganization of the state government. With Green's help, Moss carefully worked out the wording of the bills. Everything was in readiness for the coup, and on the Sunday before the opening of the 1935 legislative session, all the Democratic legislators, including the defeated senatorial candidates from Portsmouth and South Kingstown, gathered at the Governor's residence. They were told to attend a caucus at eleven on the morning of January 1 at the State House, at which time they would be told what was going to happen.

On Tuesday morning, January 1, all the Democratic legislators were brought into the scheme. Just one thing went awry. Edmund W. Flynn wanted to be the Chief Justice of the new Supreme Court. He had little use for Green personally and the feeling was mutual. Flynn was, however, a popular figure on both sides of the aisle in both houses, and he let it be known that unless he were made Chief Justice, there would be a great deal of trouble pushing the Governor's contemplated reforms through the House of Representatives, of which he was the majority leader. In the words of one member of the administration, "He held a gun to our heads." Flynn was supported by James H. Kiernan, who wanted Flynn's job as majority leader. Lieutenant Governor Quinn had been given the task of selling Gainer to the assembled Democrats in caucus, but working under the pressure of time, he was unable to convince them, and Flynn won out. No doubt, appeasement of McCoy, Flynn's Pawtucket ally, played a part in the decision also. In any event, the ethnic balance remained undisturbed and the Democratic caucus approved the scheme.

When the caucus had ended, Quinn called the Senate into its first session. The carefully planned scene was then enacted. Quinn ordered the Secretary of State, Louis Cappelli, to swear in all the senators-elect except Republicans B. Earl Anthony of Portsmouth and Wallace Campbell of South Kingstown. He had, he solemnly announced, been informed that a protest to their certification had been noted. Taken aback, Anthony and Campbell did not know what to do. Campbell's desk was replete with flowers from well-wishers and he was dumbfounded by Quinn's statement. With the Senate now evenly divided twenty to twenty and working without rules, Senator Troy stood and requested that the Lieutenant Governor appoint a special committee to procure the ballot boxes and ballots cast in certain towns at the last election. Troy's motion was seconded, as prearranged, by Senator Francis

J. Kiernan, and before the Republicans knew what happened Quinn called for a voice vote and ruled it approved. The resolution was transmitted to the House, which concurred by a roll call vote of fifty-seven Democrats to forty-two Republicans, and then signed by Governor Green, who was impatiently waiting for the bill. All this took place within a space of a few minutes. The Senate had been at ease awaiting the return of the resolution from the House, and the Republicans, realizing what was about to take place, began to leave the building in hopes of preventing a legal quorum from being presented in the Senate. Quinn, citing Chapter 24, Section 32 of the *General Laws,* which gives the presiding officers of both houses the right to compel attendance, issued warrants for the arrest of Republican Senators Daniel F. McLaughlin, Lester Simmons, and Archibald B. Kenyon, for whom the Democrats had plans. McLaughlin later left for dinner with two state troopers—the Superintendent of State Police had supplied about twenty-five troopers at the Governor's request—and Simmons was soon let off. Only Kenyon remained at the Capitol.

When the House had approved the first measure and Green had signed it, Quinn called the Senate back to order. He then appointed Senators Kiernan, Dwyer, and Kenyon to procure and count the ballots of Portsmouth and South Kingstown, to determine who had been elected senators from those towns. Waiting in Louis Cappelli's office all this time was Joe Atkins, the Republican Deputy Secretary of State, whom Cappelli had kept on. Atkins' duties had been to record the votes as counted by the State Returning Board and to take care of their security. He had the combination to the state vault, and to make sure that he remained until they were ready for him, the Democrats had stationed a State Trooper with him in Cappelli's office. Even lunch was brought to him while he waited, not knowing what was happening. After the special committee was named, Atkins was asked to open the vault. Upon the appearance of two burly state troopers, each of whom was carrying a large sledge hammer to smash it in, Atkins complied with the request. The ballots from the two disputed towns were then brought to a committee room. The discounted ballots, which had been separated from the counted ones, were mixed in with them and the entire amount recounted. The committee pored over the ballots, threw out some for improper markings, and came out with new totals. Kiernan, Dwyer, and Kenyon unanimously declared that Democrats Charles A. White, Jr. and Joseph P. Dunn had been elected from South Kingstown and Portsmouth. The special committee had actually rejected more ballots than the State Returning Board had. Prior to the special count, the votes had stood this way:

South Kingstown		*Portsmouth*	
Campbell (Republican)	1,369	Anthony (Republican)	535
White (Democrat)	1,308	Dunn (Democrat)	496
total	2,677	total	1,031

After the Senate count, the vote stood:

White (Democrat)	1,318	Dunn (Democrat)	520
Campbell (Republican)	1,292	Anthony (Republican)	510
total	2,610	total	1,030

Democrats now had twenty-two senators to the Republicans' twenty, and thus control of both houses of the General Assembly. Secretary of State Cappelli swore in the new senators and Senator Troy then moved in rapid-fire order for the consideration of the five major bills which Moss had drawn up.

The first bill vacated the office of Sheriff Andrews of Providence and the second vacated the five judgeships of the State Supreme Court. The Republican judges on the Court were granted large pensions on condition that they resign their offices by noon the following day. The first bill was passed by a voice vote and the second by a roll call vote, with Republican McLaughlin casting the lone dissenting ballot. Republican Senators Kenyon and Handy were present but did not vote. The third bill wiped out the Providence Safety Board and gave Governor Green the power to name a Public Safety Director for a thirty-day period. The fourth bill abolished the office of Finance Commissioner and created the combined office of State Budget Director and State Comptroller, to be appointed by the Governor. These also passed by voice vote. The last bill was the most voluminous. In essence it merged the some eighty state commissions into ten departments, to become effective in sixty days. From the time the Senate reconvened to hear the report of the special committee to the adoption of the fifth measure at 7:32 P.M., only fourteen minutes had elapsed. The House quickly approved the Senate measures by roll call votes, along straight party lines, and Governor Green eagerly signed them into law.

By this time it was 10:30 P.M. and the Grand Committee (less almost all the Republican senators and representatives) met to fill the vacancies of Sheriff and judges of the Supreme Court. Philip E. Quinn of Providence was elected as Sheriff of Providence County and the agreed-upon slate of judges was duly elected. Theodore Francis Green was then sworn into office as governor for a second term. The time was 12:05 A.M., and the Governor read an abbreviated inaugural address containing recommendations for much that had already occurred.

While the Grand Committee was filling the new vacancies, Higgins, in the governor's car, delivered letters to the Providence Safety Board—Everitte St. John Chaffee, George T. Marsh, and Michael Corrigan. They were informed that they had been removed from office and were therefore no longer state officials. On the following day, the new Supreme Court justices, except for Condon, who was in Washington, were sworn into office and the bloodless revolution of 1935 was over.

Instead of being reorganized under a new state constitution, as Democrats had urged for so long, Rhode Island had been made over by the determination, the cleverness, the audacity, and the persistence of the Rhode Island Democratic Party. To justify the actions that had taken place on New Year's Day, Governor Green addressed a statewide radio audience. Praising the new regime, he said that the Democratic success made him feel "the spiritual presence of the Patron Saint of the Democratic Party in Rhode Island, Thomas Wilson Dorr." It was this spirit and Dorr's "indomitable advocacy of the rights of the people" that had led the Democrats on and would continue to do so.[7]

While Democrats rejoiced, others cursed. Republicans attacked the coup as an unconstitutional, illegal, and dictatorial act. The

Providence Journal condemned the haste with which the legislature had acted on the five bills, and charged that they were "not reforms but political maneuvers and reprisals." The Rhode Island Bar Association was aghast at the treatment of the Court, despite the fact that two Republicans had been appointed to the state's highest judicial body. Fred Perkins, secretary of the Association, was particularly vehement in his denunciation of Green and the Democrats. (Many years later Perkins himself would be elevated to the Supreme Court by a Democrat, Governor Dennis Roberts, who often looked upon the bench as a convenient place to deposit potential Republican opposition.)[8]

Legally or not, the rotten-borough system had at last been beaten without benefit of a new constitution. The Democrats were now in control of both branches of the government and they believed they knew how to use their power. The state could be reorganized and, in the process, the spoils of victory could be distributed to the party faithful. The Rhode Island Democratic Party, however, had been built on a tenuous coalition of various ethnic groups. Whether the coalition could hold together was another matter. It did not take long to find out.

Flushed with their triumph on New Year's Day, the Democrats adopted new Senate rules which gave the power of committee assignments and choice of committee chairmen to the lieutenant governor. James H. Kiernan succeeded Flynn as majority leader, and by the end of January the infamous Brayton Law of 1901 had been repealed. The Governor's appointees became subject to confirmation by the Senate, not to substitution by it. Other major acts passed by the regular session of the 1935 General Assembly were a proposal for a constitutional amendment to extend voter registration through September 30, an appropriations bill for the fiscal year of July 1, 1934, to June 30, 1935, a $200,000 old-age pension bill, a resolution establishing a State Planning Board to chart the state's economic future, and a bill providing for a referendum to decide on the need for voting machines.[9]

Progress ended there, for the distribution of patronage now began to occupy most of the Democrats' time. With the office of

Finance Commissioner abolished, Green had appointed Thomas McCoy of Pawtucket to the newly created position of Budget Director and Comptroller. McCoy was more or less a political choice: he controlled about nine Democrats in the House—the balance of power—and placating him might help to ensure passage of the Governor's program. But McCoy was also an able administrator, and besides, since the budget director served at the governor's pleasure, Green could remove McCoy if he proved to be troublesome. James H. Kiernan was another, though not so serious, challenge to Green's influence in the House. House Democrats had their own battle over committee assignments, and Kiernan alienated many Democratic legislators by his dictatorial tactics and lack of finesse in handling them.

The appointment of Judges Baker and Capotosto to the Supreme Court had left vacant two Superior Court judgeships. Ethnic problems immediately arose, as Alberic A. Archambault, Felix Toupin, Patrick P. Curran, Mortimer A. Sullivan, and Luigi De Pasquale presented themselves as candidates. Green finally decided upon his old law partner Curran and former Democratic State Chairman Archambault, while, at the same time, he elevated Judge Jeremiah O'Connell to be the presiding justice of the Superior Court. These appointments made some people happy and upset others. The Senate approved the nominations and Republican Senator Handy conveniently voted on the Democratic side. (Green often reminded Handy of his debt to the Governor for placing him on the Horse Racing Commission, and when an occasional Republican vote was needed in a close contest, Handy could usually be prevailed upon to act accordingly.)[10]

The sheriffs of the five Rhode Island counties offered another source of enlarged patronage. Democratic deputies filtered through Sheriff Philip E. Quinn of Providence County, and in late January the Grand Committee vacated the other four offices of sheriff and Democrats became sheriffs in Bristol, Kent, Newport, and Washington Counties. In addition, four Republican roving clerks of the Superior Court were turned out and replaced by Democrats. As Senator Troy so aptly put it, "The people of the State (had) issued a mandate to the Democratic Party to administer the affairs of the State."[11]

More than altruism and devotion to the cause underlay the speedy passage of the skeleton reorganization bill on New Year's Day. Consolidating the departments and commissions of the state also meant the creation of many new jobs for good Democrats. The problem was to determine who was to get what. Governor Green insisted that only capable people be appointed to any position, regardless of factional influences; even McCoy's appointment had fallen within this limitation. Nonetheless, necessity dictated that Green exercise great political prudence in screening the field of candidates for the new political plums. For example, thirteen Italo-Americans in the General Assembly requested Green to appoint Ernest Santagini as State Director of Public Works. Albert J. Lamarre, McCoy's man in Pawtucket, also wanted the post, and Franco-American groups urged him on Green. The Governor, however, wanted Charles F. McElroy, chairman of the Providence City Committee, in that position. This fight alone caused much bitterness in the ranks of the Democrats. Green began to realize the seriousness of his opposition when Representative Shunney, the dog-loving Democratic representative from Woonsocket, urged that the Grand Committee fill all the posts— department heads as well as Superior and District Court judgeships—instead of allowing the Governor to do so with the consent of the Senate. This did not come about, but the possibility served as an additional caution to Green.[12]

The fight over the selection of department heads went on into February. Senate Democratic caucuses finally accepted four of Green's appointees—Thomas Kennelly as Director of Taxation and Regulation, Dr. John E. Donley as Director of Welfare, James Rockett as Director of Education, and Edward McLaughlin as Director of Public Health—but Senate Democrats forced Burton K. Harris on Green as Director of Agriculture, and Republican aid was called upon to approve L. Metcalfe Walling as Director of Labor and Charles F. McElroy as Director of Public Works. Favors in kind were of course promised to the friendly Republicans. Throughout, McCoy fought Green's appointments behind the scenes, in an effort to place his own people in several key jobs. The department heads appointed divisional chiefs and other subordinates, and were thus a lucrative source of patronage.

Patronage squabbles continued. McCoy, wanting more to say on who should fill clerkships and other offices, continued to press Green, and for more than mere political reasons. He and Walter O'Hara, one of the original owners of the new race track, wanted Pawtucket to own its public utility facilities, which would give them control of the policies of the plant and thus an opportunity to corner the utilities market in the Blackstone and Woonsocket sections of the state. Green was aware of their plans and resisted them as best he could. McCoy's controls in the House not only extended to the nine representatives but also to the House Finance Committee, chaired by Harry Curvin, who was politically beholden to McCoy. James H. Kiernan also wanted more of a voice in patronage matters, and he was disgruntled with Green for personal reasons as well. Kiernan resented Green's desire to lead all the Democrats, and he also felt that Edward J. Higgins had usurped his own rightful position as Green's personal agent. Kiernan, after all, had started to work with Green before Higgins had come on the scene. In a word, Green was having a great deal of trouble with factions in his own party. Largely for that reason, major items of the Governor's program failed to pass the regular 1935 session of the General Assembly. One was the calling of a constitutional convention and the other was the appropriations bill for the fiscal year 1935–36.

In February Governor Green had requested from the State Supreme Court an advisory opinion on the legality of legislation calling for a constitutional convention. Back in 1883 a Republican Court had ruled in the negative, but now, soon before the Assembly ordinarily adjourned, the Court unanimously stated that the legislature could summon such a convention. The Court recommended, but did not require, a referendum on the necessity of the call. The issue of a new constitution, however, was lost in a factional struggle to determine the manner of selecting delegates to such a convention if one were held. One group of Democrats, led by Quinn, wanted a nonpartisan convention to draw up the new constitution. Another group, of which the Governor was a part, really wanted the convention dominated solely by Democrats. To ensure the latter, the proposal was made that party committees nominate delegates. Although this managed to get through the House, the Senate buried the measure completely. Some Democratic senators, including Dunn of Portsmouth, were genuinely afraid that a new constitution would not be in the best interests of their small towns. Quinn, as presiding officer, could also direct the Senate away from the proposal he personally disapproved. In any event, no constitutional convention was called.[13]

No action was taken either on the annual appropriations bill. It was painfully apparent that Chairman Curvin of the House Finance Committee was holding up the bill in an attempt to force Green to come to terms with McCoy on the question of a municipal utilities system in Pawtucket. Green refused to give in, and a stalemate ensued. Two more of the Governor's pet projects, the prohibition of dual office holding and the requirement that sheriffs and clerks turn in fines and fees to the general treasury, never left the ground because Democrats, not Republicans, were now profiting from the existing system.

The regular 1935 legislative session, then, was indeed a spectacle. The first day had resulted in the Democratic take-over of the State Senate and the passage of measures which ousted Republicans from key positions. Most of the remainder of the session was spent in personal feuding over patronage, jealousies, and pet projects. The General Assembly suddenly adjourned on April 13, and Governor Green announced almost immediately that he would call a special session to reconsider measures that should have been acted upon earlier.[14]

Two days later, at the Jefferson Day Dinner, Governor Green publicly excoriated McCoy and Kiernan for opposing him in the House. A thunderous ovation greeted the Governor at the conclusion of his address, and he was verbally supported by Lieutenant Governor Quinn. Realizing he had the support of the Democratic rank and file, Green decided to meet McCoy head on. The Governor openly blamed McCoy for holding up many bills in the House and attacked him for his selfishness. He then summarily ousted McCoy as Budget Director and promoted a talented young Italo-American Democrat, Christopher Del Sesto, to his place.[15]

Green had often turned to radio to explain his position on various matters, and now he did so again to broadcast his impressions of the legislative session just concluded. He stressed the importance of the repeal of the Brayton Law and spoke of how efficient state government would become under the reorganization, but he also enumerated the legislature's failures and then proceeded to denounce the Democratic legislators who had held up bills because they wanted to use them for trading purposes. Green explained that he had removed McCoy from the position of Budget Director because he had "failed to act with the administration which was trying to procure the unconditional passage of the appropriation bill." Although McCoy had helped draft the bill, he had "sat silent while his intimate political friends and supporters wrecked the administration program." The open attack on McCoy had a salutary effect on Kiernan, and in early May he called Green the "most patient, ablest man who ever sat in the Governor's chair." McCoy was not so docile. He charged the Governor and Higgins with attempting to bribe a Democratic representative to abandon McCoy by offering a bit of direct patronage to him, a charge not without foundation.[16]

To break the back of McCoy's control of the Pawtucket bloc in the House, Governor Green chose to deal with the Republicans. Green wanted five major things passed in the special session. These were 1) the reorganization bill amplifying the original measure passed on New Year's Day, 2) an appropriations bill, 3) the establishment of a Police Commission in Providence not subject to state control, 4) the addition of two judges to the Superior Court, and 5) the removal of all the district judges and a new slate to replace them. The Republican House leaders offered to support these measures if Green would abandon his plans for a constitutional convention, allow the Republicans a greater voice in selection of key personnel in the new administrative setup, and give one of the new Superior Court judgeships to a Republican. Green agreed, the bills were passed, and Green ceased to be concerned with McCoy and his henchmen.[17]

Dealing with the opposition, a common thing among practical politicians, had been rewarding. For one thing, Green had not had to trade much, for a constitutional convention no longer seemed so important now that the Democratic Party was in control of the state. Second, and more important, by dealing with the Republicans and trading a *quid pro quo,* Green had thwarted McCoy's control of the House, which had often been more frustrating than being blocked by the Republicans. Later, under a different set of circumstances, he would be able to push McCoy even farther away. As for now, Green could be satisfied with having won a measure of control in the General Assembly. He had entered the regular legislative session in January without a majority in the Senate, and by the end of May, he had not only obtained relatively firm leadership of his party and thus of both houses, but had also learned a great deal about using the political weapons of an executive leader—patronage, the power of removal, and informal deals with the opposition party.

Green continued to maintain close liaison with the Roosevelt Administration while he dealt with domestic politics in Rhode Island. Although Federal patronage now tended to be channelled through Senator Gerry, Green used the economic situation as the means of preserving his own status with Washington. In April, 1935, Congress passed a $4 billion relief program and Governor Green led Rhode Island's successful bid to obtain funds for rivers and harbors improvements as well as other projects in the state. By mid-May $2 million of Federal funds were earmarked for Rhode Island, and construction went ahead on the works projects already accepted by the electorate. New buildings were erected at Wallum Lake, the Howard State Institutions at Warwick, Rhode Island State College, and the Rhode Island School for the Deaf. In September $7.5 million more was given to Rhode Island for public works and, as House Majority Leader Kiernan pointed out, Green deserved the credit for having obtained such a large amount for the state. Green was wise enough to take political advantage of such Federal windfalls, and he made several radio addresses emphasizing the benefits derived by the state from the New Deal and carefully linking the New Deal with his own administration in Rhode Island.[18]

In November Green again took to the air to explain the intricacies and summarize the accomplishments of the New Deal. He pointed out that with Federal aid, Rhode Island now had 150 miles of new and 780 miles of rebuilt roads, 9 miles of new cement sidewalks, 5 miles of new water pipe, 25 miles of storm and sanitary sewers, 275 newly built or refurbished public buildings, and 2 million new trees in the state forests. The Governor stressed the fact that the Federal government had adopted work relief plans along the lines he himself had established for Rhode Island at the very beginning of his state administration. The partnership of state and Federal governments, established to relieve unemployment distress, was now firmly entrenched. Green had taken full advantage of it for his own political career.[19]

At the opening session of the 1936 legislature, Green asked that the Assembly consider the welfare of the state first and at all times in their deliberations. With control of the Democratic legislators more firmly established than had been the case in 1935, the Governor managed to have some notable legislation steered through both houses. Labor, which had found renewed strength with the advent of the New Deal, was more kindly treated than ever before in Rhode Island. The Assembly passed a workmen's compensation act, a forty-eight-hour law for women and children, and an anti-injunction act for labor disputes. In addition, a retirement system for state employees was established and a state unemployment insurance act, in conjunction with the social security provisions of Federal legislation, was placed on the statute books. At long last sheriffs' and court clerks' fees had to be turned over to the general treasury instead of being kept by the sheriffs and clerks themselves. The legislature also passed resolutions for several state constitutional amendments. These would have provided for permanent registration of voters, given the governor power of the item veto in appropriations bills, established the right of initiative and referendum, and provided for absentee voting. As it turned out, none of these proposals was approved a second time in the following legislature, as required by the state constitution, and they were consequently never submitted to the people for their approval. Governor Green told a statewide radio audience that this General Assembly had concerned itself more with the welfare of the workingman—and woman—than any in Rhode Island's history.[20]

Despite the arrangements he had made with the Republicans in the special session called in 1935, Green decided to go forward in 1936 with a new plan for a constitutional convention. A bill was introduced into the Senate with no provision for a referendum on the question of holding such a convention. Many senators, particularly Democrats from small towns, objected to this deficiency and finally such a proviso was added to the bill. The Senate passed the measure when Quinn cast a tie-breaking vote. The House passed the bill on a roll call vote, 57 to 42, and the Governor set March 10 as the date for the referendum. Referenda creating compulsory holidays on New Year's Day and Columbus Day were on the ballot at the same time. The constitutional convention plan was defeated by some 12,000 votes with less than 50 per cent of the electorate, mostly concentrated in the small towns, having turned out. To some extent, the loss of the constitutional convention referendum was looked upon as a Democratic defeat. By this time, however, the entire issue of a convention was no longer important to most people and the small number of voters tends to show that the Democrats simply did not bother to go to the polls. The constitution of Rhode Island seemed destined to remain relatively intact.[21]

State politics was closely linked to the national scene in 1936. Postmaster General Farley and Green corresponded extensively over Rhode Island and national problems. During the first few months of 1936 Green tried to have a few Republicans in Rhode Island removed from the Federal payroll. Farley looked into the matter but did nothing about it. Federal patronage in the state, according to the time-honored custom of senatorial courtesy, was within the domain of Senator Gerry. That would change in 1937, when Green assumed his seat as United States senator, but for now he had to bide his time.[22]

Of course Green's trade with the Republicans in the state in May, 1935, had required him to appoint a few Republicans to posts in his own administration. In accordance with the deal, he had appointed House Republican Minority Leader Walter Curry to the Superior Court to fill one of the two seats created on the bench; Democratic Mayor Sullivan of Newport had been the other appointee. (Green was fond of pointing out that when the five Democrats and six Republicans on the Superior Court were added to the three Democrats and two Republicans on the Supreme Court, the result was an over-all bipartisan body.) In addition, as part of the 1935 trade, Green had also channeled a few choice state positions through the Republicans. These appointments in fact had upset several Italo-Franco and Portugese-American groups, whom McCoy and his lieutenant Lamarre encouraged to protest to the Governor. Most of the objections came from Pawtucket.[23]

Theodore Francis Green became a national figure in 1936 by way of the politics of the national Democratic Party. At the Democratic National Convention in Philadelphia that year Green made a seconding speech for Franklin D. Roosevelt, twenty years after he had introduced him to a Rhode Island Democratic audience at a rally when Roosevelt was Assistant Secretary of the Navy. Green was also brought to the attention of the nation when Senator Peter Gerry, who finally decided to follow his somewhat reactionary bent, resigned as Democratic National Committeeman from Rhode Island during the national convention. On the spot, Green was selected in his place by the Rhode Island delegates. This action made the front pages of many newspapers in the country. Green was to hold that position for twenty-four years.

Green was catapulted into the minds of the nationwide public, however, by way of radio. John D. M. Hamilton, chairman of the Republican National Committee, spoke in Rhode Island in mid-July, shortly after Governor Alfred Landon of Kansas had been nominated for the Presidency at the Republican National Convention. Hamilton called Landon "a man of common sense" with the qualities necessary for a President to possess. Several days later Green ripped into Hamilton in a radio speech in Providence. Turning on Landon, Green asked him question after question of public importance, with devastating effect. Green concluded his speech with a ringing tribute to Roosevelt, whom he called "a great man . . . whose idealism points the way to a healthier, saner, more prosperous, and happier life for the masses of our people."[24]

The address was excellent campaign oratory and was followed by a nationwide address on July 28 when, along with the governors of Pennsylvania, Illinois, Iowa, Nebraska, and Oregon, Green spoke on a program sponsored by the Democratic National Committee. The address was short, to the point, and well delivered. Green, leading off, called Landon "a question mark" who had "been given the biggest newspaper buildup in the history of American politics." He pointed out that under Roosevelt Rhode Island had been recovering from the effects of the depression brought on by "mistakes of the Hoover policies," and concluded by saying that "With cash in her pocket and new hope in her heart Rhode Island is on her way." His speech was well received and he had hundreds of requests from all over the country for copies to be used in other state campaigns against the Republicans. If one were to pinpoint any event which started Green on a national political career, it would have to be his July 28 radio speech.[25]

On October 3 Green announced that he was a candidate for the United States Senate. Keeping in close touch with the Democratic National Committee, Green wrote Farley his impressions of the political conditions in Rhode Island. Green expected no trouble being nominated for the Senate, but Lieutenant Governor Quinn was being opposed for the gubernatorial nomination by a rump group of Democrats led by Thomas McCoy. Green implied in his letter to Farley that O'Hara of the Narragansett Race Track was financially behind McCoy and had also given strong support to a Republican in a special election for Congress held in 1935. The Governor pointed out that the Republicans would probably nominate for governor Charles P. Sisson who, in Green's opinion, would not make as strong a run as William H. Vanderbilt, the former State Senator. Green carefully stated that Gerry was doing little good for the cause of the party of the Democrats and feared that Gerry's contemplated sale of his newspaper, possibly before the election and to Republicans, might harm the ticket.[26]

The Democrats, meeting in state convention in October, unanimously nominated Green for the Senate. McCoy's strength proved far from adequate to damage Quinn, and Quinn's friend Raymond E. Jordan was selected as the nominee for lieutenant governor. Secretary of State Cappelli and Attorney General Hartigan were chosen to run for re-election. Aime J. Forand, who won the nomination for Congress from the First District, and Congressman John M. O'Connell beat back opposition from several sources—including Christopher Del Sesto, who was strongly backed by many Italo-Americans—to win renomination from the Second District. Green had carefully shown no favoritism in that particular contest. The Democratic state ticket was thus headed by Yankee-Protestant Green, who was followed by Irish-Catholic Quinn, Yankee-Protestant Jordan, Italian Cappelli, Irish-Catholic Hartigan, and for general treasurer, Franco-American Henri Roberge. The two Congressmen on the slate were a Franco-American and an Irish-Catholic. This newest ethnic coalition made ready to do battle with the Republicans.

Republican Jesse H. Metcalf, part owner of the *Providence Journal,* was renominated for the United States Senate. Sisson was chosen as the Republican candidate for governor and the rest of the ticket was composed of relatively weak candidates. Charles Risk was renominated for Congress and Republican House Leader Sandager, who had taken Curry's place when Curry had been "promoted" by Green to the Superior Court, was selected to oppose O'Connell in the Second Congressional District.

The Rhode Island Democrats ran a well-organized campaign in 1936. The names of Roosevelt, Green, and Quinn were regularly mentioned as a sort of secular trinity. The economic benefits accruing to the state under the New Deal were constantly emphasized, and Green hammered at Metcalf's anti-New Deal voting record. Green repudiated the Hoover philosophy and stated that "the needs and wants of the people are proper matters of governmental concern." The Democratic State Committee saw to it that all those who derived material benefits from the Democratic regimes in Washington and Providence were reminded of their duty to vote straight Democratic in November. The ethnic groups in the state were catered to by specific members of each, selected by Green and Higgins.[27]

The Republicans at the state and national level had little chance of winning in 1936. The Rhode Island House of Representatives remained Democratic by four seats, but the State Senate again went Republican by six seats as Democrats lost the towns of Coventry, Johnston, North Smithfield, South Kingstown, and Tiverton, all of which they had captured, one way or another, in the 1934 election. Despite this fact, however, in January, 1937, seven Republican senators, led by friendly Harry T. Bodwell of Cranston, voted with the Democrats to organize the Senate under a "compromise agreement." That is a story in itself.

The new senator from the State of Rhode Island and Providence Plantations, Theodore Francis Green, was deluged by thousands of greetings and congratulations on his victory. At sixty-nine, Green stood on the threshold of a long and respected career in the United States Senate, in which he served until 1961. He took his place alongside four of his ancestors who had also served their country in the Congress, beginning with Jonathan Arnold of the Continental Congress. It had taken thirty years for "the gentleman from Providence" to become "the Senator from Rhode Island." His contributions to his country, state, and party in the latter capacity would match those of the years 1906 through 1936. Theodore Francis Green had indeed judged for himself, spoken for himself, and looked, always, to the future.

Chapter X

Aftermath

I turned the whole thing around!

—Theodore Francis Green

AN evaluation of the importance of Theodore Francis Green
from 1906 through 1936 must take into account his role in
national as well as Rhode Island politics. No doubt his influence
in those years at the national level was not very great. Not until
his terms as United States Senator did he make any significant
contributions in that area. True enough, Green was caught up
in the wave of progressivism which began to take hold in the nation shortly after 1900. This movement coincided with Green's
own ideas of social, economic, and political improvement in his
own state. As did the Progressives of his day, Green advocated
clean government and aid to lower-income groups. But his name
does not rank with the La Follettes and others who held strong
ideological views of what had to be done to change America.
Green never had a strong messianic impulse to revamp society.
Neither did he share the isolationist tendencies of most of the
Progressives nor the extreme nationalist feelings of some of them.
His essential moderation also kept him from advocating the ex-
tremism so often pressed for in the first quarter of this century.
Green was simply a patrician who entered politics out of a sense
of responsibility inherent in his own family tradition and culture.

If there was need to reform conditions in the country shortly
after the turn of the century, there was certainly much reason to
do the same for the situation in Rhode Island. Green's political
career up to 1937 is of relative importance almost exclusively at
the state level. His major contribution, therefore, was his influ-

ence on politics and the administration of government in the nation's smallest state. A study of his political career in Rhode Island is also an examination of the nature of the rise of the Democratic Party in a state which, like so many others, has had a political struggle waged between its rural and urban population and among its various ethnic and religious groups. Rhode Island, then, is a microcosm of the kind of national politics which has been so greatly affected by the rise of the so-called newer Americans to a higher social, economic, and political status.

The shift in power from the legislative to the executive branch of government in Rhode Island was consolidated by Theodore Francis Green during his second term as governor. The successful coup on New Year's Day, 1935, placed the control of the State Senate in the hands of the Democratic Party. The General Assembly thereupon gave the governor a real power of appointment when it repealed the Brayton Law of 1901. In so doing, the Senate surrendered its right of substituting its own nominees for those of the governor. Democratic legislators, led by Green, veered completely away from the previous Republican practice of maintaining control of the state by the dominance of the Senate. Instead of retaining command for themselves, the Democrats in the Senate and the House, handed the executive the weapon of state patronage which the Senate Republicans had previously wielded themselves.

Had the legislature not repealed the Brayton Law of 1901, the selection of new department personnel might well have remained in the Senate's collective hands. With the governor having the power of appointment, even though the Senate had to confirm his appointees, political power now tended to be concentrated in the executive branch. In a word, the governor, not a Senate party leader or even a political boss, became the actual dispenser of state patronage. The Senate thus ceased to be the all-important factor in the new administrative reorganization which eventually followed the political events of New Year's Day, 1935, and became a defensive body instead.

Political power within the Democratic Party organization shifted also in that the governor, not the party chairman, became

the most important leader of the party. Thus the growth of the
executive branch of government was at the expense of party as
well as legislative considerations. The governor now personified
the Democratic Party and led the legislature at the same time.
One proof of this shift can be seen from the fact that Governor
Green, in order to put through some of his legislative program in
his second term, was able to deal with Republican legislators and,
at the same time, publicly chastize a few leading Democrats without fear of reprisals at his party convention or at the polls. Indeed, before Green's administration such political tactics on the
part of any governor would have meant his political suicide.

The impact of Governor Green on the power of the executive
was a major contribution to Rhode Island politics and the Democratic Party in the state. Green was the first governor to act as a
successful focal point for political action on behalf of the Democratic Party. The Governor, and therefore his party in the state,
took command of the legislative program and administration. In
previous Republican years, the state legislature had been controlled by Republican Party bosses, not the governor. Green used
the expanded power of the executive to further control of a Democratic governor over his party. The few times since 1932 when Republicans have been elected to the governorship, the Democrats
have had to rally their activity around a party chairman. This has
proved to be most inadequate for maintaining a sound organization. When a Democrat occupies the governor's chair, the party has
a symbolic and actual chief. Theodore Francis Green was the first.

A second major contribution made by Green to Rhode Island
politics was the reorganization of the administration of the state.
Prior to the new administrative establishment in 1935, Rhode Island had an irregular patchquilt of commissions and departments.
With the governor having no real appointive power, the heads of
these various agencies were not responsible to him but, in the final analysis, to the party bosses who directed the process by
which they had been selected. It was no easy task for Green to
bring about a new organization of the administration of government. Shortly after the passage of the skeleton reorganization act
on New Year's Day, 1935, the General Assembly, including Democrats, began to balk at amplification of the Governor's plans.

They remembered that Green's dispensation of RFC funds in 1933 had in effect cut them off from a lucrative source of patronage and they resented any further development of the governor's powers. The facts of political life, however, precluded their doing very much about it, particularly when Green chose to barter with the Republicans for approval of his legislative program in 1935. Thus the selection of personnel in the administration of the state's government became centralized in the office of the governor. When the civil service system was incorporated into state government in later years, the legislature became even more remote from administration. The new administrative procedures which began in Green's second term brought more efficiency and organization into Rhode Island's government.

A very important contribution of Theodore Francis Green was his use of the power of his office. During the difficult days of the first part of 1933, when the economic situation called for leadership in the handling of relief for the distressed, it was necessary to have a man with the strong concept of political leadership. Green had this to begin with and a lesser man as governor between January and April, 1933, might well have caused disaster in the state. By using the medium of radio, for example, to advance his political programs he set the tone for state politicians of the future. He rallied the people when they needed rallying. They believed him when he declared his slogan was "humanity first" and they knew he meant it. Green made the office of governor a symbol for the people, not a figurehead for political bosses.

Green's successful rise in politics was due to the mixture of three ingredients. First, the web of Rhode Island's ethnic politics served as a vehicle for his eventual climb to the governorship of the state. Second, the nationwide economic depression following the stock market crash in 1929 served as a catalytic agent for the assumption of a kind of executive power hitherto unknown in Rhode Island's government. Neither of these factors, however, would have been enough to cause the combustion which propelled him so high without the third ingredient, that of Theodore Francis Green's tenacity and political astuteness.

Extensive control by native-stock Republican citizens of Rhode

Island's political life lasted into the twentieth century. It must be remembered, however, that this kind of hegemony stimulated the establishment of a firm opposition, centering first in the Irish newcomers and then gradually encompassing other ethnic groups, particularly the Italians, and then the French. The economic depression of the early thirties brought the diverse ethnic groups together for the first time on such a grand scale. In taking out their ire on the Republican Party which was in control during the beginning of the depression, most of the Irish, Italian, and French voters became thoroughly Democratic. Many of them voted for the very first time in 1932, as was true with such other smaller groups as the Negroes and the Portuguese. In essence, the immigrant minority groups united in the early thirties and looked to the Democratic Party as the savior of their very lives. Most Protestants in Rhode Island tended to be Republican, Catholics Democratic, and the third major religious group, the Jews, turned in the direction of the Democratic Party as a result of the economic debacle of 1929 and the political appeal offered by Franklin D. Roosevelt. Prior to the age of Roosevelt, most leading Jewish politicians in Rhode Island could be found on the Republican side. In their desire to associate themselves with the most successful element in the community, the Yankee Protestants, Jews tended to be Republican before 1932. Afterwards this was much less true, and by the end of World War II, Jews in Rhode Island had become mostly Democratic in political outlook. The Roosevelt era brought most Jewish citizens in political line with the non-Protestant ethnic minorities. Green rode the crest of this wave of unity.

Theodore Francis Green was a Yankee Protestant, but a Democrat by virtue of convictions he inherited from his mother's side. Although his ethnic background was more a liability than an asset during his early struggles to gain political recognition in Rhode Island, it later became advantageous to him as the non-Catholic, native-stock leader of all the elements which composed most of the Democratic Party membership. In a sense, had Green not been a Yankee Protestant, he might well never have won the governorship of the state. Patrick H. Quinn's remark in 1930 that Green owed the Democratic Party more than the party owed him had a great deal of truth in it at that time. By 1932, however, Green's background served as a unifying force for the diversified elements of the Democratic Party. One of the reasons for Green's nomination for governor in 1912 was the anticipation that his Yankee-Protestant heritage would be attractive to the non-Democratic native-stock voting population. In 1932, however, the Democrats did not need to appeal to the Yankee Protestants any longer but could well use one of them to unite their own party.

During his term as governor, Green was a neutral leader of the non-Yankee ethnic groups fighting for political status. The French could ask him to appoint members of their own group to positions of authority and the Italians could do the same for their people. At the same time, Green stood to win favor from both groups after he had won the governorship in 1932 by playing one group off against the other. In short, he was all things to all people. Although this did make him a certain number of political enemies, it helped cement most of the "mass dissatisfied" to him as their man. That he intensely believed in the rights of the people aided him to maintain his own equilibrium when his political leadership was challenged at various times by one ethnic group or another.

The Federal government, because of the depression in the thirties, passed a great deal of relief and public works legislation. For the most part this money was distributed to the people through the states, which had to accept the money formally after having their proposed projects approved by the Federal government. As governor, Green directed the procedures involved in planning the construction of various public works. Under his direction, using Federal funds, large tracts of shore property were developed for beaches, the state institutions were made more modern and in fact more humane, the state airport was made a first class field instead of the pond it had been, and the state forests replanted with new trees. In brief, Green was Governor of Rhode Island when a multitude of public works projects was carried out in the state. He directed the flow of funds into the projects he himself thought worthwhile—and indeed they were. The economic factors in the depression era enabled Green to be a real leader as governor.

Green' tenacity in political life was rewarded when he was elected in 1932. Despite his earlier defeats in 1912 and 1918 and the many slights in Democratic conventions and circles before 1930, Green held on to affiliation with the Democratic Party. Lesser men of his class might have abandoned the long road to personal victory in the Democratic Party, as some did. By not winning and yet holding on, Green eventually made himself a more important cog in Democratic politics than he would have been had he been politically victorious in elections prior to 1932. As a statewide officer before the depression, Green would have been a mere political aberration from the normal routine of state politics in Rhode Island. When depression necessitated the firm hand of the executive leader, Green became important.

Green's political astuteness in his eventual domination of the political scene was very similar to that of Franklin D. Roosevelt. His success in politics ran parallel to that of Roosevelt, on a smaller scale. Neither joined the party of his own class but cast his lot with the Democrats. They were both socially progressive, internationalist in outlook, idealistic in purpose, yet politically pragmatic in using the means to obtain those ends. Both Green and Roosevelt looked upon government as the agent to make things better for the people. Green was able to balance his idealism for better government with the realities of political life.

Green's emotional drive to gain recognition in the minds of men via the political life and to contribute something positive to the world around him was enhanced by his careful use of prudence and intuition. He was a friend of Peter Gerry, but not so friendly that any of the latter's somewhat reactionary reputation rubbed off on him. Green sympathized with the desire of Al Smith to be President but knew, somehow, that transferring his own allegiance to Roosevelt in 1932 would do him more good than harm despite the nature of Irish-Catholic influence in Rhode Island. Calling out the National Guard in a serious strike had been unfortunate for Governor San Souci in 1922, but Green was able to turn similar action on his part in 1934 to his own advantage.

Green knew he needed Thomas P. McCoy as his Irish running mate in 1930 and his Budget Director in 1935, but he also knew when it was time to cast him off. He did not permit his lukewarm attitude toward Edmund W. Flynn, the Democratic House floor leader in 1933 and 1934, to prevent Flynn's selection as Chief Justice of the State Supreme Court in 1935. In fact, Flynn's appointment practically ensured a favorable response when Green asked for a Supreme Court advisory opinion on the question of calling for a constitutional convention. Example after example could be cited to show Green's political skill. He had the intuition so necessary for the successful politician.

Theodore Francis Green was by no means admired by all people. Many, not all Republicans, disliked him intensely. Several leaders in his own party harangued him because he would not direct more patronage through them. Only political force and the threat to take more direct legal action finally thwarted one Democrat in particular. Another leader of the party in the legislature believed he had been unfairly dealt with when Green chose, instead of him, another Democrat to be his close associate and personal adviser. The political facts of life often required Green to select a member of one ethnic group over another in the same group. Although this sometimes made a political enemy of the one not favored, it usually mattered little in the long run to the entire group.

Some of our founding fathers sincerely believed that the people must be led by a natural aristocracy of the intellectual elite. Theodore Francis Green was indeed one of those aristocrats rooted in the tradition and culture of the past. Yet, he was not tied to the past and always sought improvement of the present by formulating intelligent plans for the future. Rhode Island will always have good cause to remember him. He was a symbol to its people and most Rhode Islanders came to look upon him as a gentleman, a leader, a wise politician, and an able statesman. He was indeed all of these.

Notes

CHAPTER I

[1] Howard K. Stokes, *The Finances and Administration of Providence* (Baltimore, 1903), 12–13; James Q. Dealey, *Political Situations in Rhode Island and Suggested Constitutional Changes* (Providence, 1928), 48.

[2] The chronology of events and the story of the Dorr Rebellion may be read in Arthur Mowry, *The Dorr War* (Providence, 1901); Dan King, *Life and Times of Thomas Wilson Dorr* (Boston, 1859); and the numerous accounts in the *Providence Journal* during that era. It might be noted here that Theodore Francis Green's grandfather on his mother's side, Judge Walter S. Burges, had been Dorr's closest friend and legal defender.

[3] William Kirk, *A Modern City* (Chicago, 1909), 151.

[4] See Clifford C. Hubbard, *Constitutional Development in Rhode Island* (unpublished doctoral dissertation, Brown University, 1926), 182-88; Kirk, *A Modern City*, 151.

[5] Hubbard, *Constitutional Development*, 233; Kirk, *A Modern City*, 152.

[6] Dealey, *Political Situations in Rhode Island*, 41.

[7] Kirk, *A Modern City*, 43, 46–47; Elmer E. Cornwell, Jr., "Party Absorption of Ethnic Groups: The Case of Providence, Rhode Island," in *Social Forces*, March, 1960, p. 207.

[8] *The State*, July 1, 1905.

[9] The Providence Journal Almanac, 1907 (Providence, 1907), p. 49 (hereafter referred to as *Providence Journal Almanac*); *Manual with Rules and Orders for the Use of the General Assembly of the State of Rhode Island, 1907* (Providence, 1907), p. 319 (hereafter referred to as *Rhode Island Manual*). No town or city could be divided into districts for the purpose of selecting representatives; Article V, Section 2, Rhode Island State Constitution. Not until 1910, after an amendment to the constitution had been passed by the legislature and ratified by the people, were single-member districts employed.

[10] Dealey, *Political Situations in Rhode Island*, 16.

[11] Kirk, *A Modern City*, 51, 56; *The State*, April 7, 1906.

[12] Kirk, *A Modern City*, 147–48; Dealey, *Political Situations in Rhode Island*, 35.

[13] *The State*, June 17, August 26, 1906.

[14] Hubbard, *Constitutional Development in Rhode Island*, 227–31; *Boston Journal*, January 31, 1907; *Providence Journal*, April 29, 1906.

[15] Address in Providence, May 4, 1943. All unpublished speeches and all correspondence to and from Green cited here are from the manuscript Green Papers, in the possession of Theodore Francis Green, 14 John Street, Providence.

[16] Address at Northeastern University Commencement, Boston, June 15, 1934; address in Providence, December 9, 1938.

[17] Speech in Providence, October 24, 1935; address to the National Conference of Christians and Jews, Providence, February 23, 1936; speech in Providence, May 4, 1943.

[18] Quoted in Eric F. Goldman, *Rendezvous with Destiny* (New York, 1956), 125–26.

CHAPTER II

[1] *The State*, May 19, 1906; *Providence Journal*, July 1, 1906. See also both newspapers throughout the period.

[2] *Providence Journal*, October 16, 17, 1906.

[3] *Ibid.*, September 2, 16, 1906.

[4] *Ibid.*, September 15–October 1, 1906.

[5] *Ibid.*, October 4, 11, 1906.

[6] A sample ballot was printed in the *Providence Journal*, October 23, 1906. See also *ibid.*, October 21 and November 4.

[7] *Ibid.*, October 16, 1906.

[8] *Ibid.*, October 15, 1906; *The State*, October 20, 1906.

[9] Elmer E. Cornwell, Jr., "A Note on Providence Politics in the Age of Bryan," *Rhode Island History*, 19:33–40 (April, 1960).

[10] *Providence Journal*, October 26, 1906. The *Journal* mistakenly referred to the poster as being printed in Hebrew instead of Yiddish.

[11] *Ibid.*, October 23, 1906; *The State*, October 27, 1906.

[12] *Providence Journal*, October 24, November 1, 1906; *Ibid.*, November 5, 1906; *The State*, November 3, 1906; *The Rhode Island Issue*, 7:1 (November, 1906).

[13] All election returns are from the *Providence Journal Almanac, 1907*.

[14] *Providence Journal*, December 8, 16, 1906.

[15] *Ibid.*, December 15, 16, 1906.

[16] *Ibid.*, January 1, 2, 1907.

[17] *Ibid.*

[18] See the *Journal of the House of Representatives*, January 2, March 14, 1907. See also the *Providence Tribune*, January 3, 1907.

[19] *Rhode Island Manual, 1906*, pp. 344–45; Article IV, Section 8 of the State Constitution; *Providence Journal*, January 3, 1907.

[20] *Ibid.*, January 4, 1907; *Providence Tribune*, January 2, 1907.

[21] *Rhode Island Manual, 1906*, p. 343; *House Journal*, January 4, 1907.

[22] *Ibid.*, January 4, 1907; *Rhode Island Manual, 1906*, p. 346; *Providence Journal*, January 5, 1907.

[23] *Providence Journal*, January 5, 1907.

[24] *Ibid.*, *Providence Tribune*, January 9, 1907; *House Journal*, January 8, 1907.

[25] *House Journal*, January 9, 1907; *Providence Journal*, January 10, 1907. Rule 39 read: "The standing committees shall take into consideration all such petitions, resolves, acts, bills, matters or things as may be referred to them by the House, with power to report by bill or otherwise."

[26] *Rhode Island Manual, 1906*, p. 348; *Providence Journal*, January 10, 1907.

[27] *House Journal*, January 9, 1907.

[28] *Rhode Island Manual, 1906*, p. 349.

[29] From the point of view of some, Green's idea was reactionary. The result of his law would have been to restrict the suffrage rather than enlarge it, which was the tradition of the Democratic Party. *Providence Tribune, Providence Journal*, January 10, 1907.

[30] Frank E. Fitzsimmons to Green and others, January 12, 1907; copy of Green's speech in the Green Papers; *Providence Journal*, January 16, 1907.

[31] *House Journal, 1907, passim.*

[32] *Providence Journal*, January 27, 30, 1907.

[33] *House Journal*, January 30, 1907; *Providence Journal*, January 31, 1907.

[34] *Ibid.*, February 6, 1907.

[35] *Ibid.,* February 8, 1907.

[36] *Ibid.,* February 6, 1907.

[37] *House Journal,* February 6, 1907.

[38] *Providence Journal,* February 20, 1907.

[39] *Ibid.,* February 20, 1907.

[40] *The State,* February 16, 1907; *House Journal,* February 28, 1907.

[41] *Providence Journal,* March 2, 1907; *Providence Bulletin,* March 1, 1907; *House Journal,* March 5, 1907, and the numerous verbatim copies of the incident in the Green Papers.

[42] *Providence Journal,* March 6, 17, 1907; *House Journal,* March 5, 1907.

[43] *Ibid.,* March 15, 1907; *Providence Journal,* March 17, 1907.

[44] *Ibid.,* March 8, 1907.

[45] *Ibid.,* September 26, 1907.

[46] For a more detailed account of the appropriations fight see *ibid.,* March 12–14, 1907.

[47] *Ibid.,* March 18, 28, 29, 1907; *The State,* February 16, 1907; *House Journal,* March 28, 1907.

[48] The report of the caucus has been taken from the *Providence Journal,* March 28, 1907. The proposals and arguments for the last provision can be found in the Green Papers. See also *House Journal,* March 28, 1907.

[49] *Providence Tribune,* April 4, 1907; *Providence Bulletin,* April 3, 1907.

[50] *House Journal,* April 12, 1907.

[51] *Providence Journal,* April 18, 22, 1907; *Providence Tribune,* April 19, 20, 1907.

[52] *Providence Journal,* April 24, 1907.

[53] *Ibid.*

CHAPTER III

[1] *Providence Journal,* October 9, 12, 1907.

[2] Speech made at Infantry Hall, Providence, October 19, 1907.

[3] *Providence Tribune,* October 12, 1907.

[4] Speech made at 48 Weybosset Street, October 24, 1907.

[5] *Providence Journal,* October 29, 30, 1907.

[6] *Ibid.,* November 4, 1907; James L. Jenks to Green, November 11, 1907.

[7] *Providence Journal,* June 20, 1907; *Rhode Island Manual, 1908,* p. 158.

[8] See the *Providence Sunday Tribune,* October 25, and the *Providence Journal,* October 26, 1908, for discussions of this matter.

[9] *Providence Sunday Tribune,* August 30, 1908; Duane Lockard, *New England State Politics* (Princeton, 1959), 177.

[10] For all voting results see the *Providence Journal Almanac, 1909.*

[11] See Hubbard, Constitutional Development in Rhode Island, 237; *Rhode Island Manual, 1910,* pp. 56–58; *House Journal,* April 28, 1909.

[12] Hubbard, Constitutional Development in Rhode Island, 239; *Providence Journal,* October 6, 1909.

[13] *Providence Bulletin,* October 28, 1909; *Providence Tribune,* October 28, 1909; *Providence Sunday Tribune,* October 31, 1909; *Providence Journal Almanac,* 1910, p. 82.

[14] Frank E. Fitzsimmons to Green, November 4, 1909; *Providence Journal,* November 6, 1909.

[15] *Ibid.,* February 23, August 3, 1910.

[16] *Ibid.,* August 29, 1910.

[17] *Providence Tribune,* August 29, September 2, 1910.

[18] *Ibid.,* September 19, 21, 1910.

[19] Green to Frank E. Fitzsimmons, published in the *Providence Tribune,* September 25, 1910; Grace Granger to Green, September 26, 1910; Providence *Evening Bulletin,* September 26, 1910.

[20] *Providence Journal, Providence News-Democrat,* and *Providence Tribune,* September 29, 30, 1910; Green to O'Shaunessy, September 29, 1910; O'Shaunessy to Green, October 6, 1910.

[21] *Providence Journal Almanac, 1911.*

[22] *Providence Journal,* January 8, April 20, 1911.

[23] *Ibid.,* October 18, November 6, 1911; Fitzsimmons to Green, October 19, 1911; *Providence Tribune, Newport Herald,* November 5, 6, 1911; *Providence Journal Almanac. 1912.*

[24] Lewis A. Waterman to Green, November 11, 1911.

[25] *Providence Journal,* May 26, 1912; Goddard to Green, May 26, 1912; *Providence Tribune,* May 26, 27, 1912.

[26] Speeches at Woonsocket and Manville, May 29 and Arctic, May 28, 1912; *Providence Bulletin,* May 31, 1912.

[27] *Providence Tribune,* June 12, 13, 17, 1912; *Providence Journal,* June 12, 25, 1912.

[28] *Providence Tribune,* July 25, 1912.

[29] Telegram from Theodore Roosevelt, Jr., to Green, July 3, and letter of July 31, 1912; Green to Roosevelt, July 3, 27, 1912; *Providence Tribune, Providence Journal,* October 1–11, 1912.

[30] Providence *Evening Bulletin,* October 10, 1912.

[31] *Providence Journal,* October 7, 1912.

[32] *Ibid.,* October 13, 1912; John R. Rathom to Green, October 15, 1912.

[33] *Providence Tribune,* October 11, 1912.

[34] Letter of acceptance in the Green Papers; Luke O'Connor to Green, October 16, 24, 1912.

[35] Sturges to Green, October 14, 1912.

[36] Joseph McDonald to Green, October 14, 1912; William P. Faunce to Green, October 21, 1912; William MacDonald and Walter Bronson to Green, October 14, 1912; Zechariah Chafee, Jr., to Green, October 12, 1912; R. L. Beeckman to Green, October 16, 1912; Patrick J. McCarthy to Green, October 14, 1912.

[37] Speech at Barrington, October 23, 1912, original in the Green Papers; quoted in part in the *Providence Journal,* October 24, 1912.

[38] *Ibid.,* October 23, 26, 30, 31, 1912; sample prices in Green Papers.

[39] *Providence Journal,* October 27, 1912.

[40] Speech at rally at Labor Temple, original in the Green Papers; quoted in part in *Providence Journal,* October 18, 1912.

[41] Speech at Colonial Theatre, Newport, October 27, 1912. See also the reports on the financial condition of the state, in the *Providence Journal* and the *Newport Herald,* October 27, 1912.

[42] *Providence Journal,* October 29, 1912.

[43] Speech at Woonsocket, October 29, 1912; *Providence Journal,* October 30, 1912; *Woonsocket Evening Call,* October 28, 1912.

[44] Compilation of statistics taken from voting records and private papers of Green, which contain an extensive elaboration of these points.

[45] *Providence Journal,* October 30, November 2, 1912; Legislative Reference

Bulletin number 4, March, 1911; *Acts and Resolves passed by the General Assembly,* 1912; Lockard, *New England State Politics,* 186. A study of dual office-holding made by Robert Grieve in 1912 showed that there were 289 persons employed by the state as commissioners, inspectors, medical examiners, and the like; of the 289, only four were Democrats.

[46] Speech in Centredale, November 2, 1912.

[47] Providence *Evening Bulletin,* October 18, 1912; *Pawtucket Times,* October 25, 1912; *Providence Journal,* November 1, 1912.

[48] Robert Grieve to Green, November 1, 1912.

[49] *Woodsocket Evening Call,* October 26, 1912.

[50] *Providence Journal,* July 29, November 5, 1912.

[51] *Providence Journal Almanac,* 1914.

[52] Grieve to Green, November 12, 1912; *Woonsocket Evening Call, Providence Journal,* November 6, 1912.

[53] Eleanor Green to Green, November 12, 1912.

CHAPTER IV

[1] Thomas J. Pence (director of publicity for the Democratic National Committee) to Green, August 21, 1914.

[2] Exchange between Green and Gerry, May 15, 17, 1913; M. McAyvell to Green, July 8, 1913.

[3] Memoranda in the Green Papers; *Providence Journal,* October 1, 6, 1914; J. B. S. Brazeau to Green, July 13, 1913.

[4] *Providence Tribune,* May 6, 1914.

[5] *Providence Journal,* January 22, April 26, 1913.

[6] Green to Aram Pothier, March 31, 1914; *Providence Tribune,* April 1, 1914.

[7] Providence *Evening Bulletin,* April 3, 1914.

[8] *Providence Journal,* June 7, 1914.

[9] *Providence Tribune,* June 18, August 17, 1914.

[10] *Providence Journal,* August 21, 25, 1914; *Providence Tribune,* August 24, 1914.

[11] Providence *Evening Bulletin,* August 31, 1914.

[12] Green to T. W. Gregory, September 2, 1914; Green to Patrick Quinn, September 19, 1914; *Providence Tribune,* September 21, 1914.

[13] For the following political events, see the *Providence Journal* and the *Tribune* for the month of October, 1914.

[14] *Providence Journal,* October 20, November 3, 1914.

[15] Speeches in the Green Papers.

[16] *Providence Journal Almanac,* 1914.

[17] Green to Beeckman, November 4, and Beeckman to Green, November 6, 1914; T. W. Gregory to Green, January 6, 1915.

[18] *Providence Tribune,* January 11, May 24, August 4, 17, 30, 1915; *Providence Journal,* July 22, August 30, September 17, 1915.

[19] For an account of Rhode Island politics and the political maneuvers discussed in the following paragraphs, see the *Providence Journal,* January through October, 1916.

[20] *Ibid.,* October 28, 1916.

[21] Letter from Republican National Committee, September 19, 1916; Jerome M. Fitzgerald to Green, October 1, 1916.

[22] Providence *Evening Bulletin,* June 20, 1916; *Providence Journal,* September 28, 1916; Charles Bates Dana to Green, October 2, 1916; Green to Dana, October

13, 1916. Some other Brown graduates were also offended. Rathbone Gardner protested such activity, as did Zechariah Chafee, Jr. See *Providence Journal*, October 6, 15, 1916.

[23] The correspondence between Faunce, Hughes, Green, and the other principals in this incident is contained in the Green Papers. The dates are October 10 to October 16, 1916.

[24] Election returns from *Providence Journal Almanac*, 1917.

[25] Green to Beeckman, November 6, 1916; Beeckman to Green, November 27, 1916; W. D. Jamieson to Green, November 6, 1916.

[26] *Providence Journal*, August 16, 1918.

[27] Lewis McGowan to Green, September 4, 1918; Green to McGowan, September 8, 1918.

[28] *Providence Journal*, September 9, 1918; Edward M. Sullivan to Green, September 9, 1918.

[29] Frederick W. Tillinghast to Green, September 9, 1918.

[30] Green to Sullivan, September 10, 1918; telegram from Patrick Quinn to Green, September 12, 1918.

[31] Green to Sullivan, September 14, 1918.

[32] Record of telephone call in the Green Papers, September 21, 1918.

[33] *Providence Journal*, September 22, 1918.

[34] Memorandum in the Green Papers, September 27, 1918.

[35] *Providence Journal*, October 3, 4, 1918.

[36] *Ibid.*, October 5, 1918.

[37] Green to Josephus Daniels, October 2, 1918.

[38] Beeckman to Franklin Roosevelt, May 15, 1917; Roosevelt to Beeckman, May 18, 1917; Clark Burdick to Beeckman, May 23, 1917; Josephus Daniels to Beeckman, June 18, 1917.

[39] John R. Rathom to Daniels, June 26, 1917; Beeckman to Daniels, June 27, 1917; Captain Beach to Chief of Bureau of Ordnance, December 17, 1917.

[40] *Providence Journal*, October 21, November 4, 1918.

[41] *Ibid.*, October 8–November 5, 1918.

[42] Wilson's speech before Congress, May 27, 1918; *Providence Journal*, October 9-27, 1918.

[43] Telegrams from Scott Ferris to Green, October 25, 26, 1918; Providence *Evening Bulletin*, October 27, 1918.

[44] *Ibid.*, October 24, 31, November 2, 1918.

[45] Telegrams from Green to W. D. Jamieson, November 4, 1918, and Jamieson to Green on the same day.

[46] Election returns from *Providence Journal Almanac*, 1919.

[47] *Providence Journal*, November 6, 1918.

CHAPTER V

[1] Exchange between Alberic A. Archambault and Green, March 20, 21, 1919; Green to W. D. Jamieson, December 3, 1919.

[2] Roosevelt to Green, August 24, November 8, 1920, March 21, 1921; Green to Roosevelt, August 31, November 6, 1920.

[3] *Providence Journal Almanac, 1921.*

[4] Green to Wilson, November 3, 1920.

[5] Green to William H. Short, November 29, 1920.

[6] Bill S126, March 29, 1921; *Providence Tribune*, March 30, 1921; Chafee to

Green, October 24, 1921; Green to Chafee, October 31, 1921.

[7] For accounts to the Democratic state convention, see the *Providence Journal,* October 4, 1922; for the Republican convention, see the issue of October 12.

[8] See David Patten, *Rhode-Island Story* (Providence, 1954), 69–74.

[9] Election returns from *Providence Journal Almanac, 1923.*

[10] For the events in the state Senate for 1923 and 1924, see the *Providence Journal, the Providence Tribune,* and C. C. Hubbard, "Legislative War in Rhode Island," in *National Municipal Review,* 13:477–80 (1924).

[11] Green to Hughes, October 18, 1923.

[12] *Providence Tribune,* January 14, 1924; *Providence Journal,* January 10, 22, 31, 1924.

[13] Green to Clarke Potter, March 26, 1924.

[14] *Providence Tribune,* April 21, 1924; *Providence Journal,* April 26, 1924.

[15] It was generally believed that Pelkey was responsible for the bombing, which he wanted as a diversionary tactic to get the Republicans out of the State House. He was indicted for the alleged conspiracy but never tried. See Patten, *Rhode-Island Story,* 108–9.

[16] Typed copies of the reports as well as Green's handwritten instructions are in the Green Papers.

[17] Green to Royal S. Copeland, June 9, 1924; Copeland to Green, June 14, 1924. Russell Murphy, a florist with political ambitions, was Green's agent on several of these surveys. Green had few prominent state Democrats working for him at this time. James Kiernan, who went with Green later, was at that time backing Mayor Gainer.

[18] *Providence Journal,* September 23, 1924.

[19] Providence *Evening Bulletin,* September, 30, 1924.

[20] *Providence Journal,* October 1, 1924.

[21] *Providence Journal Almanac,* 1925.

[22] *Providence Journal,* April 19, 23, and throughout the summer, 1928.

[23] James H. Kiernan to Green, July 6, 1928; see also memoranda in the Green Papers, July 31, 1928.

[24] *Providence Tribune, Providence Journal,* September 14, 1928. See also memoranda in the Green Papers, containing the letters urging his candidacy. It is not unlikely that they were drafted by Green himself.

[25] *Providence Journal,* October 10, 1928.

[26] *Ibid.,* October 30, 1928.

[27] *Providence Journal Almanac,* 1929.

[28] Green to Russell Murphy, January 26, 1929; J. Q. Dealey to Green, February 6, 1929.

CHAPTER VI

[1] *Providence Journal,* January 23, 1930; Green to William C. Pelkey, January 23, 1930; Desk Diary of Green, July 23, 1930 (hereafter cited as Diary).

[2] Diary, December 12, 1929.

[3] *Providence Journal,* March 4, 1930; original draft in Green Papers.

[4] *Providence Journal Almanac, 1930.*

[5] *Providence Journal,* March 22, April 3, 1930.

[6] *Ibid.,* March 22, 1930; Diary, March 24, 1930.

[7] Gerry to Green, March 10, 22, June 7, 10, 26, 1930.

[8] Green to Edward Bullock, March 14, 1930; Bullock to Green, July 9, 1930.

[9] *Providence Journal,* January 10, 1930; Charles M. Hall to Green, February 21, 1930.

[10] Hall to Green, May 17, 27, and Green to Hall, May 20, 27, 1930.

[11] Joseph Maresca to Green, June 10, and Green to Maresca, June 11, 1930; Hall to Green, June 10, 1930.

[12] Diary, January 5, March 24, June 12, 26, 1930; survey reports in the Green Papers.

[13] Providence *Evening Bulletin,* August 5, 1930.

[14] *Rhode Islander,* August 8, 1930.

[15] Diary, August 6, 1930; *Providence Journal,* August 7, 1930.

[16] *Ibid.,* August 29, 1930.

[17] *Ibid.,* August 30, 1930.

[18] Providence *Evening Bulletin,* September 5, 1930; Diary, September 9, 1930.

[19] *Providence Journal,* September 8, 12, 1930.

[20] Diary, September 2, 8, 9, 26, 27, 1930.

[21] *Providence Journal,* October 2, 1930.

[22] Cooney to Green, October 2, 1930; Providence *Evening Bulletin,* October 2–4, 1930.

[23] Interview with Edward J. Higgins; Cooney to Green, October 4, 1930.

[24] *Providence Journal,* October, 10, 23, 1930.

[25] Figures preserved in the Green Papers; J. Howard McGrath to Green, January 20, 1930; Green to Henry D. Hamilton, October 10, 1930.

[26] *Providence Journal,* October 19, 22, 1930; *Providence News-Tribune,* October 20, 25, 1930; Providence *Evening Bulletin,* October 28, 1930; *Rhode Islander,* November 1, 1930.

[27] *Providence Journal,* November 2, 1930; telegram from Eddie Dowling to Green, October 1, 1930; Dowling to Green, October 17, 1930.

[28] *Providence News-Tribune,* October 29, 1930.

[29] *Ibid.,* October 31, 1930; *Pawtucket Times,* November 3, 1930.

[30] *Providence Journal,* October 28, 1930.

[31] *Ibid.,* October 27, November 3, 1930.

[32] *Ibid.,* November 3, 1930; Green to Case, October 18, 1930.

[33] Case to Green, October 21, 1930; *Providence Journal,* October 20, 1930.

[34] *Ibid.,* October 21, 27, 1930; Green to Case, October 21, 1930.

[35] Case to Green, October 29, 1930; *Providence Journal,* November 2, 1930.

[36] *Pawtucket Times,* October 29, 1930; Providence *Evening Bulletin,* October 30, 1930; *Providence Journal,* October 20, 1930.

[37] *Ibid.,* November 4, 1930.

[38] *Providence Journal Almanac, 1931.*

[39] Vernon C. Norton to Green, November 6, 1930. Green and Gerry ran about even in the Italian districts of the state; report in the Green Papers.

[40] Interview with Edward J. Higgins, December 19, 1960; McGrath to Green, December 30, 1930; *Providence Journal,* November 21, 1930.

CHAPTER VII

[1] *Providence Journal,* November 1, 1931.

[2] *Ibid.,* November 24, 1931.

[3] *Ibid.,* November 25, 26, 1931.

[4] Diary, June 30, December 12, 18, 1931.

[5] *Ibid.,* January 27, 1932.

[6] *Providence Journal,* February 9, 28, 1932.

[7] Memoranda in the Green Papers.

[8] Frederick H. Allen to Green, February 16, 1932; Green to Allen, February 13, 1932.

[9] Patrick H. Quinn to Green, March 30, April 1, 1932; Diary, April 8, 1932.

[10] *Ibid.,* April 4, 19, 1932; James H. Kiernan to Green, April 5, 1932.

[11] *Ibid.,* April 16, 19, 1932.

[12] Allen to Green, April 5, 1932; *Providence Journal,* May 3, 1932.

[13] *Ibid.,* May 17, August 1, October 23, 1932; Diary, June 9, 1932.

[14] *Providence Journal,* July 8, 1932; Green to Samson, July 11, 1932; Samson to Green, July 12, 1932.

[15] *Newport News,* July 8, 1932; James A. Farley to Green, July 18, 1932; *Providence Journal,* July 19, 1932.

[16] *Ibid.,* July 21, August 7, 15, 26, 1932; Providence *Evening Bulletin,* July 21, 1932; *Providence News-Tribune,* August 26, 1932.

[17] Diary, August 25, 29, 30, 1932; *Providence Journal,* August 27, September 7, 15, 16, 1932; *Newport News,* September 6, 1932.

[18] *Providence Journal,* October 8, 1932.

[19] *Ibid.,* October 10, 1932; Providence *Evening Bulletin,* October 14, 1932.

[20] *Providence Journal,* October, October 15-17, 1932.

[21] *Ibid.,* October 18, 1932.

[22] *Pawtuxet Valley Daily Times,* October 20, 1932; *Le Jean-Baptiste,* October 20, 1932.

[23] *Providence Journal,* October 22–24, 1932; *Pawtuxet Valley Daily Times,* October 22, 1932.

[24] Green to Mrs. R. B. Williams, October 24, 1932.

[25] *Providence Journal,* October 25, 26, 1932; *Pawtucket Times,* November 3, 1932.

[26] Providence *Evening Bulletin,* October 29, 1932.

[27] *Providence Journal,* October 28, November 3, 1932.

[28] Providence *Evening Bulletin,* November 2, 3, 1932.

[29] *Ibid.,* October 23, 1932; *Time,* November 7, 1932.

[30] *Providence Journal Almanac, 1933.*

[31] *Providence Journal,* December 15, 1932.

CHAPTER VIII

[1] Many accounts of events depicted in this chapter have been gleaned from the *Providence Journal,* from January 1, 1933, to June 30, 1934. I have given specific citations only where it seemed necessary. Much information was also obtained from Edward J. Higgins and his files as well as several other persons, most of whom preferred to remain unnamed.

[2] All references to House and Senate bills cited in this chapter may be found in the *House Journal,* volume 30, and *Senate Journal,* volume 28, both for 1933.

[3] *Providence Journal,* January 6, 1933.

[4] *Ibid.,* January 10, 1933.

[5] *Ibid.,* February 8, 1933.

[6] *Ibid.,* April 7, May 2, 1933.

[7] *Ibid.,* February 1, 5, 7, 1933.

[8] *Ibid.,* February 9, 1933.

[9] *Ibid.,* February 13, 1933, and memoranda in the Green Papers.

[10] *Ibid.,* February 16, 1933.

[11] *Ibid.*, March 1, 1933.

[12] *Ibid.*, March 5, 1933.

[13] *Ibid.*, March 21, 22, 1933.

[14] *Ibid.*, March 24, 1933.

[15] *Ibid.*, March 26–April 2, 1933.

[16] *Ibid.*, April 11, 12, 18, 1933.

[17] *Ibid.*, April 24, 1933.

[18] *Ibid.*, April 27, 28, May 2, 1933.

[19] *Ibid.*, February 10, 1933; *House Journal*, March 10, 14, 1933.

[20] *Ibid.*, March 22, April 1, 1933.

[21] *Ibid.*, April 27, 1933.

[22] *Ibid.*, May 2, 15, 17, 1933.

[23] For the following events, see *ibid.* and the House and Senate *Journals* for June, 1933.

[24] From May 23, 1933, to December 31, 1933, the federal government supplied $1,383,806 for relief to Rhode Island unemployed. From January 1, 1934, to June 30, 1934, the amount was $1,407,955. See *Providence Journal*, January 6 and July 8, 1934.

[25] *Ibid.*, throughout October, 1933.

[26] *Ibid.*, June 7, December 6, 1933.

[27] *Ibid.*, September 10, November 22, December 7, 20, 1933.

[28] Green to Everitte St. John Chaffee, January 4, 1934.

[29] *Providence Journal*, January 17, 21, 24, 1934.

[30] *Ibid.*, January 27, February 29, 1934.

[31] *Ibid.*, February 21, March 9, 28, 1934.

[32] *Ibid.*, May 12, 1934.

[33] *Ibid.*, May 5, 19, 20, 30, June 5, 1934.

[34] *Ibid.*, January 4, May 19, 1934.

[35] *Ibid.*, June 12, September 10, 1934.

[36] *Ibid.*, September 8, 9, 1934; radio speech, September 10, 1934, draft in the Green Papers.

[37] *Providence Journal*, September 10–16, 1934.

[38] *Ibid.*, September 12, 13, 1934.

[39] *Ibid.*, September 19, October 8, 1934.

[40] *Ibid.*, March 31, 1933.

[41] Radio speech, September 24, 1934, draft in the Green Papers.

CHAPTER IX

[1] Much of the information contained in this chapter relative to the politics of the Democratic Party in 1934, 1935, and 1936 was obtained in interviews with several interested parties. See also the *Providence Journal* throughout the period. Many explanations of the behind the scenes manuvers may also be found in the private papers of Theodore Francis Green, in the form of memoranda, notes, and other communications.

[2] *Providence Journal*, October 11, 23, 24, 29, 1934; interview with Judge Robert E. Quinn, February 10, 1961. I am indebted to Judge Quinn for giving his views of the political events of 1934–35.

[3] Radio speeches, October 21, 25, 28, November 2, 1934, in the Green Papers.

[4] *Providence Journal*, September 23, 1934; interview with Quinn.

[5] *Ibid.; Providence Journal*, November 9, 1934.

[6] For coverage of the events of January 1, 1935, see the *Providence Journal*, January 2, 1935, and the Senate and House *Journals*, January 1, 1935.

[7] Radio speech, January 2, 1935.

[8] *Providence Journal*, January 4, 11, 12, 1935.

[9] Direct references to House and Senate action may be seen in *House Journal*, volume 35, and *Senate Journal*, volume 33.

[10] *Providence Journal*, January 10, 1935.

[11] *Ibid.*, February 2, 1935.

[12] *Ibid.*, January 24, February 9, 1935; memoranda in the Green Papers.

[13] *Providence Journal*, February 5, 1935; Zechariah Chafee, Jr., *The Constitutional Convention that Never Met* (Providence, 1938). This pamphlet contains much useful chronological information relative to the entire problem of the constitutional convention in Rhode Island.

[14] *Providence Journal*, April 14, 1935.

[15] *Ibid.*, April 15, 1935.

[16] *Ibid.*, May 6, 16, 1935.

[17] Memoranda in Green Papers. The go-between in the deal with the Republicans was Republican house leader Curry's law partner. McGrath and Higgins worked for the Democratic side.

[18] James H. Kiernan to Green, September 26, 1935.

[19] Radio speech, November 19, 1935.

[20] House Journal, January 7, 1935; Providence Journal, May 2, 1935.

[21] Chafee, *Constitutional Convention*, part II; *Senate Journal*, January 2, 1936; *House Journal*, January 15, 1936 .

[22] Correspondence between Farley and Green, January through March, 1936.

[23] Numerous letters in the Green Papers attest to the complaints he received from several organizations representing ethnic groups. Almost all of them mentioned in the correspondence the name of McCoy or Lamarre.

[24] *Providence Journal*, July 17, 1935; radio speech, July 22, 1936.

[25] Radio speech, July 28, 1936.

[26] Green to Shawcross, October 3, 1936; Green to Farley, September 26, 1936.

[27] Ratification speech, October 11, 1936; *Providence Journal*, October-November, 1936.

Bibliography

UNPUBLISHED MATERIAL

Green, Theodore Francis. Private collection of letters, memoranda, diaries, and speeches.

Hubbard, Clifford Chesley. "Constitutional Development in Rhode Island." Unpublished doctoral dissertation, Department of Political Science, Brown University, 1929.

PUBLIC DOCUMENTS

Acts and Resolves, General Assembly, Providence, Rhode Island, 1907, 1933–1935, and 1935–37.

Journal of the House of Representatives, General Assembly, Providence, Rhode Island, 1907, 1933 through 1936.

Journal of the Senate, General Assembly, Providence, Rhode Island, 1907, 1933 through 1936.

Providence Journal Almanac, Providence, Rhode Island, 1905 through 1936.

Rhode Island Manual, Providence, Rhode Island, 1905 through 1936.

NEWSPAPERS

Providence Bulletin.
Providence Journal.
Providence News-Democrat.
Providence Tribune.
The Rhode Island Issue.
The State.
The United League News.
Woonsocket Evening Call.

BOOKS

Chaffee, Zechariah, Jr. *The Constitutional Convention that Never Met.* Providence: The Book Shop, 1939.

Chaffee, Everitte St. John. *The Amateurs.* Providence: The Adams Company, 1953.

Dealey, James Quayle. *Political Situations in Rhode Island.* Providence, 1928.

Kirk, William A. *A Modern City.* Chicago: University of Chicago Press, 1909.

Lockard, Duane. *New England State Politics.* Princeton: Princeton University Press, 1959.

Patten, David. *Rhode Island Story*. Providence: Providence Journal Company, 1954.

Stokes, Howard Kemble. *The Finances and Administration of Providence*. Baltimore: Johns Hopkins Press, 1903.

ARTICLES

Edwards, William H. "Senator Theodore Francis Green," *Harvard Law School Bulletin*, VIII (1957), April, pp. 6–7.

"Elder Statesman Looks at the World Today," *United States News*, XLVI (February 13, 1959), pp. 82–6.

Fox, J. Dewitt. "The Scintillating Senator Theodore Francis Green," *Life and Health* (August 1957), pp. 10 ff.

Garvin, Lucius F. C. *Century*, LXVI (1903), p. 310.

Green, Theodore Francis. "A Man Should Never Stop Work," *The Sunday Oregonian Parade* (April 12, 1959), p. 2.

Hubbard, Clifford Chesley. "The Legislative War in Rhode Island," *The National Municipal Review*, XIII (1924), pp. 477–80.

Lockett, Edward B. "The Debonair, Doughty Senator Green," *New York Times Magazine* (February 10, 1957), pp. 12 ff.

Smith, Beverly. "The Incredible Senator Green," *The Saturday Evening Post* (January 5, 1957), pp. 13 ff.

Stedman, Murray S. and Susan W. "'The Rise of the Democratic Party of Rhode Island," *New England Quarterly* (September, 1951).

Steffens, Lincoln. "Rhode Island, a State for Sale," *McClure*, XXIV (1905), p. 337 ff.

Williamson, Chilton. "Rhode Island Suffrage Since the Dorr War," *New England Quarterly* (March, 1955).

Index